The Snarling Muse is the first stu[dy to] look at the "golden age" of Engl[ish] political satire—the ministry of S[ir] Robert Walpole—in light of the [close] relationship that was developing [at that] time between literary and graphic political satire. While taking into consideration the individual genius of writers like Pope, Gay, Swift, and Johnson, Carretta analyses the nonliterary resources available to the eighteenth-century English satirist. Contemporary political theory and rhetoric, for example, are key considerations that lead us to understand how political satirists treated anomalies such as the officially unsanctioned position of prime minister. The shift in the writing of history—from didactic uniformitarian history to historicism, the theory that each political event is unique— also influenced the exceptional poetry and prints in the time of both Pope and Churchill.

Most significantly, however, Carretta isolates the tremendous capacity of the visual arts to illuminate the development of political verse satire. He explores the common fund of Renaissance iconography inherited by eighteenth-century artists and writers, including, for example, translations and adaptations of emblem books. He discusses how the gradual breakdown of inherited traditions allowed satirists to make recognizable deviations from received forms. The conservative yet innovative nature of these passing traditions gave early Georgian England the most memorable period of political satire in English history. By investigating the shared iconographic vocabulary of verbal and visual satirists, as well as by discovering links with political rhetoric and historiography, Carretta contributes a fruitful and welcome interdisciplinary approach to eighteenth-century English studies.

The Snarling Muse

The Snarling Muse

VERBAL AND VISUAL POLITICAL SATIRE FROM POPE TO CHURCHILL

Vincent Carretta

UNIVERSITY OF PENNSYLVANIA PRESS

PHILADELPHIA · 1983

Credits

An earlier version of part of chapter 1 appeared in *Studies in English Literature* 21 (Summer 1981): 14–28, and is reproduced here by permission of the William Marsh Rice University. An earlier version of part of chapter 3 appeared in the *Journal of English and Germanic Philology* 77 (April 1978): 212–31, and is reproduced here by permission of the University of Illinois Press. Small sections of chapters 2 and 5 appeared, respectively, in *The Scriblerian* 10 (Spring 1978): 81–84, and in *Modern Philology* 77 (1979): 56–57, and are reproduced here by permission, respectively, of the editors and of The University of Chicago Press.

Illustration numbers 1, 3, 4, 5, 9, 12, 15, 16, 18, 19, 20, 21, 22, 26, 28, 29, 32, 34, 35, 36, 43, 44, 46, 47, 49, 50, 51, 54, 58, 59, 60, 62, 63, 64, 67, and 68 are reproduced by permission of the Trustees of the British Museum. Illustration numbers 6, 8, 10, 11, 14, 17, 23, 24, 25, 27, 30, 31, 33, 38, 40, 45, 48, 52, 53, 55, 56, 57, 61, 65, 66, 69, 70, 71, 72, and 73 are reproduced courtesy of the Library of Congress. Illustration numbers 2, 7, 13, 37, 39, 41, and 42 are reproduced by permission of the Folger Shakespeare Library.

Library of Congress Cataloging in Publication Data
Carretta, Vincent.
    "The snarling muse."
    Extension of the author's thesis—University of Iowa.
    Bibliography: p.
    1. Satire, English—History and criticism.
2. English poetry—18th century—History and criticism.
3. English wit and humor, Pictorial.   4. Politics and
literature—Great Britain.   5. Art and literature—
Great Britain.   6. Politics in art—Great Britain.
I. Title.   II. Title: Visual and verbal satire from
Pope to Churchill.
PR565.H5C37   1983   827'.5'09   83-6979
ISBN 0-8122-7885-2

Printed in the United States of America

For Pat

Poets and print designers, too, frame many of the same images. Books like Peter M. Daly's *Literature in the Light of the Emblem* and Ernest B. Gilman's *The Curious Perspective* are two of the most recent contributions to the strong emphasis on verbal-visual relationships in seventeenth-century studies.[5] To take just one example, the influence of the emblematic tradition on the other arts is widely accepted for that period. The emblematic tradition, however, as Paulson reminds us in *Emblem and Expression*, did not end in 1700. Editions, translations, and adaptations of earlier emblem books were published in the eighteenth century, keeping the earlier patterns of imagery available to satirists, who increasingly made secular and particular the religious and general forms they inherited.

Let us just briefly consider one example of how an artist could borrow from the history painting and emblematic traditions to create an occasional political satire. Hogarth's *Henry the Eighth and Anne Boleyn* (ca. 1728–29) at first appears to be simply a history painting on the subject of Henry's marriage to Anne Boleyn. In that context, the seated figure leaning on the throne is Cardinal Wolsey, his facial expression revealing his concern for his future and his pose indicating his political ambition to take the throne himself. But most viewers at the end of the 1720s would have recalled the frequent Opposition comparisons of Walpole to Wolsey. The context becomes occasional as well as historical. It may be emblematic at the same time. Compare the Wolsey figure in Hogarth's print to the central figure of Julius Caesar in plate 42 of *The Doctrine of Morality* (1721, reissued 1726 as *Moral Virtue Delineated*), an unacknowledged English edition of Otto Van Veen's *Moralia Horatiana* (1607). Caesar's facial expression and pose in this emblem entitled "Fear is the constant Companion of Greatness" are strikingly similar to those of the Wolsey-Walpole figure in the Hogarth engraving. The prose explanation of the emblem tells us that the picture is intended to be "a most effectual Cure for the Ambitious" (p. 84). Hogarth makes an occasional political statement that at the same time remains a general truth about human nature.

Hogarth's conception and execution of *Henry the Eighth* assume that his audience share with him historiographic traditions inherited from the Renaissance. For his engraving to be rhetorically successful, Hogarth must have viewers who accept or at least recognize three premises: a secular typology "abstracted" from its religious origins; the closely related concept of exemplar history; and the belief in uniformitarianism that underlies the other premises. The belief that human nature is uniform through the ages permits one to search history for exemplars with whom contemporaries may be compared. Historical figures can thus either "point a moral, or adorn a tale." Furthermore, a man like Wolsey in the past can be a type of Walpole in the present. The present becomes more knowable, even predictable, when we apply lessons from the past.

1. William Hogarth, *Henry the Eighth and Anne Boleyn*

Art shared all these Renaissance traditions with her sister poetry. The conservative yet innovative nature of these passing traditions gave verbal and visual satirists in early Georgian England the means to produce the greatest period of political satire England has ever experienced. Happily, as we shall see, the means were unusually well suited to the kind of political power Walpole exercised.

The Snarling Muse begins with a study of *Windsor Forest* (1713) because I want to discuss the iconographic and historiographic traditions before

2. *The Doctrine of Morality*; or, *A View of Human Life, According to the Stoick Philosophy,* plate 42

showing how Pope and his contemporaries turned these weapons against Walpole. I want to establish the casualness with which a poet could assume his audience's familiarity with and acceptance of his premises. When Pope sought to praise Queen Anne and to attack the impending Hanoverian Succession, he carefully composed *Windsor Forest* as if it were a history painting in verse. Because he wanted to emphasize the constitutional issues involved in the debate over succession, Pope selected allegorical and even emblematic pictorial metaphors to portray Anne and the Stuart line as the only true successors to Elizabeth I. He invests Anne with the iconography of religious and nationalist patriotism that surrounded England's most glorious queen.

Similarly, when the ministry of Sir Robert Walpole and his opponents clashed over constitutional issues in the 1730s, the competing prints and broadside poems tapped a fund of allegorical and emblematic metaphors inherited from the Renaissance. Such metaphors dominate the prose of Lord Bolingbroke, William Pulteney, and the Opposition journal *The Crafts-man*, as well as the poetry of Pope, Swift, Gay, Johnson, and James Thomson. Other such images in prose and verse have close ties with contemporary graphic satire, particularly the work of Hogarth. Bolingbroke, Pope, and their friends encouraged the production of general satire by emphasizing constitutional issues, or measures, rather than personalities, or men, in their opposition to Walpole. They argued that Walpole's measures would be proper objects of attack no matter who was carrying them out. As a result, the Opposition frequently expressed their political, secular, and partisan assaults in imagery adapted from earlier traditions of apolitical history painting and religious emblem books. For example, Pope's *Epistle to Bathurst* is based upon the Opposition rhetorical strategy of attacking measures as well as men.

Essential to the Opposition rhetorical practices aimed at the ministry of Walpole was the belief that history should be studied for didactic purposes, a belief founded on the assumption that human nature is uniform throughout all periods of time. This belief in uniformitarianism justified the parallels Walpole's enemies drew in verse and prints between present times and the past. Moreover, the notion that George II and his allegedly corrupt minister Walpole were modern counterparts of earlier historical figures like Tiberius or Sejanus encouraged the production of satire based on these classical models or subjects, such as Pope's *Imitations of Horace* or the print *The Downfall of Sejanus*.

After the fall of Walpole from power in 1742 and the death of Pope in 1744, the organized Opposition rhetorical strategy of emphasizing policies rather than persons collapsed. Indeed, many members of the former Opposition quickly took office and adopted the very practices they had been attacking for years. The growing importance of political personalities rather than constitutional principles as the basis for political conflicts parallels a corresponding increase in personal caricature in poetry and prints of the 1740s and 1750s. The narrowly partisan nature of these works (by authors such as Charles Hanbury Williams or the pseudonymous Porcupinus Pelagius) makes them unfamiliar today to any but the most specialized eighteenth-century scholars, yet their contribution to the development of caricature and satire should not be overlooked. In addition, the 1740s and 1750s marked the beginning of the gradual replacement of didactic uniformitarian history by historicism, or the theory that each historical event is unique.

These developments in satire and historiography help to explain the differences between the poetry and prints of Pope's times and those of Churchill's. As a result of historicism, the past was becoming less accessible to satirists as a means for attacking the present. Increasingly, contemporary events had to be explained, rather than illustrated with parallels from earlier times. Consequently, prose rather than verse became the primary vehicle for discussing politics. These changes from the 1720s and 1730s become clear when we compare the relationship between *The North Briton* and Churchill's poetry with that between *The Craftsman* and Pope's satire.

Although Pope might be considered the hero of *The Snarling Muse*, this is not a Pope book: he is offstage in chapter 2 and out of the theater in chapters 6–8. I concentrate on Pope in the first five chapters because he did best what so many others were at the same time trying to do. I investigate verbal and visual political satire by using Pope as a focal point, or test case. I am less interested here in pursuing particular sources and influences of a poet's images (usually that sort of thing is simply impossible to prove) than I am in showing why verbal and visual satirists had so much in common in the kinds of shapes they contrive. This book is primarily concerned with the iconography political satirists shared from 1714 to 1764 and is not intended to be a comprehensive survey of political satire during the first six decades of eighteenth-century England. Consequently, of the thousands of political engravings, pamphlets, and poems I studied before writing this book, I have chosen to discuss a representative few to support my argument.

A book that treats political rhetoric, poetry, engravings, and historiography—even though they are intimately related—is difficult to organize. For example, a strictly chronological ordering of the engravings would be more disjunct than the iconographic one I chose. Thus, the discussion of the colossus image in chapter 2 traces the figure from the seventeenth century to the 1740s, but chapter 3 discusses engravings of the 1720s and 1730s. I decided that, especially for readers less familiar with the prints than I, a thematic principle of organization would be best. Each chapter, with one exception, treats both verbal and visual political satire and is organized thematically, or imagistically. The exception is chapter 7, the discussion of the mid-century shift in historiography, which requires an extended treatment before the reader can appreciate how it affected satire. Indeed, historically the shift was well under way before Bute's coming to power caused political satirists to discover how unavailable the rhetorical strategy of the 1730s had become by the 1760s.

Like anyone who writes about Pope's political satire, I am greatly indebted to Maynard Mack, who in *The Garden and the City* first made me aware that

> whatever its motives, Pope's career in political satire began at a period when a remarkable instrument of satirical communication lay ready to his hand. This was the extensive vocabulary of disaffection minted by the writers of the *Craftsman* and kept bright by continual rubbing in the Opposition press generally, as well as, in some cases, the parliamentary debates themselves.[6]

Mack, too, was one of the first to discuss, albeit briefly, the importance of graphic satire in political satire.

The fullest treatment of political graphic satire is Herbert Atherton's *Political Prints in the Age of Hogarth*, a book that demonstrates the usefulness of the engravings to historians of politics like himself.[7] Atherton remarks that "students of literature [have not] attempted any analysis, even though prints share much in common with literary satire." Since I came to the engravings trained as a literary historian, I hope to complement Atherton's perspective with my own.

Studies such as Atherton's or my own of the low, or popular, art form of the political engraving naturally complement studies like Ronald Paulson's *Emblem and Expression* and Morris Brownell's *Alexander Pope and the Arts of Georgian England* of high, or elite, art of the period. I detect, though for different reasons, the same shift from emblematic to expressive representation in popular engravings that Paulson traces in higher art. My discussion of Pope's relationship to prints supplements Brownell's handling of Pope's artistic interests and connections.

From a literary perspective, *The Snarling Muse* complements three recent books: Bertrand Goldgar's *Walpole and the Wits*, Howard Weinbrot's *Augustus Caesar in "Augustan" England*, and Thomas Lockwood's *Post-Augustan Satire*.[8] Although Goldgar's book chronologically overlaps part of mine, it seeks answers to very different questions. It is a straightforward, chronological literary history of the period 1722-42 and does not discuss visual political satire. Neither does Weinbrot's *Augustus Caesar in "Augustan" England*, a thorough study of the literary history of Horatian imitations and the changing view of Augustus Caesar in the eighteenth-century. The later half of my study overlaps the earlier sections of Lockwood's *Post-Augustan Satire*, but our approaches are very different. He does not cover visual satire, does not restrict himself to political satire, and emphasizes literary rather than extra-literary influences on the development of verse satire.

I wish to thank the Newberry Library, the Folger Shakespeare Library, the William Andrews Clark Memorial Library (University of California, Los Angeles), and the American Council of Learned Societies for fellowships that helped make research for *The Snarling Muse* possible and pleasurable. I am indebted as well to the late Wilmarth S. Lewis, who kindly allowed me to study the prints in his Lewis Walpole Library. I owe a special debt of gratitude to the members and staff of the Institute for Research in the Humanities of the University of Wisconsin-Madison for giving me the setting and services needed to complete the research and writing of the first draft of this book. Two Summer Research Fellowships from the University of Maryland enabled me to revise that version in light of the thoughtful readings and helpful comments given me by Morris Brownell, Robert Hume, Paul Korshin, David Lampe, F. P. Lock, Bernard Reilly, and Deborah Stuart.

Publication of this book was partially supported by a Book Subsidy Award from the General Research Board of the University of Maryland.

University of Maryland   VINCENT CARRETTA
College Park

CHAPTER I

Anne and Elizabeth: The Poet as Historian and Painter in *Windsor Forest*

No man can have in his mind a conception of the future, for the future is not yet. But of our conceptions of the past, we make a future.—Hobbes, *The Elements of Law*

There Kings shall sue, and suppliant states be seen
Once more to bend before a British QUEEN.
   —*Windsor Forest*

Alexander Pope's *Windsor Forest* may seem an odd work with which to begin a study of verbal and visual political satire in early Georgian England. It is not a formal satire, though parts of it are satiric, and it is quite far removed chronologically from most of the works I deal with in this study. But precisely because *Windsor Forest* is not one of the many satires against Sir Robert Walpole and his successors we can isolate some of the traditions of history writing and image making that lay ready for the later satirists in poetry and prints. Such traditions can be viewed more clearly without the distorting lens of satire. Much of the effectiveness of Opposition attacks on Walpole in the 1730s depended upon the continuing survival of widely shared assumptions about history, art, and literature, not yet exclusively the property of any one political faction.

In *Windsor Forest* Pope demonstrates how easily a political poet of the early eighteenth century could create a Tory history-painting in verse by combining classical historiography with seventeenth-century Whig notions about the development of England's constitution.[1] Pope's easy adaptation of traditional views of history, the Whig interpretation of history, and available methods of pictorial representation in the service of a Tory view of England in 1713 anticipated the strategy and tactics Bolingbroke devised against Sir Robert Walpole twenty years later. The cyclical structure of Pope's poem reflects the patterns of rise and fall classical and Renaissance historians detected in earlier unstable political systems. The reign of Anne becomes in *Windsor Forest* the last of a series of restorations in the cyclical history of England. Because human nature was thought to be uniform wherever and whenever it was studied in secular history, English affairs of the present could be compared profitably with English affairs of the past: consequently, Anne's reign could be seen as a restoration to the immemorial constitution of pre-Norman times, which had last been recognized under Elizabeth's rule.[2] Throughout the poem, Pope's assumptions about history create the complex system of allusions his audience would have recognized as the material of poetry and history writing. Just as he blames William III by allusions to William I, he praises Anne by allusions to Elizabeth.[3] *Windsor Forest* is essentially a panegyric celebrating the restoration of England to the limited monarchy of Elizabeth.[4]

Windsor Forest opens with a description of the forest as it is at the beginning of the eighteenth century. Pope makes "the oak forests of Windsor a synecdoche for England," and he assigns a double role to Windsor Forest, "for the Forest is both a principle and a place."[5] "Thy Forests, *Windsor!* and thy green Retreats, / At once the Monarch's and the Muse's Seats" (1–2) are introduced to us as a place very like the garden found in *Paradise Lost*:

> The Groves of *Eden*, vanish'd now so long,
> Live in Description, and look green in Song:
> *These*, were my Breast inspir'd with equal Flame,
> Like them in Beauty, should be like in Fame.   (7–10)

The essential characteristic of this modern-day Eden is the *concordia discors* Earl R. Wasserman discusses. Pope has no doubt about what caused this simulacrum of paradise, a paradise combining aspects of both Eden and Arcadia: "And Peace and Plenty tell, a STUART reigns" (42). But:

> Not thus the Land appear'd in Ages past,
> A dreary Desert and a gloomy Waste,
> To Savage Beasts and Savage Laws a Prey,
> And Kings more furious and severe than they.   (43–46)

The Windsor Forest, and by extension, the England of 1710, has been regenerated. By describing the present forest-England in the terms he does, Pope forces the reader to recognize that his poem portrays not so much a new England as an old England restored. And this is only the first of many instances of cyclic restoration that help to organize the poem.

These cyclical restorations reflect the assumption, probably as old as history writing itself, that human nature remains the same throughout history. In the eighteenth century, this concept called uniformitarianism was often identified with Polybius, the classical historian who had observed that it is "the mental transference of similar circumstances to our times that gives us the means of forming presentiments of what is about to happen."[6] His more recent follower, Machiavelli, stresses in the *Discourses* the pattern of continually repeating cycles in history. Two centuries later Bolingbroke describes this same pattern: "There are certain general principles, and rules of life and conduct, which always must be true, because they are conformable to the invariable nature of things. He who studies history . . . will soon distinguish and collect them, and by so doing will form himself a general system of ethics and politics on the surest foundations, on the trial of these principles and rules in all ages, and on the confirmation of them by universal experience."[7]

Uniformitarianism justifies the poet-historian Pope's implicit criticism of William III through his description of William the Conqueror (42−84). Both kings could be seen as foreign usurpers of the English throne and their actions comparable, in accordance with what has been called "the exemplar theory of history": the actions of men in one historical period may be usefully compared to the actions of men in an earlier or later period.[8] In addition, both kings had been personally unpopular. Had Pope been accused of attacking William III through his treatment of William the Conqueror, he could simply have smiled and blamed such "confusion" on his reader's fancy.[9] "Confusion" of this sort was very likely because Pope's readers, familiar with classical historiography and the English tradition of the immemorial constitution, were likely to have seen William I as a type in the poem of William III. When Pope describes the Normans (43−92), he tells us not only what England was like after the Conquest, but also what she was like before it. From the opening of this section Pope clearly "recreates the traditional view of the tyrannies exercised by the Norman kings, especially as they were illustrated in the formation of the New Forest as a royal hunting ground by William I."[10] Pope's emphasis on the religious and political tyranny of William I indicates that he relied on Walter Mapes' twelfth-century account of the creation of the New Forest, which he probably found in Camden's *Britannia* (1695, p. 115): "The Conqueror took away much land from God and men, and converted it to the use of wild beasts, and the sport of his dogs; by which he demolish'd 36 Mother-churches, and drove away the poor inhabitants."[11]

Line after line of this section makes obvious the terror and cruelty imposed by the Norman conquerors. But what do we learn of the natives in that immemorial time before the Conquest? What was destroyed is described in Arcadian and classical terms:

> The Fields are ravish'd from th'industrious Swains,
> From Men their Cities, and from Gods their Fanes:
> The levell'd Towns with Weeds lie cover'd o'er,
> The hollow Winds thro' naked Temples roar;
> Round broken Columns clasping Ivy twin'd;
> O'er Heaps of Ruin stalk'd the stately Hind;
> The Fox obscene to gaping Tombs retires,
> And savage Howlings fill the sacred Quires.   (65–72)

Elwin and Courthope observe that these lines "suppose a much statelier architecture than belonged to the rude village churches of the Saxons." [12] Perhaps Pope here, particularly by referring to the Arcadian "Swains" and the classical pre-Norman architecture, alludes to one of the constitutional myths Coke and others used during the seventeenth century—the legend of the eponymous Brutus founding Britain. According to this myth, which Pope later turned to for political purposes, [13] English political institutions were directly derived from the classical age and were only later adopted by the conquering Saxons. Several lines later Pope tells us that the true Britons presumably antedated the Saxons, for these victims of the Normans were those "Whom ev'n the *Saxon* spar'd" (77).

In *Windsor Forest*, Pope leaves little doubt that William the Conqueror's tyranny is a direct result of his usurping power and destroying the balance that already existed in the pre-Norman government. Pope implies that the English government before the Conquest was very much like the eighteenth-century government Addison describes in *The Spectator* as "Mixt Government," with its constituent elements of nobles and commons. [14] William the Conqueror destroyed liberty by destroying the balance of power and moving the government toward a dictatorship:

> Aw'd by his Nobles, by his Commons curst,
> Th' Oppressor rul'd Tyrannick where he durst,
> Stretch'd o'er the Poor, and Church, his Iron Rod,
> And serv'd alike his Vassals and his God.   (73–76)[15]

Sharing with Pope the common assumptions of uniformitarian and exemplar history, a contemporary reader could justifiably suspect a reference to William III in the lines just quoted. The late king was often seen by his opponents as another foreign usurper of the English throne and a tyrant who interrupted the smooth transition of power England's constitution required. In an earlier version of the poem, Pope made the reference to William III even more likely with a couplet deleted before publication: "Oh may no more a foreign Master's Rage / With Wrongs yet Legal, curse a future Age!" [16] That same suspicious contemporary reader might well see this suppressed couplet in conjunction with the lines on William I as a comment on the impending Hanoverian succession. Pope's reader would have found Jean Bodin's application of uniformitarianism in 1566 to be still valid: "from these ["accounts of days long past"] not only are present-day affairs readily interpreted but also future events are inferred, and we may acquire reliable maxims for what we should seek and avoid."[17]

In *Windsor Forest* the imposition of the "Norman Yoke" initiates the degenerative phase of the historical cycle.[18] The downward movement is caused by the destruction of the pre-Norman balanced government, and the resultant loss of liberty reduces the native Britons to a brutal existence. Pope's representation of the conquered Britons reflects contemporary political theory as set down by Addison: "It is odd to consider the Connection between Despotic Government and Barbarity, and how the making of one Person more than Man, makes the rest less."[19]

But the tyranny the Normans supposedly imposed was not thought to be permanent: William I was a conquerer, but only temporarily. William upset the old order, but he did not institute a new one. With the passage of time, the cycle of history regenerated the original constitution. Following the tradition of Camden, Pope asserts that God punished William and his sons and that "Succeeding Monarchs heard the Subjects Cries, / Nor saw displeas'd the peaceful Cottage rise" (85–86). Pope failed, like seventeenth-century historians, to account satisfactorily for the supposed absorption of the conquerors by the conquered. Perhaps he intended to emphasize the unpopularity of William by implying that simply the change of rulers had to be a recognizable improvement.

Whatever the cause of the assimilation, eventually "Fair *Liberty, Britannia's* Goddess, rears / Her chearful Head, and leads the golden Years" (91–92). Although the personification need not refer to anyone at all, alert contemporary readers who suspected an earlier reference to William III might identify "Fair *Liberty*" with another monarch, the obvious choices being Queen Anne and especially Queen Elizabeth. The Twickenham editors' suggestion that "*Liberty*" "is perhaps to be identified with Queen Anne" has never before been questioned.[20] I think it more likely, however, that "*Liberty*" is intended as an allusion to both Elizabeth and Anne, linking them with each other just as William I and William III are linked earlier in the poem. The linking of Anne with Elizabeth had been conventional for at least a decade before *Windsor Forest*. Lady Mary Chudleigh makes the connection in "To the Queen" in *Poems on Several Occasions* (1703), and Sir Richard Blackmore does so in *Eliza: An Epick Poem* (1705).

Pope praises Anne by identifying her with Elizabeth and thus balances the blame he gives William III. This reference to Elizabeth-Anne marks the return of the classical historical cycle to the immemorial constitution.

Before both queens assumed the throne the constitution had been upset and liberty lost. When both queens put the constitution back in practice, liberty was restored.

The assumption that the restoration of true constitutional rule will bring about a restoration of liberty accords with historical theory available to Pope. For the eighteenth century, Polybius and Machiavelli were the direct classical sources for understanding the English constitution Addison describes and defends. According to Polybius, the only way to halt and reverse the process of degeneration begun by governmental imbalance is to return the state to its first principles. Machiavelli calls this restoration a *ricorso*. Swift was certainly aware of this concept in 1709: "The Nature of Things is such, that if Abuses be not remedied, they will certainly encrease, nor ever stop til they end in the Subversion of a Common-Wealth. As there must always of Necessity be some corruptions; so in a well-instituted State, the executive Power will be always contending against them, by *reducing Things* (as Machiavel speaks) *to their first Principles*: never letting Abuses grow inveterate, or multiply so far that it will be hard to find Remedies, and perhaps impossible to apply them."[21]

Swift's *A Discourse of the Contests and Dissentions between the Nobles and the Commons in Athens and Rome, with the Consequences they had upon both those States* expresses what was a commonly held view of the historical development of the English constitution: "Since the *Norman* Conquest, the Balance of Power in *England* has often varied, and sometimes been wholly overturned; the Part which the Commons had in it, *that most disputed Point in its Original, Progress and Extent*, was, by their own Confessions, but a very inconsiderable share. . . . About the middle of Queen Elizabeth's Reign, I take the Power between the Nobles and the Commons to have been in more equal Balance, than it was ever before or since."[22] This balance, last achieved in the reign of England's previous queen, is established again under England's current queen. If I am correct in suggesting that the appearance of "Fair *Liberty*" implies the restoration of England to the state of the constitution before the Norman Conquest, Pope probably wanted his readers to associate the *ricorso* under Anne with that under Elizabeth, and to see both queens as representatives of "*Liberty*."

The identification of the "Goddess" in *Windsor Forest* with Elizabeth becomes even stronger when we look at the Arcadian interlude this figure introduces into the poem, and by implication into English history. The cycle of the seasons (93–164) comprises a micro-cycle of death and rebirth reflecting the macro-cycle of classical cyclic history with which Pope organizes the whole poem. The order restored to nature reflects the social and political order restored by the "Goddess," "Fair *Liberty*." Even Pope's use of the historical present tense in the Arcadian passage allows him to refer to either Anne or Elizabeth. Indeed, the last lines of this section combine the present with the past tense and remind us strongly of imagery popularly associated with Elizabeth and more recently with Anne:

> Let old *Arcadia* boast her ample Plain,
> Th' Immortal Huntress, and her Virgin Train;
> Nor envy *Windsor!* since thy Shades have seen
> As bright a Goddess, and as chast a Queen;
> Whose Care, like hers, protects the Sylvan Reign,
> The Earth's fair Light, and Empress of the Main.   (159–64)[23]

Pope may well have intended the Lodona episode that follows to be taken as yet another manifestation of the cyclic pattern of the poem. If so, the Lodona passage recapitulates what has gone before, this time in terms of classical myth. Although one should always be wary of the limits of allegorical approaches to eighteenth-century literature, let us consider where such an approach to the Lodona story might lead.[24] Pope's readers could easily associate "*Diana*" with Elizabeth. The tradition of Elizabeth as Diana was extremely strong during her reign—a tradition that Pope certainly was likely to have been aware of.[25] What better image of the classical cycle of uniformitarian history than the goddess Diana with her ever-changing yet ever-restored symbol of the moon? "Diana stray'd" in Windsor Forest, Pope may be saying, during the brief interlude of Elizabeth's golden age of constitutional rule. But the land she led was not as steadfast and incorruptible as its ruler Diana-Elizabeth. "Lodona . . . is the goddess without her divinity . . . England, the nation and its people."[26] Straying beyond the bounds of the forest, just as England strayed from its original principles after Elizabeth's reign, Lodona-England becomes the victim of lust and irrational passion:

> It chanc'd, as eager of the Chace the Maid
> Beyond the Forest's verdant Limits stray'd,
> *Pan* saw and lov'd, and burning with Desire
> Pursu'd her Flight; her Flight increas'd his Fire.   (181–84)

A sadder, wiser, and no longer innocent Lodona-England is restored to the symbol of British Destiny, the "great Father of the *British* Floods" (219).

The Lodona episode then is Pope's mythic representation of the evils that befell England when she transgressed the bounds of the original constitution that had earlier been restored under Elizabeth. Pan, god of lust, pursuing Lodona represents the political excesses that embraced England in the seventeenth century. Lodona's fall has no lasting consequences, for she is returned to the true course of British Destiny after the Stuart Restoration of 1660, which leads finally to the glory of Anne. Such a mythic representation of England between Elizabeth and Charles II reflects Swift's account of the years 1603–60:

> But then [at Elizabeth's death], or soon after arose a Faction in *England*, which, under the name of *Puritan*, began to grow popular, by molding up their new Schemes of Religion with *Republican* Principles in Government; who gaining upon the *Prerogative*, as well as the Nobles, under several Denominations, for the Space of about Sixty Years, did at last overthrow the Constitution; and according to the usual Course of such Revolutions, did introduce a Tyranny, first of the People, and then of a single Person. [27]

Pope repeats the pattern of fall and restoration later in the poem, but in more strictly historical terms. Thus, after

> A dreadful Series of Intestine Wars,
> Inglorious Triumphs, and dishonest Scars.
> At length great *ANNA* said—Let Discord cease!
> She said, the World obey'd, and all was *Peace!*   (325–28)

Between Lodona and "great ANNA" lies the passage that describes the retired *beatus vir*:

> Happy the Man whom this bright Court approves,
> His Sov'reign favours, and his Country loves;
> Happy next him who to these Shades retires,
> Whom Nature charms, and whom the Muse inspires,
> Whom humbler Joys of home-felt Quiet please,
> Successive Study, Exercise and Ease.
>
> .   .   .   .
>
> Such was the Life great *Scipio* once admir'd,
> Thus *Atticus*, and *Trumbal* thus retir'd.   (235–58)

The Twickenham editors point out, "If these early lines refer to [Sir William] Trumbull's retirement in the Forest, [they] are puzzling, for there is no evidence that Trumbull attempted poetry."[28] Recently, a more convincing case has been made that the subject of these lines is Lansdowne, who wrote poetry in praise of James II and his queen, and who retired for a number of years after 1688.[29] But the lines also may be intended to refer to the role of philosopher in general, and to Pope in particular. Pope's contemporaries might have recognized him in his guise of retired philosopher, a role that enabled him to play both the honest poet and the disinterested historian at the same time. In 1715 he wrote to Martha Blount, "I am so much in the taste of rural pleasures, I had rather see the sun than any thing he can shew me, except yourself. . . . on the contrary a true town life of hurry, confusion, noise, slander, and dissension, is a sort of apprenticeship to hell and its furies."[30]

Pope has been able to sing "the golden Years" (92) of England's past and present, but realizing that only Lansdowne can "touch the fair Fame of *Albion's* Golden Days" (242) to come, he pauses to look at his own roles of philosopher and poet-historian. He, like Lansdowne, "O'er figur'd Worlds now travels with his Eye. / Of ancient Writ unlocks the learned Store, / Consults the Dead, and lives past Ages o'er" (246–48). The poet-historian observes from the outside the Court of which he is not a part. His position allows him to be objective about the actions of other men. In later poems Pope uses this position as justification for his role of satirist-historian. Pope's assertion of objectivity in *Windsor Forest*, if accepted by the reader, invests his celebration of Anne with a credibility that could not be achieved by a politically motivated poet.

Immediately after he tells us of the necessity of retirement for the poetic imagination—"Nor *Po* so swells the fabling Poet's Lays" (227)—Pope asks that he be carried back to the retirement that will allow him to complete the poem:

> Ye sacred Nine! that all my Soul possess,
> Whose Raptures fire me, and whose Visions bless,
> Bear me, oh bear me to sequester'd Scenes,
> The bow'ry Mazes and surrounding Greens;
> To *Thames*'s Bank which fragrant Breezes fill,
> Or where ye Muses sport on *Cooper*'s Hill.   (259–64)

At this point, however, the poet of retirement briefly anticipates the need for a poet of action to inaugurate the vision of the future. As both poet and secretary at war, Lansdowne was the perfect analogue to an earlier Elizabethan poet who was also a man of action: "*Surrey*, the *Granville* of a former Age: / Matchless his Pen, victorious was his Lance" (292–93). In the account of history that prefaces the appearance of "great ANNA," Pope again carefully stresses the cyclic pattern of history. Thus the martyr Henry VI is followed by the war-making oppressor Edward IV, just as "sacred *Charles*" is followed by the unrest and warfare of Cromwell and William III. Perhaps intended to parallel the Lodona episode, the fall and restoration of England under Anne is followed immediately by the appearance of "Old Father Thames." From line 330 to virtually the end of the poem his is the vatic voice of British Destiny.

This British Destiny is repeatedly expressed in terms of a combined classical and English historiography. The references are unmistakable to a future England restored architecturally, religiously, and constitutionally to its pre–Norman Conquest condition:

Behold! *Augusta*'s glitt'ring Spires increase,
And Temples rise, the beauteous Works of Peace.
I see, I see where two fair Cities bend
Their ample Bow, a new *White-Hall* ascend!

. . . .

There Kings shall sue, and suppliant States be seen
Once more to bend before a *British* QUEEN.   (377–84)

All is possible because the cycle of history has restored an analogue to Elizabeth in the form of Anne. Although Pope now makes explicit the parallel
between Anne and Elizabeth he has been suggesting throughout *Windsor
Forest*, twentieth-century readers may not fully appreciate the importance
and the subtlety of the compliment he pays Anne. But few of Pope's
contemporaries would have failed to recognize the appropriateness of comparing Elizabeth with Anne, who on 23 December 1702 had officially
announced "that it was her Majesty's Pleasure, that whenever there were
occasion to Embroider, Depict, Grave, Carve or Paint her Majesty's Arms,
these Words, SEMPER EADEM, should be us'd for a *Motto*: it being the
same that had been us'd by her Predecessor Queen *Elizabeth*, of glorious
Memory."[31] The sharing of the motto itself expresses the same themes of
continuity and restoration Pope uses in his poem.

The reference to the ultimately unfulfilled wish for "a new *White-Hall*"
is not only a reference to the projected reconstruction of the building
destroyed in 1698, but it is also an architectural metaphor for the restoration of the principles of the traditional constitution. The new building
symbolizes the *ricorso* necessary to restore the England of Anne to its pre-
Norman condition, only temporarily restored in the reign of Elizabeth.
Just at the place where London and Westminster with its Parliament
meet—at the curve of the Thames, suggestive of the rainbow image of
harmony—Whitehall, seat of the Court, will be rebuilt. That England
under Anne is a restoration rather than a new beginning is emphasized by
Pope's choice of the archaic "Augusta" and "Albion" in talking of the
future. Similarly, the restoration of England to its original condition will
lead to *ricorsi* in other lands:

Oh stretch thy Reign, fair *Peace!* from Shore to Shore,
Till Conquest cease, and Slav'ry be no more:
Till the freed *Indians* in their native Groves
Reap their own Fruits, and woo their Sable Loves,
Peru once more a Race of Kings behold,
And other *Mexico's* be roof'd with Gold.   (407–12)

But the poet-historian able to sing "the golden Years" of Elizabeth and
Anne must be replaced by George Granville, Lord Lansdowne, better suited

to sing the "Golden Days" of England's future restored in the wake of the Peace of Utrecht:

Here cease thy Flight, nor with unhallow'd Lays
Touch the fair Fame of *Albion*'s Golden Days.
The Thoughts of Gods let *Granville*'s Verse recite,
And bring the Scenes of opening Fate to Light.   (423–26)

In keeping with the cyclical structure of the poem, the poet-historian Pope returns to his rural retirement and to the restored Windsor Forest with which the poem began. Implicit in the ending is the hope that the cycles of England's formerly unstable political history will be replaced by the linear progression through space and time of an England restored to her first principles of government. Pope's political use of contemporary historiography parallels his political use of history painting. He uses contemporary historiography and art theory to combine a cyclical with a linear representation of England's political development in *Windsor Forest*.

A number of twentieth-century critics have discussed the pictorial elements in the poetry of Pope, noting especially his colorful descriptions and scattered emblematic passages.[32] Norman Ault, for example, estimates that Pope uses a color-word on the average of once in every seven lines of *Windsor Forest*, and Robert J. Allen points out "the satiric imagery drawn from history-painting" in Pope's first-published *Imitation of Horace*.[33] For the most part, however, modern treatments of Pope's pictorial inclinations deal with details rather than the extent to which his knowledge of history painting and the emblematic tradition influenced the conception and organization of his poetry.[34] Here and in the following chapters I shall try to explain why Pope chooses the kinds of images he does and how he uses those images to organize his political poetry.

Windsor Forest is the only sustained verbal history-painting of Pope's poetic career. It is his first attempt at using political material in verse and also his only attempt at creating political panegyric.[35] After the Homeric translations, Pope's political poems are all satiric. The association of *Windsor Forest* with contemporary history-painting should not be surprising in light of the fact that poetry and painting were considered virtual twins.

In the Renaissance art treatises, which appeared first in Italy and France and later in England, Horace's words *ut pictura poesis* were constantly taken out of their original context to serve as justification for identifying painting with poetry. Classical authority for the relationship of the two arts was also found in the statement by Simonides that painting is mute poetry.[36] These doctrines underlay the theory of Paolo Lomazzo, whose *Trattato dell'Arte de la Pittura* (1584) became the first direct Italian influence on English artists when Richard Haydocke partially translated it in 1598. Thus, when Dryden, in order "to say something farther of [painting] and to make some observations on it, in relation to the likeness and agreement which it has with poetry, its sister," wrote his *A Parallel Betwixt Painting and Poetry* (1695), he applied the same rules to both arts.[37] Each was to represent heightened Nature in order to instruct through pleasure while observing the dramatic unities.

A basic difference between the arts was recognized, however, as early as 1637, when Franciscus Junius emphasized in his *De pictura veterum* that words could describe an action through the course of time while painting could only treat a point in time. Anticipating Gotthold Lessing's distinction between painting as a spatial and poetry as a temporal form, Junius stressed that the painter must very carefully illustrate that significant moment in a narrative "where it most concerneth him."[38] Dryden was well aware of this important difference between the two arts, as was Shaftesbury, who dealt with the subject in his unpublished "Second Characters." To Dryden the temporal limitation of painting was not necessarily a disadvantage, however: "I must say this to the advantage of painting, even above tragedy, that what this last represents in the space of many hours, the former shows us in one moment. The action, the passion, and the manners of so many persons as are contained in a picture are to be discerned at once, in the twinkling of an eye."[39]

The significant moment of *Windsor Forest* is its occasion, the Peace of Utrecht. To celebrate this event, Pope skillfully combines the temporal advantages of poetry with the spatial virtues of history painting. We may better see just how visual a poem *Windsor Forest* is if we compare it with the contemporary *Allegory of the Protestant Succession*, painted by Sir James Thornhill (Serjeant Painter to the King, 1720–32) in the Great Hall of Greenwich Hospital from 1708 to 1727.[40] Fortunately, we have two explications of Thornhill's painting, one by Richard Steele in 1714 and the other written by the artist himself, perhaps in 1730.[41] Here is Steele's description of the central figures in the painting:

> In the middle of the Oval are represented King *William* and Queen *Mary* sitting on a Throne under a great Pavilion or Purple Canopy, attended by the four Cardinal Vertues, as *Prudence, Temperance, Fortitude* and *Justice.*
>
> Over the Queen's Head is *Concord* with the *Fasces*, at her Feet two Doves, denoting mutual Concord and innocent Agreement, with *Cupid* holding the King's Scepter, while he is presenting *Peace* with the Lamb and Olive Branch, and *Liberty* expressed by the *Athenian* Cap, to *Europe*, who laying her Crowns at his Feet, receives them with an Air of Respect and Gratitude. The King tramples Tyranny under his Feet,

which is exprest by a *French* Personage, with his Leaden Crown falling off, his Chains, Yoke and Iron Sword broken to pieces, Cardinal's Cap, triple crown'd Mitres, etc. tumbling down. Just beneath is *Time* bringing *Truth* to Light, near which is a Figure of Architecture, holding a large Drawing of part of the Hospital with the Cupola, and pointing up to the Royal Founders, attended by the little *Genii* of her Art. Beneath her is *Wisdom* and *Heroick Virtue*, represented by *Pallas* and *Hercules*, destroying *Ambition, Envy, Covetousness, Detraction, Calumny*, with other Vices, which seem to fall to the Earth, the place of their more natural Abode.

Thornhill intended to adapt the conventional European tradition of history painting to glorify Whiggery and the Protestant succession that would soon bring George I to the throne, and to identify William and Mary rather than the Tory heroine Anne with the British triumph over the French that had been formalized by the Treaty of Utrecht. In contrast with Thornhill's painting, Pope's poem appears to have been intended as a complete rebuttal of the Whig version of recent history. The clear and distinct differences between Whig and Tory views of political events reflected the fact "that whatever the complexities of the body politic in the early years of the eighteenth century, its life-blood was the existence and conflict of two major parties."[42]

Pope indicates early in the poem that his is a Tory, perhaps even Jacobite allegiance, when he announces "Rich Industry sits smiling on the Plains, / And Peace and Plenty tell, a STUART reigns" (41–42). His satiric thrusts by means of exemplar history aimed at William III reinforce the impression that he found the legally ratified Protestant succession distasteful. He is direct in aligning himself with the Tories, but he wisely refuses to be more than suggestive about any Jacobite sympathies he may have had.[43]

Although Pope's poem and Thornhill's painting are widely divergent in content, they were quite similar in rhetorical intentions. Both were created as pieces of political propaganda, and the form chosen by the poet is very like that employed by the artist. In *Windsor Forest* Pope sees poets as rivals to history painters, handling the same subjects and executing them in the same emblematic manner. At one point he explicitly compares the two types of creators and concludes that the poetic product is longer-lasting than the pictorial:

With *Edward*'s Acts adorn the shining Page,
Stretch his long Triumphs down thro' ev'ry Age,
Draw Monarchs chain'd, and *Cressi*'s glorious Field,
The Lillies blazing on the Regal Shield.
Then, from her Roofs when *Verrio*'s Colours fall,

And leave inanimate the naked Wall;
Still in thy Song shou'd vanquish'd *France* appear,
And bleed for ever under *Britain*'s Spear.   (303–10)

The combination of emblem and allegory is as important to Thornhill's painting as it is to *Windsor Forest*, particularly as the poem rises to the emblematic prophetic vision of "Old Father *Thames*." For example, the malevolent forces overcome by "fair *Peace*" are expressed in the same allegorical and essentially pictorial manner in the poem as they are in the painting. In turn, poet and painter may have been inspired by Virgil (*Georgics* 3:37–39, and *Aeneid* 1:293–96):

Exil'd by Thee from Earth to deepest Hell,
In Brazen Bonds shall barb'rous *Discord* dwell:
Gigantick *Pride*, pale *Terror*, gloomy *Care*,
And mad *Ambition*, shall attend her there.
There purple *Vengeance* bath'd in Gore retires,
Her Weapons blunted, and extinct her Fires:
There hateful *Envy* her own Snakes shall feel,
And *Persecution* mourn her broken Wheel:
There *Faction* roar, *Rebellion* bite her Chain,
And gasping Furies thirst for Blood in vain.   (413–22)

With his repetition of the imperative "Behold!", "Old Father Thames" emphasizes the visual nature of his prophecy:

Behold! th'ascending *Villa*'s on my side
Project long Shadows o'er the Chrystal Tyde.
Behold! *Augusta*'s glitt'ring Spires increase,
And Temples rise, the beauteous Works of Peace.   (375–78)

Here new works of architecture symbolize the harmony of the future just as the "Figure of Architecture" does in the *Allegory of the Protestant Succession*. With his reference to the rainbow image, conventional emblem of Concord, Pope reiterates the notion of his poem as history painting in lines meant to link Anne with Elizabeth:

I see, I see where two fair Cities bend
Their ample Bow, a new *White-Hall* ascend!
There mighty Nations shall inquire their Doom,
The World's great Oracle in Times to come;
There Kings shall sue, and suppliant States be seen
Once more to bend before a *British* QUEEN.   (379–84)

We, too, are to see foreign kings kneeling before Anne as they had done before Elizabeth. Perhaps the rainbow image, associated with Elizabeth in the famous "Rainbow" portrait, is intended to strengthen the association Pope makes between the two queens.[44]

The scenes Pope draws are basically static, reflecting the temporal limitations placed on history painting. Their spatial quality may be made to encompass *"Peru"* and "other *Mexico*'s," but the emblematic description of "Old Father Thames" and the allegorical prophecy he utters stop the action of the poem. Maynard Mack refers to the static nature of *Windsor Forest* and its relationship to the tradition of Renaissance painting when he notes that Pope "follows the convention of Tudor and Stuart allegorical painting, where monarchs regularly lead and control figures of 'Peace and Plenty,' together with more orthodox members of the classical Pantheon. Behind his tableau lies also, we may guess, the tradition of emblematic pageants (this is a Windsor landscape after all, and the monarch is its climax) such as were acted at court and put on for royal progresses in the reigns of Elizabeth and James."[45]

Mack's likening *Windsor Forest* to "the tradition of emblematic pageants" is apt because the poem combines the spatial qualities of Thornhill's history painting with the temporal implications of a progress piece. As we have seen, the poem's action consists of the transmission of the British constitution from time immemorial to the reign of Anne. Allegorically, the heroine is "Fair *Liberty, Britannia*'s Goddess" (91), who takes the historical form of Elizabeth and Anne. A sense of stasis infuses the poem as a result of the historical assumptions underlying the work. The concepts of uniformitarianism and exemplar history give a feeling of continuity and repetition to the action as it moves through time.

Frequently, Pope interrupts the temporal progress of the poem in order to achieve a more strictly spatial, pictorial effect. Thus, after stating in the past tense that "Th' Oppressor rul'd Tyrannick where he *durst*" (74), Pope paints a scene in the historical present tense, the scene of the death of the Conqueror's son, William Rufus, in a hunting accident:

> But see the Man who spacious Regions gave
> A Waste for Beasts, himself deny'd a Grave!
> Stretch'd on the Lawn his second Hope survey,
> At once the Chaser and at once the Prey.
> Lo *Rufus*, tugging at the deadly Dart,
> Bleeds in the Forest, like a wounded Hart.   (79–84)

Similarly, Pope exhorts us to envision the scenes depicting the various seasons, a motif commonly found in Renaissance history painting, including that of Thornhill:

> See! from the Brake the whirring Pheasant springs,
> And mounts exulting on triumphant Wings;

3. Queen Elizabeth as Diana, Seated in Judgment Upon the Pope, As Calisto After Her Transgression (B.M. 12)

> Short is his Joy! he feels the fiery Wound,
> Flutters in Blood, and panting beats the Ground.
> Ah! what avail his glossie, varying Dyes,
> His Purple Crest, and Scarlet-circled Eyes,
> The vivid Green his shining Plumes unfold;
> His painted Wings, and Breast that flames with Gold?   (111–18)

Pope's use of the essentially static, spatial quality of history painting reinforces a sense of timelessness in the poem. There is forward movement and yet repetition in the action of the poem. The "characteristically Renaissance way of understanding the presence of pagan gods in a modern setting"[46] is employed to underscore this sense of timelessness in Pope's poem in the same way the appearance of pagan gods extends the implications of the allegory in Thornhill's painting.

Poet and painter draw their subjects in their official roles. William and Anne are more important as symbols than they are as individuals. Their

4. Romeyn de Hooghe, *Europe in Rouw* (B.M. 1420)

positions are stressed more than are their personalities. The emphasis on role rather than particular person is due in part to the tradition behind the composition of state portraits. Moreover, the placement of William and Mary in heaven and the thinly veiled allusions to Anne and the divine fiat reflect the common post-Reformation substitution of civic for theological subjects in paintings.[47]

Pope and Thornhill had more immediate political motivations, however, for treating their subject matter as they did. Each sought to defend and justify the reign of his favorite sovereign. Whereas Pope saw the reign of William and Mary as an interruption in the smooth flow of English history, Thornhill wanted to emphasize the traditional and conservative aspects of the reign of William and Mary, even though their coming was called a Glorious Revolution. The timelessness implicit in the painting's spatial quality seemed to support the Whig belief that the Protestant succession was a natural and appropriate continuation of British history, as normal as the representations of the seasons and the pagan gods surrounding William and Mary.

By creating a history painting in verse, Pope combines the timeless quality of the pictorial form with a sense of continuous action. Through exemplar history, Pope paints the development of the "ancient constitution" as one of both change and restoration. Pope defends Anne and the Stuart succession by portraying them as the result and reiteration of previous British history. He exploits the spatial nature of history painting when *Windsor Forest* reaches its climax with the emblematic vision of "Old Father Thames," establishing a structural pattern that Pope returns to often in his later, satiric, political poetry.

Except for the *New Dunciad*, however, Pope turns increasingly to a pictorial tradition different from history painting. Frequently the development of satiric prints is to history painting what mock-epic is to epic poetry. Thus, while Pope chose to use the conventions of the state portrait and history painting to depict the Tory theme of his political panegyric, there was already an alternative tradition available to him. James II and his consort were the objects of many nasty, personal attacks in the period immediately after their "abdication."[48] Primarily Dutch-inspired, popular prints sought to separate the man James II from his previous position as one way to increase public support for William and Mary. Turning the concept of history painting on its head, the prints showed James II as a man rather than a ruler, even to the point of casting doubt on the virtue of his wife and on the paternity of his son. Popular engravings, with their mixture of personal and emblematic expression, were aimed at a less-cultured audience than were history paintings, offering verbal satirists a greater variety of pictorial imagery to choose from.

This tradition of popular engravings goes back to the last half of the sixteenth century in England. One of the earliest such prints is an antipapal satire listed in the *British Museum Catalogue* (no. 12) as "Queen Elizabeth as Diana, Seated in Judgment Upon the Pope, As Calisto After Her Transgression." Produced in 1558 by Peter Miricenys, this is a Dutch print adapted from an engraving of Calisto brought before Diana. The naked Elizabeth, seated on her throne, is surrounded by female figures holding the heraldic shields of England's Protestant allies. Before the queen, the struggling pope is uncovered by allegorical figures of Time, identifiable by his emblematic hourglass and scythe, and Truth, a naked woman. Under the pope's seat are several hatching eggs, including one marked *"Inquisition."* This print, with its combination of images drawn from classical, historical, allegorical, emblematic, iconographic, and heraldic sources, is a good example of the richness of visual imagery poets of the eighteenth century shared with artists of popular engravings in the Renaissance.

The richness of imagery inherited from the Renaissance may be seen also in prints on the death of William III, prints that anticipate in theme and manner of representation what Pope does in *Windsor Forest*. For example, *Europe in Rouw* ("Europe in Mourning," B.M. 1420), by Romeyn de Hooghe, is an allegorical frontispiece to a Dutch tract of 1702. The print shows a weeping Europe, threatened by a Fury with fetters and a torch, lamenting to Jupiter the death of William III. As the tract itself explains, England and Europe will be saved from French tyranny by a return to Elizabethan rule, implicitly under Anne.[49] In Romeyn de Hooghe's 1702 print celebrating Anne's accession, *Heh Hoog-en Lager-Huys Van Engeland* ("The Upper and Lower Houses of Parliament in England," B.M. 1424), we see Anne on her throne, supported by Prosperity with her cornucopia and by infant genii holding heraldic shields and emblems of Justice and Commerce.

Pope's mingling in his poetic imagery of the visual conventions he inherited, first seen in *Windsor Forest*, becomes especially interesting when we watch him and his fellow satirists try to maintain the balance between particular and general satire so that their topical verse is transformed into more lasting literature. The visual resources available to verbal satirists during the 1730s and 1740s can best be seen in the graphic side of the war conducted against the government by Pope and his contemporaries.

CHAPTER II

"Measures Not Men": Political Rhetoric and Visual Satire, 1720–42

Our disputes were formerly, to say the truth, much more
about persons than things; or, at most, about particular
points of political conduct, in which we should have soon
agreed, if persons and personal interests had been less
concerned, and the blind prejudice of party less prevalent.
Whether the Big-endians or the Little-endians got the better,
I believe no man of sense and knowledge thought the
constitution concerned; notwithstanding all the clamor raised
at one time about the dangers of the church, and at another
time about the danger of the protestant succession. But the
case is, at this time, vastly altered.
    —Bolingbroke, *A Letter on the Spirit of Patriotism*, written
1736, published 1749

If I can but fill my Nitch,
I attempt no higher Pitch.
Leave to D'ANVERS and his Mate,
Maxims wise, to rule the State.
POULTNEY deep, accomplish'd ST. JOHNS,
Scourge the Villains with a Vengeance.
Let me, tho' the Smell be Noisom,
Strip their Bums; let CALEB hoyse 'em;
Then, apply ALECTO's Whip,
Till they wiggle, howl, and skip.
    —Jonathan Swift, *An Epistle to a Lady*, 1733

To understand fully the nature of engraved attacks on Sir Robert Walpole
and his ministry we must consider the kind of visual satire dominant before

he came to power. The popular title of Hogarth's first major print—*An Emblematical Print on the South Sea Scheme* (1721)—suggests that we see the engraving in light of the emblematic and allegorical traditions eighteenth-century print designers and buyers inherited.[1]

Although the viewers of popular engravings were often uneducated, they were frequently quite sophisticated in their knowledge of iconography. For example, the continued use of pageant-wagons in the Lord Mayor's Day parade kept before their eyes conventional medieval and Renaissance imagery, as well as more recent allegorical figures. "After all, with a few words of explanation by the speakers in the pageants, Restoration audiences were expected to integrate the visual iconography of Commerce and classical and Christian mythology."[2]

Although the pageantry of the Lord Mayor's Day parade declined during the first sixty years of the eighteenth century, the processions continued to be mounted. We have the illustrated pageant books for Elkanah Settle's pageant of 1708, which was never staged because of the death of Prince George of Denmark, Queen Anne's consort, and we know that in 1761 the pageants were fully revived. Between those dates, evidence of elaborate civic pageantry is scanty. But public displays of classical and allegorical iconography were readily available in other forms, at least to the English aristocracy, as illustrated in James Thornhill's engraving of the fireworks used to celebrate the Peace of Utrecht.[3]

The lower classes of English society were exposed to iconography in varying degrees of sophistication, from the esoteric pageantry of Masonic parades to the more exoteric imagery of funeral processions, trade-guild pageants, or events such as the procession planned (but never carried out) by the Whigs in 1711 to celebrate the anniversary of Queen Elizabeth's accession to the throne. All of these visual traditions were available to satirists. Let us consider briefly just two popular visual traditions that found their way into engraved and verbal political satire—the puppet show and playing cards.[4]

Increasingly popular in England since the sixteenth century, puppet shows brought polite art to the masses. In addition to Biblical and legendary plots inherited from the Middle Ages, puppet booths at fairgrounds throughout the eighteenth century performed adaptations of contemporary polite theater and included allegorical, historical, and mythical figures in their shows. Plots were drawn from chapbooks and popular ballads as well. A short list of some titles and the dates of their known eighteenth-century performances indicates the range of puppet theater: *The Creation of the World* (1712, 1717, 1733, 1756); *Queen Elizabeth* (1726, 1761); *Whittington* (1737, 1739, 1748, 1762); *The Last Year's Campaign* (Victory of Malplaquet) (1710); *The Universal Monarch defeated; or, The Queen of Hungary Tri-*

5. William Hogarth, *An Emblematical Print on the South Sea Scheme* (B.M. 1722)

umphant (1737); *The Seige of Troy* (1712, 1731, 1734); and *Mother Shipton, and the Downfall of Cardinal Wolsey* (1728). One of the "Smithfield Muses" brought to "the ear of Kings" in Pope's *Dunciad* would have been that of puppetry.

Puppet imagery finds its way into poetry before the eighteenth century. Addison wrote a Latin mock-epic on puppets in 1698, "Machinae Gesticulantes, anglice A Puppet Show"; and as early as 1682 Shadwell's *A Lenten Prologue refus'd by the Players* applies puppetry to politics: "Behind the curtain, by court-wires, with ease / They turn those pliant puppets as they please."[5] Swift uses the puppet metaphor for political ends in *Mad Mullinix and Timothy* (1728), as does Pope in *The Impertinent* (1733) and *An Epistle to Dr. Arbuthnot* (1735). The anonymous author of *The C{ourt} Unmasqu'd; or, The State Puppet-Show* (London, 1734) anticipates Pope's later use of the levee in the *Dunciad*:

. . . for lo! my *Minions* throng,
Thicken in Form, and justling crowd along,
In *suppliant Posture* at my *Shrine* they bow,
Rise with my *gracious* Nod, or *tumble low*."   (P.6)

And the anonymous *Politicks in Miniature; or, The Humours of Punch's Resignation. A Tragi-Comi-Farcical-Operatical Puppet-Show. With a New Scene of
Punch's Levee and the surprising Metamorphosis of his Puppets* (London, 1742)
combines a levee scene with the depiction of Walpole as Punch, the puppet-
master (or "Prompter," as he appears in *Arbuthnot*), an image we shall see
repeated in political engravings.

At least as widely known as the puppet theater was what might well be
called the iconography of playing cards. Engraved satires whose imagery
was modeled on the visual conventions of card decks had been aimed at
James II, and the tradition of satiric cards continued into the eighteenth
century. One example is the 1709 engraving *Queen Anne Triumphing Over
Popery and France* (B.M. 1492), of which the design forms the ace of hearts.
The 1720 *April-Kaart of Kaart Spel Van Momus Naar De Nieuwste Mode*
("April Card; or, Momus's Game at Cards after the Newest Fashion," B.M.
1642) is a satire on the South Sea Scheme. A fine example of the iconogra-
phy of playing cards used against Walpole is George Bickham's 1740 *The
{Cha}mpion; or, Even{ing} Adver{tiser}* (B.M. 2453).

Playing-card imagery appears in several political poems of the early
eighteenth-century. Gay's "A Ballad on Quadrille," first published in the
1728 Pope-Swift *Miscellanies*, uses the card metaphor to make a very general
political comment in a poem about how *"Satan"* (l. 5) "Sent forth his Spirit
call'd *Quadrille*" (6) to corrupt England:

Sure Cards he has for ev'ry Thing,
    Which well Court-Cards they name,
And Statesman-like, calls in the King,
    To help out a bad Game;
But if the Parties manage ill,
    The King is forc'd to lose *Codille*, etc.   (14–19)[6]

By the 1730s the card-game metaphor is used to attack Walpole, as in
the anonymous *The State Dunces. Inscribed to Mr. Pope. Part II. Being the Last*
(London, 1733):

DUNCES of *meaner Rank* now claim my Song.
Tho' not so *great* in Rank, not *less* in Fame,
Nor of *less use* in playing APPIUS' [Walpole's] *Game*;
All right *Court Cards* and ready at *Command*,
For if his *Game* you rightly understand,
The KNAVES are still the *best Cards* in his Hand.   (P. 14)

6. George Bickham, *The {Cha}mpion; or, Even{ing} Adver{tiser}* (B.M. 2453)

The metaphor returns in the anonymous *The Norfolk Gamester; or, The Art of Managing the Whole Pack, Even King, Queen, and Jack* (London, 1734), a collection of anti-Walpole poems on cribbage (e.g., "The N[o]R[fol]k Game of Cribbage; or, The Art of Winning All Ways") and chess ("The Game of Chess Verssify'd from the Craftsman"). But satirists were not restricted to purely popular traditions for visual sources.

There was also the double tradition of emblem books, which appealed to sophisticated and illiterate alike, because, as Mario Praz observes:

there is a contrast of tendencies in the use of the emblem. On one side emblematics, following in the tracks of hieroglyphics, aims at establishing a mode of expression which only a few may understand; in a word, an esoteric language. On the other hand, it aims at being a way of making ethical and religious truths accessible to all, even to the illiterate and to children, through the lure of pictures. That is, it follows the tradition of the *Biblia pauperum*, rather than the hieroglyphics, thus fulfilling in the seventeenth century the function performed by the bas-relief of the cathedrals in the Middle Ages.[7]

This double tradition of the emblem books did not disappear in the eighteenth century, as is commonly thought; emblem books were still produced, and the vitality and techniques of the tradition were absorbed by social and political satirists who expressed them in prints and poetry.[8] The integration of esoteric with exoteric meanings was well suited to the satirists' object of clothing offensive content in acceptable garb.

Andrea Alciati, an Italian lawyer, created the first emblem book in 1531, establishing the form and name of the genre. From then on, most emblem books can be considered as varying degrees of plagiarism of Alciati's original, itself largely a compilation of conventional figures, such as that of Fortune with her wheel. In their purest form, emblem books are collections of pictures accompanied by verbal explanations. The major difference between emblem books and later graphic satire is that emblem books are far less limited by the need for verisimilitude. The emblem and its explanatory verse were not occasional works produced to comment on contemporary events. In emblem books the picture is very often of an object whose allegorical significance is apparently arbitrary.[9] However, the conservative nature of the emblematic tradition restrained writers of emblem books from becoming idiosyncratic.

When satirists began to adopt emblems and to adapt them to their illustrations of contemporary social and political events, they found that the conventional arbitrariness of the emblematic tradition lent their occasional pieces a sense of timelessness and generality. We see an increasing mixture of emblematic with naturalistic details in satiric engravings of the early eighteenth century. The study of the development of the imagery in political satire then becomes an investigation of the changing proportions of emblematic and naturalistic representations found in both verse and engravings.

This combination of emblematic and naturalistic elements may be seen in Hogarth's *An Emblematical Print on the South Sea Scheme*, one of the most original English "Bubble" prints illustrating the collapse of the South Sea Company stock and its aftermath.[10] Most of the bubble prints listed in the *British Museum Catalogue of Political and Personal Satires* are either foreign in origin or Anglicized versions of French or Dutch engravings of the French stock collapse of 1720. In that year Paris panicked when the speculative stock bubble of the Scotsman John Law's Mississippi Company burst. There followed a flood of prints satirizing the discrepancy between the illusion and reality of, in Pope's words, "blest Paper Credit." [11] These French and Dutch prints served as models for English engravers later in the same year when the South Sea Company stock bubble also burst.

The South Sea Company had been organized to sell stock in order to take over at first part and later all of the national debt, on the assumption that the company would monopolize the trade with the Spanish New World guaranteed by the Asiento Treaty. Directors of the company systematically bribed government officials to get preferential treatment and avoid supervision. The madness of speculation swept England, and stock companies were begun "for exploiting services, inventions, and new trades: improvement in the coaling trade from Newcastle; large-scale funeral furnishing; chains of pawnbrokers; mines and exploitation in 'Argin' for gum arabic, ambergris and ostrich feathers, in 'The Isle of May' for salt, and in every part of discovered and undiscovered America." The list is only partial; soon stocks were advertised for sale in companies that had not yet decided what the money would be used for. [12]

The value of South Sea Company stock reached its peak of about £1,000 in the summer of 1720, but by the end of the year it fell to less than half that and took the ministry with it. An investigation into the scandal opened in 1721 and revealed widespread corruption in financial and government circles. Rumors extended the blame even to George I, who was officially governor of the company. When the bubble burst, stockjobbers, or sellers of stock, firmly established themselves on the list of conventional British villains. Walpole's alleged protection of as many important figures as possible who were involved with the company earned him a permanent association with the scandal as well as the title "Skreen-Master General."

Such, then, is the economic and political context of Hogarth's *An Emblematic Print on the South Sea Scheme*. As its title indicates, the print is unabashedly emblematic. We are struck also by the blatantly nonnaturalistic location: there was never such a place as this in London. "In an incredible study of perspective (even for him), he has placed the Guildhall at one side, the London Monument at the other, and St. Paul's and other London buildings between, each with its own vanishing point." [13] However, the structures Paulson identifies here are not realistically depicted in the engraving. We can identify the Guildhall because Hogarth has placed one of the gigantic statues actually found in the building on the roof of the edifice. As in typical emblematic representations, the allegorical significance of Gog, or Magog, and the Guildhall are more important than is verisimilitude. The monument on the right both is and is not the anti–Roman Catholic London Fire Monument. On Hogarth's structure foxes, or perhaps wolves, have replaced the dragon on the real monument. The form of the monument in the print is similar enough to the actual one that we do not doubt the allusion, but Hogarth's commemorates the South Sea Company: "THIS MONUMENT WAS ERECTED IN MEMORY OF THE DE-STRUCTION OF THIS CITY BY THE SOUTH SEA IN 1720."

An emblem, albeit an unusually complex one, *The South Sea Scheme* is accompanied by Hogarth's own explanatory verse:

See here the Causes why in London,
So many Men are made, and undone,
That Arts, and honest Trading drop,
To Swarm about the Devils Shop, (A)
Who Cuts out (B) Fortunes Golden Haunches,
Trapping their Souls with Lotts and Chances,
Shareing em from Blue Garters down
To all Blue Aprons in the Town.
Here all Religions flock together,
Like Tame and Wild Fowl of a Feather,
Leaving their strife Religious bustle,
Kneel down to play at pitch and Hustle; (C)
Thus when the Sheepherds are at play,
Their flocks must surely go Astray;
The woeful Cause that in these Times,
(E) Honour, and (D) honesty, are Crimes,
That publickly are punish'd by
(G) Self Interest, and (F) Vilany;
So much for Monys magick power
Guess at the Rest you find out more.

The last of these vigorously Hudibrastic lines reminds us of the double tradition of "emblematics"; while much in the print is explained by the verse, even more is left unexplained. In addition, Hogarth's debt to the didactic pictorial tradition of emblem books is reflected by the important role of religious elements in the verse and illustration. These religious elements include allusions "to the familiar motifs of the scourging of Christ, the casting of dice for Christ's robe, and the like."[14] But the religious dimension of this print is more than simply a matter of elements; the sum of those elements expresses a remarkably spiritual commentary on the madness of the South Sea Bubble.

At the center of the engraving stands the image of the god worshipped by the speculating madmen, the goat, conventional emblem of lust and the devil, which here expresses the larger idea of generalized *Cupiditas*. Lust in this print is not just of the flesh, although that variety is illustrated by a pair of the riders on the goat's merry-go-round. The more universal lust de-picted is that brought out by "Monys magick power," which encourages

"(G) Self Interest, and (F) Vilany" in the mob beneath their god. By dominating the sky, the goat takes the place of the sun, which is pointedly obscured by the gathering clouds. As idol of the people, the goat has replaced the sun, the familiar image in the emblem books of God and the all-seeing eye of Providence. [15]

The distant steeple of St. Paul's reminds us that this is a world ruled by *Cupiditas* and perhaps not even seen by Providence. In such a world, the Devil reigns, and men are the prisoners of Time because they bind themselves on the wheel of Fortune. The merry-go-round and the wheel to which "honesty" is tied are images of the wheel of Fortune. That Fortune herself is at the mercy of the Devil is clear from the view of "the Devils Shop, (A)" where the demonic figure is a combination of Satan and Father Time with his scythe. [16] Hogarth's clever conception of Satan–Father Time "Who Cuts out (B) Fortunes Golden Haunches" recalls the fact that as the summer of 1720 passed there was less and less of the South Sea Company's fortune to distribute. The importance of Fortune is indicated throughout the illustration by the heavy emphasis on those who gamble by "Trapping their Souls with Lotts and Chances." Even marriage has become an official gamble in the building labeled "*Raffleing for Husbands with Lottery Fortunes in Here*" and surmounted by the horns of cuckoldom. The horns link such treatment of marriage with the values represented by the similar horns on the heads of Satan on the left and the goat in the center, as well as by the pointed ears of that traditional emblem of deceit, the fox, on the right.

Hogarth includes images of proper behavior, but all of these normative standards are undercut. Formally balancing "the Sheepherds [who] are at play, / [While] Their flocks must surely go Astray," in the left-hand corner, is the allegorical figure of Trade languishing in the shadows in the lower-right corner of the print. Anticipating the distinction the Opposition to Walpole later made between wealth gained from trade and money reaped by financial speculation, Hogarth stresses the idea that credit schemes destroy trade. Below the merry-go-round and just left of the center of the print, the man with his hands in the air is either the only person who expresses dismay at the scene around him or the greediest of men, with his hands extended in hopes of gain. The alphabet on his hornbook identifies him as a teacher, but his rage, or his avarice, like that of an impotent satirist, is useless in the world gone mad. His arms upraised in disgust or greed merely make it easier for the dwarf next to him to pick his pocket.

Just right of center, beneath the merry-go-round, is a more complicated allusion to a normative standard. The depiction of honesty about to be broken on the wheel is an allusion to Jacques Callot's *La Roue*, but it is also probably intended as an ironic allusion to a similar image of Fortune subdued on her wheel. [17] Viewers of Hogarth's engraving, who were familiar

7. Henry Peacham, *Fortuna maior*

with emblem books, would have recognized the resemblance to such emblems as that of *Fortuna maior* in Henry Peacham's *Minerva Britanna* (London, 1612; p. 194). The meaning of Peacham's emblem is indicated by the
first four lines of its caption:

> Heere Povertie, doth conquered Fortune bind,
> And under keepes, like HERCULES in aw,
> The meaning is, the wise and valiant mind,
> In Povertie esteemes not Fate a straw.

The same idea is expressed in *Sapiens supra Fortunam, Emblema* 2 of *Emblemata Florentii Schoonhovii* (Amsterdam, 1648?).

By alluding to emblems expressing Man's proper relationship to Fortune, Hogarth underscores the insanity of a world whose values are upside
down. The inversion of values is further illustrated by the man with a ladder
near the center of the print. Probably intended as an ironic visual allusion to
the medieval image of the Ladder of Virtue, the ladder in *The South Sea
Scheme* will enable the man only to get closer to his goat.[18] Similarly, the
proper value of marriage is undercut by Hogarth's toying with perspective

to make the porch on which the women stand appear to be on the point of collapse. The shaft supporting the goat's merry-go-round, like the cross on St. Paul's, has a sinister bent, as if to emphasize the instability of the values it represents.[19] Indeed, the remarkable distortion of perspective throughout the engraving is probably intended to express formally the perversion of values so clearly indicated by Hogarth's iconography.

Framing the mad scene below them are the figures of the foxes, the goat, and Gog, or Magog. The crazy speculators are shown as if they were already in the pit of Hell, surrounded by smiling images of malevolence. In light of the many religious connotations in the print, Gog, or Magog, calls to mind the passage in *Revelation* which prophesizes that the hosts of Gog and Magog will lay siege to the city of God's people after Satan has been released from his dungeon.[20] Gog, or Magog, in the print has reason to smile, because in the godless world etched by Hogarth there is no danger that heavenly fire will consume the giant.

Hogarth is so successful in his use of general, emblematic iconography that *The South Sea Scheme* is readily understood on the medieval third level of interpretation—the moral. But his satire is at the same time undeniably topical; thus, the presence of the emblematic Satan–Father Time in the Guildhall, center of City politics, reminds viewers of contemporary rumors about governmental complicity in the South Sea Scandal. Although almost overwhelmed by their emblematic surroundings, there are a number of naturalistically presented figures on the ground. Some may even be caricatures. For example, the human face on one of the horses may be intended as a personal caricature, but time has removed the likelihood of positively identifying the model. Although emblematic and allegorical representations were more frequent in this period than were personal caricatures, the latter did exist as a tradition from which artists and writers could draw. The cross-eyed portrait of Daniel Defoe in George Bickham's engraving *The Whigs Medly: The Three False Brethren* (1711), or the well-known simian likeness of Pope in *Fronti Fides No. 1* (1728) (B.M. 1812) are two of the best examples of early eighteenth-century caricature.[21]

Since the late eighteenth century, some scholars have identified the fat man with upraised arms and a teacher's hornbook at his side as John Gay, and some have said the dwarf next to him is Alexander Pope.[22] I believe these identifications are incorrect. As Paulson notes, "Hogarth's only known connection with Pope . . . is through two prints that may not be his . . . plus one in which Pope is not directly attacked."[23] But if for the sake of argument we assume the dwarf to be Pope, the other figure is not likely then to be Gay. The early commentators thought the hornbook referred to the *Fables* Gay wrote for William Augustus, the duke of Cumberland, but William was not born until April 1721. If the dwarfish pickpocket is indeed Pope, then John Arbuthnot is probably his victim. Like Gay, Arbuthnot was notorious for his girth. Arbuthnot's important involvement with the South Sea Bubble and his former occupation of schoolteacher were objects of satire in Colley Cibber's *The Refusal*, first acted in February 1721.[24] However, the identification of these figures in Hogarth's print with real people is tenuous at best and grounded far more on wishful thinking than on any true evidence.

Further lessening the likelihood that Hogarth had Pope or anyone else specifically in mind when he composed this pair of figures is the probability that Hogarth borrowed the pickpocket and his victim from an earlier print. Frederick Antal has already identified a group of figures in Bernard Picart's *A Monument Dedicated to Posterity* (B.M. 1629) (originally a French print but "Englished" in 1720) as the source for Hogarth's gambling clergymen.[25] But Antal failed to notice the importance to Hogarth of the larger group of figures that forms a triangle at the right-hand side of Picart's print, with the stockjobber as its apex and a pocket-picking dwarf as one of its corners. This grouping bears a striking resemblance to the figures that form a similar triangle at the lower left-hand side of Hogarth's *The South Sea Scheme*. The corner of Hogarth's formal triangle is marked by one of two pickpockets robbing the fat victim; the schoolteacher's other pocket is apparently being robbed as well by the man on his right. Picart's print also has a pair of pickpockets, but in the original model for *The South Sea Scheme* group, the dwarf's victim is himself a thief, robbing the man who whispers in his ear. Hogarth has replaced the stockjobber who holds out papers to the crowd in Picart's engraving with the blatantly emblematic Satan—Father Time clutching Fortune's flesh at the apex of the triangle in his own print. Hogarth has taken Picart's devil out of the clouds and placed him in the Guildhall.

Hogarth's substitution of the Devil for Picart's more naturalistic figure of the stockjobber reflects his concern to keep *An Emblematical Print on the South Sea Scheme* as general and allegorical as possible. His transformation of Picart's stockjobber is consistent with his adaptation of the gamblers in *A Monument Dedicated to Posterity*: in both instances he renders the realistic emblematic. The more naturalistically represented figures in Hogarth's print, including those often thought to have been intended as personal caricatures, are overwhelmed by their emblematic surroundings. But Hogarth in this print is no servile follower of earlier artists; he readily transforms and inverts traditional imagery as he adapts earlier, general, religious iconography for his topical, social, and political satire. Unrestricted by the emblematic tradition, Hogarth exploits and even extends it to make universal and spiritual his occasional and political comment on the events of 1720.

8. Bernard Picart, *A Monument Dedicated to Posterity* (B.M. 1629)

Still very much alive in 1726, when Bolingbroke helped to organize Walpole's opponents, were the poetic and pictorial traditions we have been discussing in relation to *Windsor Forest* and the *South Sea Scheme*. Since reliable narrative histories of Walpole's twenty years in power are readily available, I shall limit my discussion here to the rhetorical strategy of the Opposition, reflected in *The Craftsman* and prints of the period from 1720 to 1742. In the following chapters we shall look at specific examples of how Pope and others transferred the Opposition's rhetorical tactics in prose and pictures to poetry.

In the past twenty years, the warmest debate among historians of eighteenth-century England has been over to what extent Sir Lewis Namier's analysis of the British political structure at midcentury is applicable to the first forty years of the century.[26] Some of Namier's followers seek to apply to the first half of the century his thesis that issues and professed political principles had virtually no influence on the structure of English politics at the accession of George III. They argue that throughout the eighteenth century political principles were essentially irrelevant; only personalities, family relationships, and the "insatiable ambition for power"[27] really influenced politicians.

Disagreeing with the Namierites are historians who argue that political conflicts not only expressed a drive for power, but were also "concerned with real issues, involving the conflict of sincerely held principles."[28] These non-Namierite historians spend a great deal of time describing the positions of the Opposition and arguing that the ideology found in Bolingbroke's writings was sincere. Recently Quentin Skinner has argued convincingly that whether only one side is correct probably does not really matter. The Namierites may be right in seeing the members of Walpole's Opposition as insincere and self-interested when they mouthed their principles and chose their issues. Recognition of those principles and issues is essential to understanding political behavior in the early eighteenth century, but the question of sincerity is not relevant to a discussion of the nature of the imagery and presentation of history in Opposition prose, prints, and poetry.

Bolingbroke and others expressed a "politics of nostalgia."[29] The loose coalition of Tories, Jacobites, and discontented Whigs who fought Walpole revealed an uneasiness about the "Financial Revolution" that was occurring in early eighteenth-century England.[30] Pope makes frequent references to the shift from power based on land ownership to power based on financial speculation, or "paper credit." Many outside the ministry argued that Walpole must be overthrown (and, by implication, the "Financial Revolution" reversed) so that "The *old Country Interest* of the best Families in the Kingdom (which hath lately been almost swallow'd up by *Stock-jobbers* and *Monied-Upstarts*) will return to its former natural Channel" (*Craftsman*, no.

151). They feared that oligarchic rule would result from the acquisition of overwhelming economic influence by a small group of Walpolean supporters (*Craftsman*, no. 304).

This economic fear explains much of Pope's animus toward Peter Walter, who was instrumental in transferring wealth from the land to upstarts like himself:

> These are the talents that adorn them all,
> From wicked Waters ev'n to godly—
> Not more of Simony beneath black Gowns,
> Nor more of Bastardy in heirs to Crowns.
> In shillings and in pence at first they deal,
> And steal so little, few perceive they steal;
> Till like the Sea, they compass all the land,
> From Scots to Wight, from Mount to Dover strand.
>
> (*The Second Satire of Dr. John Donne*, 79–86)

Political, religious, and social traditions were in disarray, and little legitimizing ideology was left to counterbalance the amoral use of law: "Then strongly fencing ill-got wealth by law, / Indentures, Cov'nants, Articles they draw" (93–94).[31] To the Opposition the unconstitutional actions of Walpole were intended to institutionalize the results of the new economic developments depicted in Hogarth's *South Sea Scheme*.

Bolingbroke and his allies created the weekly journal *The Craftsman* as their most important vehicle for attacking ministerial policies. In the first issue they announced their intention to expose "how craft predominates in all professions" and especially in "the mystery of statecraft." Behind the persona of Caleb D'Anvers, fictitious author of most of *The Craftsman*, they incessantly castigated Walpole and the results of England's "Financial Revolution" while espousing their own "politics of nostalgia." The birth of *The Craftsman* followed a series of meetings among Daniel and William Pulteney, Chesterfield, Bathurst, Pope, Arbuthnot, Swift, and Gay at Bolingbroke's country estate, Dawley.[32] With the aid of the two Pulteneys, Bolingbroke published the first issue on 5 December 1726, and the journal remained the primary propaganda organ aimed at Walpole for the next twelve years.[33] In its weekly issues important works such as Bolingbroke's "Vision of Camilick," his *Remarks on the History of England*, and his *Dissertation upon Parties* first appeared. For the sake of convenience, I shall assume that all the ideas and arguments in *The Craftsman* reflect those of Bolingbroke, since identifying the individual author of each number is probably impossible.[34] In addition to being a reliable expression of Bolingbroke's thoughts, *The Craftsman*, with its wide circulation and high level of literary quality, is the most attractive source for studying the point of view of the Opposition.[35]

The kind of opposition to the ruling government that Bolingbroke and his allies practiced was technically unconstitutional. To deal with this problem, Bolingbroke devised a brilliant rhetorical strategy, accurately described here by Quentin Skinner:

> the essence of Bolingbroke's *coup* lay in matching this principle [of patriotism] to his party's practice in just such a way as to be able to imply to the Whigs, with maximum plausibility, that their own Ministry was pursuing at least two policies [maintenance of a standing army and the corruption of Parliament] known to every good Whig to be peculiarly liable to endanger English political liberties. This made it possible to leave the correspondingly strong impression that to oppose these precise policies was, in the circumstances, to be concerned, above all with the idea of preserving English political liberties. But to be concerned with the preservation of English political liberties was what was meant at the time by being a true patriot. This in turn enabled Bolingbroke and his party to claim with maximum plausibility that they were genuinely motivated by the spirit of patriotism. And this provided them with the element of justification which . . . was essential if they were to be able to continue with the successful pursuit of their otherwise unconstitutional policy of conducting a "formed opposition" to the King's chosen Ministry.[36]

Such justification was essential for an effective political program of opposition because the Tory party, as it had been known from the Exclusion Crisis to the death of Anne, no longer posed a threat to assume power in the second quarter of the eighteenth century.[37] Bolingbroke's strategy initiated a fight over who had inherited the legacy of the Glorious Revolution, much as modern American political parties might argue over who inherited the tradition of Lincoln. Bolingbroke managed to turn the charge of unconstitutional behavior back onto the ministry of Walpole by arguing that the former conflict between Whig and Tory parties was no longer an accurate description of current political reality. He succeeded in shifting the argument to one over who were the true Whigs and therefore the true patriots. According to *The Craftsman*, the political war in the reign of Walpole was fought not between Whig and Tory but between False Whig and True Whig.

The struggle over the inheritance of the Glorious Revolution was reflected in the contention between *The Craftsman* and ministerial writers (e.g., in the *London Journal, Free Briton, Courant, British Journal,*

Reed's Journal, Weekly Register, Flying Post, and the *Hyp Doctor*) over the tradition of late-seventeenth- and early-eighteenth-century Whig political theory.[38] For example, *Cato's Letters* (1724), published originally by the two "eighteenth-century Commonwealthmen" John Trenchard and Thomas Gordon, were quoted approvingly by both sides (e.g., *Craftsman*, nos. 268, 269, 275, 278, 288, etc.). The main teachings of these and other early Whig theorists expressed the same political principles that underlie *Windsor Forest*: repeatedly, the Polybian ideal of a balance of powers is endangered by the corruption Machiavelli warned against. But whereas Pope stressed force, the Whig "Commonwealthman" emphasized financial corruption or standing armies as the greatest threat to the constitutional balance of powers. These Whig writers, such as Andrew Fletcher, Walter Moyle, and John Trenchard, warned of more subtle and usually internal threats to English liberty than the usurpation by William I Pope describes in *Windsor Forest*. In succeeding chapters I will show that Pope adopted the "Commonwealthman" emphases in his later political poetry in ways Bolingbroke had done in the 1720s.

Bolingbroke, in his attempt to claim the legacy of 1688, embraced the Whig belief that the preservation of the ancient constitution depends on maintaining the balance of powers within the government and that that balance is threatened by corruption and standing armies. Throughout *The Craftsman*, and especially in the *Remarks on the History of England* and the *Dissertation upon Parties*, Bolingbroke argued that these true Whig ideals were upheld by the Opposition alone. He contended that he and his allies expressed the spirit of liberty, while Walpole and his party represented the spirit of factionalism: "'A spirit of liberty will be always and wholly concerned about national interests, and very indifferent about personal and private interests. On the contrary, a spirit of faction will be always and wholly concerned about these, and very indifferent about the others'" (*Remarks, Letter* 2). To counter ministerial charges that the Opposition were in reality unreformed Tories and Jacobites, Bolingbroke answered that not only was the force of Jacobitism negligible, but now virtually every Englishman accepted the Revolution of 1688 and the House of Hanover:

> The spirit of jacobitism is not only gone, but it will appear to be gone in such a manner as to leave no room to apprehend its return. . . .
>
> The whole bulk of the people hath been brought by the revolution, and by the present settlement of the crown, to entertain principles which very few of us defended in my younger days. The safety and welfare of the nation are now the first and principal objects of regard. (*Remarks, Letter* 2)

Indeed, Bolingbroke asserted that the threat the old royalist Tory party had formerly posed to liberty and the proper constitutional balance of powers still existed, only now in the form of Walpole and his followers, who called themselves Whigs, but who, Bolingbroke charged, sought to augment the power of the Crown by making excessive claims for prerogative and by advocating the practice of corruption:

> Let me conjure them, in the name of modesty, to call themselves Whigs no longer. It is time they should lay that appellation aside, since it will not be hard to prove, from the general tenor of their writings, that the maxims they advance, the doctrines they inculcate, and the conduct they recommend, lead to the destruction of civil liberty, as much as the political lessons of Sibthorpe, Manwaring, or archbishop Laud himself. They and their followers declared themselves directly against liberty. (*Remarks, Letter* 7)

Whig and Tory had been rather easily distinguished in the previous century. Perhaps the most succinct definition of the seventeenth-century Whig and Tory Parties is one Bolingbroke gives in the *Dissertation*:

> The power and majesty of the people, an original contract, the authority and independency of parliament, liberty, resistance, exclusion, abdication, deposition; these were ideas associated, at that time, to the idea of a whig, . . .
>
> Divine hereditary, indefeasible right, lineal succession, passive obedience, prerogative, non-resistance, slavery, nay, and sometimes popery, too, were associated in many minds to the idea of a tory.

But by the 1730s "the bulk of both parties are really united; united on principles of liberty, in opposition to an obscure remnant [the Jacobites] of one party, who disown those principles, and a mercenary detachment [the faction of Walpole and his ministerial followers] from the other who betray them" (*Works* 2 : 23–29). Bolingbroke here manages to link Walpole with the Jacobites.

Part of the coup Skinner praises was Bolingbroke's redefinition of the political structure under the administration of Walpole: "nothing can be more ridiculous than to preserve the nominal division of whig and tory parties, which subsisted before the revolution, when the difference of principles, that could alone make the distinction real, exists no longer; so nothing can be more reasonable than to admit the nominal division of constitutionists and anti-constitutionists, or of a court and a country-party, at this time, when an avowed difference of principles makes this distinction real" (*Works* 2 : 168). Of course, in their opposition to ministerial corruption of Parliament, Bolingbroke and his supporters proved themselves to be the "constitutionist country-party."

We have already touched on the tactical use of history in discussing the Opposition's strategy of removing the mantle of the Glorious Revolution from Walpolean Whigs and placing it on their own shoulders. J. P. Kenyon has pointed out that "the English approach to political thought was strictly legalistic and historical; roughly speaking, oldest was best, and the antecedents of any doctrine were almost as important as its intellectual validity."[39] To cast themselves as the true heirs of the Whig revolution of 1688 required an early form of what we would now call revisionist history.

Bolingbroke took the Renaissance concepts of uniformitarianism, exemplar history, and the ancient constitution and applied them unrelentingly against Walpole. In *The Craftsman*, no. 7, Bolingbroke reminds the reader what is to be done with the historical accounts he will find in this journal: "The Application of Passages of the *Roman* Story to our Times is become so common and trite a Way of satirizing the Persons of the present Age, that no Man, who has a tolerable Genius, or the least Invention of his own, will condescend to do it, . . . The Author need never be at the Trouble to make the Application. Every Child in the Street knows well enough upon whom to fix it." The very nature of the Opposition program compelled Bolingbroke to attack Walpole by means of historical precedent. Bolingbroke sought to prove that the present ministry had broken with English political traditions in ways that would lead to the loss of liberty in the 1730s. If he could show that Walpole's measures were the same that had earlier threatened the constitution, Bolingbroke could convincingly defend the need and legitimacy of an opposition. His case would be even stronger if he could give examples from other lands and other times to illustrate the constant dangers of Walpolean measures.

Bolingbroke used two traditional political fictions to emphasize the dangers—past, present, and future—of various ministerial actions: "the King can do no wrong," and the Opposition attacks "measures not men." The first of these justified the attack on Walpole's ministry, "for as the Maxim of our Law, that *the King can do no wrong*, has no other Meaning, than that his Ministers ought to be accountable for all Mismanagement and Male-Administration [*sic*], so it is highly unreasonable to point any Reflections against the Prince himself" (*Craftsman*, no. 7). Bolingbroke repeatedly sought to distinguish between attacks on the king, which would be undeniable treason, and attacks on the deeds of the king's ministers. He was careful to note that he was attacking the deeds, "the measures of a *Minister*," rather than the man himself. To attack Walpole personally would have been in effect to attack the king's prerogative to choose his own minister. The king chose the man to be his minister; the man in his role as minister chose the measures. Besides, when the minister was as corrupt as the Opposition alleged Walpole to be, "[*The Craftsman*] had enough to say of the *Minister*, and lay under no Necessity of attacking the *Man*" (Dedication to the volumes collected in 1737). The political importance of the doctrine "measures not men" was illustrated in 1741 when the Jacobite William Shippen and his followers refused to vote for Walpole's removal from office on the grounds that the motion constituted an assault on the king's prerogative. At times, *The Craftsman* accepted the fiction that somehow policies could be changed without changing the men behind them: "It is a good, old-fashion'd Observation of my Lord *Bacon* that when *Ministers* have render'd Themselves odious to the People, by *impoverishing* and oppressing Them, the best Remedy is to conciliate their Minds by an *Alteration of Measures*" (no. 202). Here, by stressing that this is an "old-fashion'd Observation" of a recognized authority, Bolingbroke again reiterated the identification of his position with English political tradition.

Occasionally, however, Bolingbroke and the other "Patriots" acknowledged that the doctrine of measures not men was more a convenient rhetorical tactic than a rule to be strictly observed. Even Bolingbroke admitted that *The Craftsman* must be more careful to follow the rule, "for He ought most certainly to confine Himself to *Things*, and meddle with *Persons* as little as possible."[40] Similarly, the journal itself said it tried to distinguish between the private and public capacities of politicians: "We thought it necessary to oppose *some Measures* . . . and *Those*, who were carrying them on, might esteem This a *personal Attack*; but it was an Attack on their *publick Characters*; and if we now and then dropt a little cursory Allusion to some particular Circumstances, which had no Relation to their *ministerial Capacity*, it was *descriptive* only, and contain'd no Reflections on their *moral Characters*, as private Men" (Dedication to the volumes collected in 1731). The assailants of Walpole's ministry certainly realized that individuals as well as practices would have to be changed (e.g., *Craftsman*, no. 373), but in general the concept of "measures not men" was followed. Perhaps the emphasis was on measures rather than men because the Opposition and ministry were really disputing constitutional issues in the 1730s, and it was rhetorically more effective to emphasize actions and beliefs than to descend to attacking merely morals and personalities. In his political poetry Pope repeatedly seeks to maintain a balance between general and personal satire.

The Opposition had to be concerned not only with being politically effective, but also with avoiding legal prosecution. Pope, for example, had to consider the possibility of being charged with criminal libel for his allusions to William III in *Windsor Forest*, because, as Laurence Hanson reminds us, "the common law held that just as it was possible to libel a dead man, since his descendants might be moved to breaches of the peace against the offender, so it was possible to libel a dead sovereign, or the State itself, which never dies." But for Pope in 1713 the danger of prosecution was remote, whereas the legal threat to Walpole's opponents was very immediate during the 1720s and 1730s. Thus, in the first four years of publication, eight issues of *The Craftsman* provoked warrants for libel. An opposition journal had to be careful in an age when "a seditious libel . . . was one likely to bring into hatred or contempt, or to excite disaffection against, the King and his heirs, the government, the Houses of Parliament, or the administration of justice, or to incite people to alter anything in Church or State by other than lawful means."[41] Bolingbroke had good legal as well as political reason to argue that his was the voice of true Whig principles and that the ministry of Walpole posed a threat to the English constitution.[42] In 1731 a Middlesex grand jury indicted William Rayner for publishing the pamphlet *Robin's Game; or, Seven's the Main. Being an Explanation of Caleb D'Anvers' Seven Egyptian Hieroglyphicks prefix'd to the Seven Volumes of the Craftsman.* At the same time, the print *Robin's Reign; or, Seven's the Main* (B.M. 1822) itself was indicted, one of the rare times the government tried to censor a print. Rayner was eventually convicted, but apparently no action was taken against the designers and engravers of the print. Political writing was obviously a more dangerous occupation than was political engraving.

In *The Importance of the Guardian Considered* (1713) Swift listed several of the standard satiric techniques used to evade arrest for libel: "First, we are careful never to print a man's name out at length; but as I do that of Mr. St——le: So that although every body alive knows who I mean, the plaintiff can have no redress in any court of justice. Secondly, by putting cases; Thirdly, by insinuations; Fourthly, by celebrating the actions of others, who acted directly contrary to the persons we would reflect on; Fifthly, by nicknames, either commonly known or stamped for the purpose, which every body can tell how to apply."[43] To this recipe for legally safe satire, Bolingbroke contributed a large fund of readily recognizable allegories, allusions, and parallels through his historical justification of the anti-ministerial cause. His continuous appeal to the political tradition supposedly underlying the program of Walpole's enemies greatly encouraged verbal and graphic satirists to turn to other traditional ways of expressing the ideology of Bolingbroke and his supporters. Bolingbroke's need to evade libel laws, coupled with his assertion that his was a position supported by historical precedent, helped create the greatest age of English satire. Satirists had political as well as legal motivations to make their works at once general and particular. The verbal and graphic attempts to reflect a purposely timeless political ideology often resulted in equally timeless literary and artistic productions. Just as Bolingbroke sought to

The Stature of a
Great Man   or the English   Colossus.

Why Man, he doth bestride ye narrow World | Men at some times are Masters of their fates
like a Colossus, and we petty Men | The fault, dear P——y is not in our Stars,
Walk under his huge Legs, & peep about | But in ourselves, that we are Underlings.
To find our selves dishonourable Graves. | Shakespear.

10. *The Stature of a Great Man; or, The English Colossus* (B.M. 2458)

11. *The Cardinal in the Dumps: The Preferment of the Barber's Block, With the Head of the Colossus* (B.M. 2454)

12. *Idol-Worship; or, The Way to Preferment* (B.M. 2447)

catured because the emphasis is on his position rather than his personality. This fact is expressed in the lines adapted from Shakespeare's *Julius Caesar* that accompany the print:

"Why Man, he doth bestride ye narrow World
Like a Colossus, and we, petty Men
Walk under his huge Legs, and peep about
To find out Selves, dishonourable Graves.
Men at some times are Masters of their fates:
The fault, dear P[ultene]y, is not in our Stars,
But in our Selves, that we are Underlings."

Shakespeare

The Stature of a Great Man; or, The English Colossus is alluded to in *The Cardinal in the Dumps: The Preferment of the Barber's Block With the Head of the Colossus* (B.M. 2454), an engraving published in July 1740 to celebrate Admiral Vernon's success at Porto Bello and the supposed humiliation of Cardinal Fleury. Vernon's victory increased public discontent with the pacific foreign policy of Walpole, whose colossal head appears on a pole in this engraving.

In another colossus print, *Idol-Worship; or, The Way to Preferment* (B.M. 2447), also published in 1740 (and advertised in *The Craftsman*), the charge of parliamentary subservience is coupled with another attack on Walpole's position as prime minister.[46] But the quotation accompanying the engraving implies that the king shares the blame with Walpole for having created an unconstitutional monster:

And Henry the KING made unto himself a great IDOL, the likeness of which was not in Heaven above, nor in the Earth beneath; and he reared up his Head unto ye Clouds, and extended his Arm over all ye Land; His Legs also were as ye Posts of a Gate, or as an Arch stretched forth over ye Doors of all ye Publick Offices in ye Land, and whosoever went out, or whosoever came in, passed beneath, and with Idolatrous Reverence lift up their Eyes, and kissed ye Cheeks of ye Postern. "Chronicle of the Kings, page 51."

The colossus image finds its way into Opposition poetic satire as well. *The Mi{ni}st{eria}l Light* (London, 1741), a collection of prose and verse, includes "The Sturdy Beggars: Their Prayer to the Colossus of the Sun" and "The Colossus: A Tale." The latter could serve as a design for a print:

He was Brazen all over, from Head to the Foot,
Gold burnish'd his Face, and Posteriours to boot;
However they worshipp'd, before or behind,
The Rays from each Part struck them instantly Blind.

13. Henry Peacham, *Minerva Britanna*

With an earthquake, Fortune destroys this colossus set up as a false god.

These colossus poems and prints could have been inspired by the correspondent in *The Craftsman*, no. 62, who offered advice to a would-be painter of ministerial foreign policy: "How could one form a Picture to remember such a *Heap of Absurdities*? . . . Image to yourself the *Map of Europe*, and where the *Streights of Gibraltar* are described, place the Figure of the *great Man* you design to vindicate, like a *Colossus*, stradling across *those* Streights, with *Ships* sailing between his Legs, and he p—ss——g upon them as they pass; sinking some, and spoiling the Cargo of others; the Fortress of Gibraltar trampled upon and demolished under one of his Feet."

Caleb D'Anvers returned to the subject of colossus imagery in *The Craftsman*, no. 98, which contains "an Account of the triumphal Edifices, Arches and other magnificent Preparations, which were made at *Antwerp*, in the Year 1549, for the Reception of *Philip* Prince of *Spain*." One of these "*triumphal Monuments*" is the colossus of Antwerp, "a vast and prodigious GIANT, being no less than *three and twenty Feet high*." The figure was created to celebrate the conquest of the giant "*Antigonus*" by "*Salvius Brabon*," an early version of Bolingbroke's "Patriot King." For "*political*

Instruction" D'Anvers proceeds to interpret this statue, as he says, "in a *mythological* and *figurative* Sense" because he "cannot suppose they [the creators of such works] design'd that Posterity should understand them in a *literal* Sense, since there are few of those venerable Fables, which do not evidently contain some valuable Piece of History or excellent Moral."

The application to Walpole is soon apparent. D'Anvers says that the colossus "*Antigonus* seems to intimate to us that the Province, where the City of *Antwerp* now stands, was formerly infested by some insolent, cruel, over-grown, rapacious *great* Man (a GIANT in *Wickedness* rather than in *Stature*) who lorded it over his Fellow-Subjects and delighted in persecuting Those, who refused to comply with or even to murmur at his *grievous Demands* and *Impositions*."

In turn, all the colossus depictions may be traced back to the emblem books of the seventeenth century where we find the figure in Henry Peacham's *Minerva Britanna* (London, 1612).[47] The verse explanation of this emblem indicates that the designer of *Idol-Worship* was being traditional when he linked the king with the colossus:

The Monuments that mightie Monarches reare,
COLOSSO's statiies, and Pyramids high,
In tract of time, doe moulder downe and weare,
Ne leaue they any little memorie,
The Passenger may warned be to say,
They had their being here, another day.

Peachum's emphasis on the colossus figure as an image of transience and vanity was repeated in *The Craftsman's* giant of Antwerp, whose "*wooden Sceptre* [implied] that his Power would not *last long*." The designer of *The Night Visit; or, The Relapse: With the Pranks of Bob Fox the Jugler, while Steward to Lady Brit, display'd on a Screen* (1742) (B.M. 2559) maintained the association between the colossus and transience in the penultimate scene on the screen. Published just a month after Walpole's resignation, this print shows the previously impressive colossus falling to the earth, figuratively expressing the title, "The Flight," of this segment of the engraving.

Just as Hogarth transformed conventional emblems and adapted them to a contemporary setting in *The South Sea Scheme*, Opposition rhetoricians in prose and prints adapted the emblematic colossus figure to the political struggle against Walpole. By particularizing the image so that it was readily identifiable with the prime minister, his opponents managed to attack a specific minister without losing a sense of continuity with the past. Readers and viewers were meant to recognize that Walpole's preeminence in 1740 was as temporary and futile as any other image set up by a glory-hungry king. The lack of caricature reinforced the Opposition tactic of attacking measures not men.

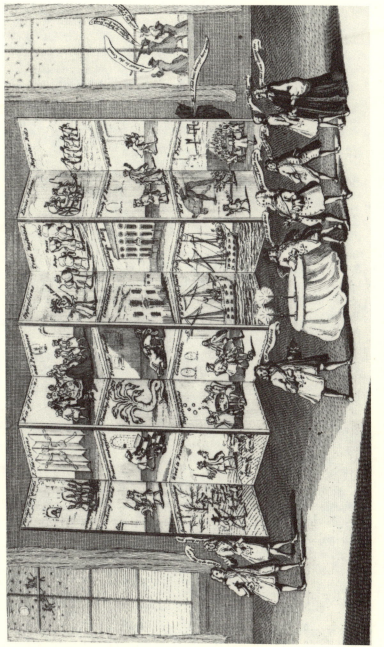

14. *The Night Visit; or, The Relapse: With the Pranks of Bob Fox the Jugler, while Steward to Lady Brit, display'd on a Screen* (B.M. 2559)

Besides reflecting the Opposition's ideological ties with the past and the tactic of attacking measures not men, the use of emblematic and allegorical forms of expression served as a sort of secular, political *Biblia pauperum*. Political truths, as Bolingbroke and his supporters saw them, could be taught through traditional iconography to even the illiterate masses. And in light of the influence of the crowd during the Sacheverell affair, the Excise Crisis, and the Jew Bill uproar, the masses were worth manipulating. In the following chapters we shall find that poets too were aware of the rhetorical effectiveness of emblematic satire. During the tumultuous reaction to Walpole's proposed Excise Bill in 1733, *The Craftsman*, no. 345, contended that prints and emblems were the most common forms of expressing popular dissatisfaction:

> When the People find Themselves generally aggrieved, They are apt to manifest their Resentment in satyrical Ballads, Allegories, By-sayings, and ironical Points of low Wit. They sometimes go farther, and break out into hieroglyphical Expressions of their Anger against the *Person*, whom They conceive to be the Projector of any Injury done, or intended to be done Them. . . . One cannot walk the Streets without hearing some *little, gibing Piece of Wit*, or seeing some *Droll-Emblem*, design'd to express the general Dislike of the People to *this Sort of Taxation*.

This issue goes on to mention several of the more popular prints and drawings, including the woodcut of *Britannia Excisa* (B.M. 1936), which was given the following account:

> As I was sauntering some Days ago through *Lincoln's-Inn-Fields*, I saw a Groupe of People, who seem'd to be exceedingly delighted with a *little, political Ditty*, chaunted out to them in a rough Base, and containing several humourous Reflections on *this Project* [i.e., the Excise Bill]; which was represented to them on a wooden Cut, (by Way of Frontispiece) under the Figure of a *devouring Dragon*, with several Heads. *This Monster* drew a Chariot; in which sat a very *portly Person*, receiving prodigious Sums of Gold, which issued from one of the Mouths of the *Beast*, and shower'd directly into his Lap. The *Chaunter* and his *Audience* seem'd extremely pleased with each other, and did not part till He had disposed of all his Goods.

To celebrate the antiministerial triumph in the Excise Crisis, *The Craftsman* published an "Advertisement" intended to associate the Opposition cause with England's greatest pictorial satirist:

> *In a few days will be publish'd, The* Projector's LOOKING-GLASS, *or, The last dying Words and Confession of* Sir ROBERT MARRAL, *premier*

Exciseman of Great Britain, *who was burnt in* Fleet-street *on* Wednesday *the* 11th *Instant; taken faithfully from his own Mouth at the Place of Execution. To which will be prefix'd his Effigies, drawn upon the Spot and curiously engraven by* Mr. H—g——th. (*Craftsman*, no. 355)

As far as we know, Hogarth never engraved such a print.

Prints such as *The Stature of a Great Man; or, The English Colossus* that exploited the tactic of parallel history presumably were aimed at a more literate audience. A good example is Hogarth's *Henry the Eighth and Anne Boleyn* (ca. 1728–29). The occasion for this print was Colley Cibber's production of Shakespeare's *Henry VIII*, which enjoyed great popularity when performed in October 1727 to celebrate the coronation of George II. Hogarth compared Walpole to Wolsey to emphasize Walpole's alleged designs on the throne, which it was believed would be thwarted by the succession of a new king. But Walpole soon proved as useful to George II as he had to George I. *The Craftsman* often exhibited Wolsey as a type of the evil, corrupt prime minister, a type used not only by Hogarth but also by the anonymous designer of "a satire on Sir Robert Walpole comparing him with Cardinal Wolsey" (B.M. 1925). Engraved around the frame of the medallion are the words "Wolsey and his successor here in one behold, both serv'd their masters both their country sold."

Wolsey was also frequently used as a type of the overreaching minister doomed to fall, whose infamous career and end paralleled and predicted Walpole's. Thus, the two ministers are joined in the anonymous *Are These Things So? The Previous Question, From An Englishman in his Grotto, To A Great Man at Court* (London, 1740): "No! with the Curs'd your Tomb shall foremost stand, / The GAVESTON'S and WOLSEY'S of the Land" (p. 11).

The visual tradition of funerary monuments which underlies these verses reappears in *A Draught of the Pillar found in the rubbish of Whitehall humbly Inscribed to the Norfolk Steward* (B.M. 2561), a 1742 print celebrating the downfall of Walpole. As the translation of the Latin inscription on the ram's skin makes clear, the Ionic column is ostensibly dedicated "to the perpetual Infamy of / Thomas Wolsey," whose crimes are also those of Walpole. To each of the ram's limbs are attached purses entitled "Places," "Secret Service," "Pensions," "Bribes," "Commendums," and "Privy Seals." The inscription ends with a reminder of the didactic function of history: "Passenger go on; Courtier, learn and be cautious." As Johnson's lines in *The Vanity of Human Wishes* (99–128) demonstrate, Wolsey remained a type of the overbearing minister well after Walpole's fall.

Caricature, which Ernst Kris and E. H. Gombrich point out seeks "to reveal the true man behind the mask of pretense and to show up his 'essential' littleness and ugliness," would not have served the Opposition's purposes. They sought to show that England was endangered by Walpole's

15. *A Draught of the Pillar found in the rubbish of Whitehall Humbly Inscribed to the Norfolk Steward* (B.M. 2561)

16. Frontispiece to *A Dissertation upon Parties* (B.M. 2150)

unconstitutional "greatness" and not by his personal failings, by his prominence rather than by his incompetence. If anything, the prints we have been
considering enhance Walpole's political stature; by its nature caricature
diminishes the importance of its subject. "'Look here,' the [caricaturist]
seems to say, 'that is all the great man consists of.'"[48] Certainly by the
mid-1730s the proper distinction between naturalistic representation and
the distortion of caricature was well enough known for Swift to refer to it in
A Character, Panegyric, and Description of the Legion Club (1736):

> How I want thee, humorous *Hogart?*
> Thou I hear, a pleasant Rogue art;
> Were but you and I acquainted,
> Every Monster should be painted;
> You should try your graving Tools
> On this odious Group of Fools;
> Draw the Beasts as I describe 'em,
> Form their Features, while I gibe them;
> Draw them like, for I assure you,
> You will need no *Car'catura*;
> Draw them so that we may trace
> All the Soul in every Face.   (219–30)[49]

But Walpole's opponents recognized that the more traditional mode of
representation we looked at in Hogarth's *South Sea Scheme* was better suited
to their satiric ends, as illustrated in the untitled frontispiece (B.M. 2150)
to Bolingbroke's *A Dissertation upon Parties*. Like the *South Sea Scheme*,
Bolingbroke's frontispiece combines emblematic with naturalistic representation. Walpole is seated at the top of a pyramid formed by clouds, a
conventional image of instability. Behind him is blindfolded Fortune with
her wheel. To Walpole's right are a fox and Mercury, god of commerce and
thieves. The female Genius of Political Corruption holds a mitre in her left
hand to represent the importance of ecclesiastical corruption to Walpole's
political power. She distributes money to the supplicants below, including
one whose pen indicates how he supports the Great Man. At the center of
the engraving is the Hydra of Corruption and in the left foreground is
Liberty, weeping over the scene behind her. The full richness the double
tradition of emblematics and naturalism afforded political satirists in the
1730s may be discovered in the figure on Walpole's left. Walpole leans on a
seated man, who in turn leans on a crutch, and whose bag of money suggests
he may be Plutus. Dressed in the breastplate of the Jewish High-Priest
(similar to one of the clerical gamblers in the *South Sea Scheme*), the figure
seems as well to be emblematic of religious greed and corruption. The
crutch, which supports the figure directly and Walpole indirectly, is an

emblematic representation of one of the bases for Walpole's rule. Moreover, the crutch is a naturalistic detail that identifies the figure as Bishop Benjamin Hoadly, whose lameness and reliance on a crutch were the satiric objects of prints like *Guess at My Meaning* (B.M. 1503). Once we make the naturalistic identification that supplements the emblematic value of the figure, we can recognize another way Hoadly served Walpole as a crutch: Lord Hervey considered Hoadly, along with his fellow clerics Francis Hare and Thomas Sherlock, to be one of Walpole's three most effective apologists.[50]

The naturalistic representation of Walpole in the emblematic context of Bolingbroke's frontispiece and in the historical context of Hogarth's print of *Henry the Eighth and Ann Boleyn* reflects a trend toward an emphasis on particular but not normally caricatured people in the imagery of the 1730s. In *The South Sea Scheme* the two central figures are virtually overwhelmed by the emblematic setting. We can detect a certain tension between measures and men in many of the engravings in the 1730s, and this tension reappears in Pope's Horatian imitations. Poets and designers of prints have increasing difficulty in reconciling traditional, generalized forms with particular people. Pope's most frequent solution is to revert to the structure of *Windsor Forest*; he would use a final emblem to summarize the particulars found earlier in the poem. Perhaps the best way to understand this trend in imagery is to look at another print. Although it is very little known, the frontispiece of *A Tryal of Skill Between a Court Lord, and a Twickenham 'Squire* (London, 1734), a poem by an anonymous author, is representative of the changes that had taken place since the South Sea Bubble engravings. The print is referred to but not reproduced by William K. Wimsatt.[51]

A sixteen-page satire on Hervey's upbringing, education, effeminacy, politics, and literary pretensions, *A Tryal of Skill* was published as a response to Hervey's earlier attacks on Pope in *Verses Address'd to the Imitator of the First Satire of the Second Book of Horace* (written in collaboration with Lady Mary Wortley Montagu), as well as in his *An Epistle from a Nobleman to a Doctor of Divinity*. As *A Tryal of Skill* makes clear, its frontispiece was intended to complement visually the words of the text:

> With a capricious, thoughtless Head,
> By Malice, not by Reason, led,
> The Prince of Poets* he [Hervey] arraigns,
> To manifest his shatter'd Brains.
> But on the Head-Piece of this Book
> Whoever does sedately look,
> May see the Novice's Disaster;
> The Poet galls the Poetaster.

*Mr. Pope   (Pp. 12–13)

17. Frontispiece to *A Tryal of Skill Between a Court Lord, and a Twickenham 'Squire*

Although the engraving is indeed crudely executed, it is of considerable interest to students of Pope, politics, and prints. The amount of information Wimsatt leaves out suggests that he did not actually see a copy of the print. For example, there is a label coming from Pope's mouth that indecorously reads "You write: you Sh——te." In addition, there should be no doubt that ink spots appear on Hervey's face. They obviously come from the quill pen at the end of Pope's sword.

The scene alludes to the most famous duel of the 1730s, that between William Pulteney and Lord Hervey in January 1731.[52] Earlier in the month Hervey had written a "Dedication" to William Yonge's *Sedition and Defamation Display'd: In a Letter to the Author of the Craftsman*. Yonge's pamphlet contained an unflattering characterization of one of the *Craftsman*'s patrons (obviously intended to be identified as Pulteney). Thinking Hervey the author of the whole pamphlet, Pulteney responded with *A Proper Reply to a Late Scurrilous Libel, Intitled Sedition and Defamation Display'd*, a small part of which accuses Hervey of, among other personal failings, sexual ambiguity. Hervey challenged Pulteney to a duel, and although both men acquitted themselves well, with slight wounds received on each side, the duel was used as part of the satiric attacks on Hervey for the rest of his life.

The epigraph to *A Tryal of Skill* is taken from *Tit for Tat; or, An Answer to the Epistle to a Nobleman* (London: Printed and sold by J. Dormer, at the Printing-Office, the Green Door, in *Black* and *White* Court in the *Old Bailey* (Price Six-Pence.) M.DCC.XXXIV.)[53] There is a minor misquotation in the sixth line:

> But can your Arm a Weapon lift,
> To battle P——ney, P——pe, or S——ft?
> In an ill Hour the Task you chose,
> Bep——s'd in Rhime, be——it in Prose:
> 'Tis Act the Second of the Farce,
> Just as you duell'd, you write Verse;
> A vanquish'd Hero in the Field,
> And on Parnassus forc'd to yield:
> Let P——pe or P——ney be the Man,
> You quit your Sword, or drop your Pen.

Whereas the poet wished only to emphasize that Pulteney and Pope were linked in their opposition to Hervey, the designer of the print virtually identified Pope with Pulteney. The clothed fox definitely establishes the allusion to the earlier duel because Henry Fox had been Hervey's second in that conflict. Also, the outdoor scene recalls the setting of the earlier duel in St. James's Park.

By associating Pope with Pulteney, the designer emphasized the political implications of the poetical conflict between Pope and Hervey in the early 1730s. The designer was also prophetic in making such a connection between the poet and the Opposition politician. In the Sporus portrait published the following year, Pope used many of the same images and phrases to satirize Hervey that Pulteney had first made popular in *A Proper Reply*.

The engraving illustrates Ronald Paulson's thesis, in *Emblem and Expression*, that the eighteenth century marks the transition from emblematic to expressive art. We need not decipher the historical allusions to recognize the print as emblematic of the motto "The pen is mightier than the sword." More specifically, the design may be intended to illustrate Pope's line "What? arm'd for *Virtue* when I point the Pen" published a year earlier in *Sat.* 2:1:105. If so, the allusion would help explain why Pope wears his coat in a duel while his opponent is undressed. In the original duel fought between Hervey and Pulteney both men were in their shirt-sleeves, even though they met in January. Strenuous dueling demanded unencumbered agility. Hervey is dressed realistically in the 1734 print while Pope is attired as if to symbolize the ease with which he will dispatch his political and literary enemy. The poet is seconded by the emblematic figure of the naked Hercules, a conventional seventeenth-century representative of either heroic virtue or eloquence.[54] In this print both associations are appropriate to the victorious poet. His antagonist is seconded by the equally conventional vulpine image of deceit and evil.

But if we "read" the print from left to right, much as Paulson suggests we study Hogarth, there is a clear shift from the purely emblematic Hercules to the emblematic-expressive figure of the fox. Recognition of the historical allusion to Henry Fox renders the emblem a visual pun on a particular person's name, which expresses the inner nature of the politician Namier described as "the most rapacious of eighteenth-century statesmen."[55] Such an emblematic-expressive depiction anticipated the shift toward the caricatures and animal figures commonly found in prints after 1740.

This engraving is a good example of the variety of forms available to artists and writers during the reign of Walpole. The central figures, basically naturalistic, are no longer overwhelmed by their surroundings. A balance is maintained among the emblematic, the realistic, and the caricatured in this print. Throughout most of this chapter I have been emphasizing the generalizing effect the Opposition rhetorical strategy tended to have, but we must not overlook noteworthy changes from earlier patterns of imagery. Although Bolingbroke and his fellow writers repeatedly asserted their rhetorical concern to change only actions, they certainly never forgot that in practical politics men and measures are intertwined.

Indeed, the failure to combine the particular with the general—a recognizable Walpole in the position of a colossus—could render a political satire ineffective, or even worse. So Pope discovered when he failed to make what may have been references to Walpole specific enough in the *Epistle to Burlington*, perhaps his first Opposition piece.[56] With Timon, Pope created an effective emblem but an unsuccessful piece of political rhetoric; he did not succeed in adapting the earlier form to the contemporary situation. He expressed the measures he opposed, but he did not identify the men clearly enough. He was vulnerable to the accusation that he had attacked his benefactor, the duke of Chandos, rather than Walpole. In a letter prefixed to the third edition of the *Epistle to Burlington*, Pope indicated that he had learned his lesson:

> Even from the Conduct shewn on this occasion, I have learnt there are some who wou'd rather be *wicked* than ridiculous; and therefore it may be safer to attack *Vices* than *Follies*. I will leave my Betters in the quiet Possession of their *Idols*, their *Groves*, and their *High-Places*; and change my Subject from their *Pride* to their *Meanness*, from their *Vanities* to their *Miseries*: And as the only certain way to avoid Misconstruction, to lessen Offence, and not to multiply ill-natur'd Applications, I may probably in my next make use of *Real* Names and not of Fictitious Ones.

In that next poem, the *Epistle to Bathurst*, Pope would prove just how good an Opposition rhetorician he had become by showing how well he could balance measures with men.

CHAPTER III

The *Epistle to Bathurst* and the South Sea Bubble

Ye wise Philosophers explain
What Magick makes our Money rise
When dropt into the Southern Main,
Or do these Juglers cheat our Eyes?
    —Swift, "The Bubble"

Why Bathurst? Of the four poems we now refer to as the Epistles to *Several Persons*, only *Of the Use of Riches, an Epistle to Allen Lord Bathurst*, presents us with the problem of deciding why Pope addressed this moral essay to this particular Opposition peer. Lord Burlington was the appropriate recipient of a poem on taste, especially on architectural taste; in Pope's eyes, no one was worthier than Martha Blount of being offered as a standard against which to measure the characters of women; and Cobham, just dismissed from government office for having opposed a ministerial measure, was the perfect reader of a poem on the rewards of virtuous retirement. But why Bathurst for this epistle?

F. W. Bateson's headnote on Bathurst is not very helpful: "In *Sober Advice from Horace*, 158, Bathurst is described as 'Philosopher and Rake.' His easy morals were notorious, but the philosophy does not seem to have amounted to much more than worldly wisdom."[1] We must consider the political as well as moral life of Bathurst if we are to discover why Pope addressed the poem to him.[2] The poem may have been far more occasional than has previously been thought. Published on 15 January, the day before Parliament convened in 1733, Pope's *Epistle to Bathurst* might well have appeared to many of its first readers as a party piece recapitulating from the Opposition's point of view the political issues of the day.

Almost from the opening of the poem, Pope establishes the political context of this moral essay:

Like Doctors thus, when much dispute has past,
We find our tenets just the same at last.

Both fairly owning, Riches in effect
No grace of Heav'n or token of th'Elect;
Giv'n to the Fool, the Mad, the Vain, the Evil,
To Ward, to Waters, Chartres, and the Devil.   (15–20)

The proper names may at first seem merely to identify particular individuals, but Opposition journalists had long and successfully striven to give to
certain names associations linked with issues or figures besides the persons
named. Pope's lengthy footnotes on these names, particularly to Chartres,
indicate that he was aware of the connections readers could make between
the appearance of such a scoundrel as Chartres here and previous representations of him in Opposition prints and prose.

Bateson remarks in the headnote that "political bias may have reinforced Pope's indignation" at Chartres because the latter was a tool and
defender of Walpole (p. 85). But Chartres was a much more useful figure for
the Opposition than that. For them he could be used as a surrogate for
Walpole. By quoting Arbuthnot's "Epitaph on Chartres," in a footnote
added in 1735, Pope purposely emphasizes the similarities between the tool
and its master, Walpole. The attributes given Chartres would have reminded readers of attacks on Walpole that had been unrelenting for years.
Walpole was often described as having "insatiable Avarice" and "matchless
Impudence." By stressing how corrupt Chartres was without having been a
minister, Pope, through Arbuthnot, forces his readers to remember the
man who had amassed even more by virtue of his governmental position:

Nor was he more singular
in the undeviating *Pravity* of his *Manners*
Than successful
in *Accumulating WEALTH*.
For, without TRADE or PROFESSION,
Without TRUST of PUBLIC MONEY,
And without BRIBE-WORTHY Service,
He acquired, or more properly created,
A MINISTERIAL ESTATE.[3]

Readers of *The Craftsman* would have known to whom to apply the lesson of
Chartres:

Oh Indignant Reader!
Think not his Life useless to Mankind!
PROVIDENCE conniv'd at his execrable Designs,
To give to After-ages
A conspicuous PROOF and EXAMPLE,
Of how small Estimation is EXORBITANT WEALTH
in the Sight of GOD,

18. *To the Glory of Colonel Don Francisco, upon his Delivery out of Goal* [sic] (B.M. 1841)

By his bestowing it on the most UNWORTHY of
ALL MORTALS.

Pope's connection of Chartres with Walpole would not have been the
first time the two men had been memoralized together. Sometime before
May 1730 the print *To the Glory of the R^t. Honble. S^r. Robert Walpole* (B.M.
1842) was published to celebrate his domestic and foreign achievements.
Unfortunately for the ministry, the Opposition reprinted the engraving,
and on 13 June *The Craftsman*, no. 206 (rptd. in Mack, *The Garden and the
City*, pp. 290–97), published a satiric explication of it. Three weeks later
The Craftsman, no. 209, called its readers' attention to a parody of the
original that had been produced in May—*To the Glory of Colonel Don
Francisco, upon his Delivery out of Goal* (sic) (B.M. 1841).[4]

The parody celebrated the premature release from imprisonment for
rape of Francis Chartres, whose capital offense had been pardoned. *The
Craftsman* suggested that the print celebrating Walpole was plagiarized
from the one commemorating Chartres and that the criminal and the
minister were intimately related: "I have been told that it was originally
design'd for *this Gentleman* [Chartres]; but that the Authors were induced,
by the Hopes of a *better Reward*, to transform it, as it was very easy to do,
into a Panegyrick on his *Friend, Confident* and *Patron*." Several pages later, in
the course of an explication of the print, a translation of the Latin verses
accompanying the engraving links Walpole and Chartres as brothers in
crime, with the minister clearly bearing the blame for letting such an arch-
villain free:

> Though yet, most noble Sir, 'tis not your Charter,
> Who have deserv'd a Rope, to wear a Garter;
> Yet have you gain'd the great Man's chief Affection,
> And scap'd the Gallows twice by his Protection.
> Go on! Despair not! On those Arts depend,
> Which first advanc'd, and still support your Friend,
> Common to both; and as they rescued Thee,
> Grown ripe for Vengeance, from the fatal Tree,
> Exert the same, to save a sinking Brother;
> For one good Turn, you know, deserves another.

Pope's lengthy note on Chartres would recall to his readers' minds the
identification of the rapist with the minister that had already been established by the Opposition.

Similarly, the personal failings of John Ward and Peter Waters, or
Walter, had implications that extended far beyond the men themselves.
Pope used Walter as another surrogate for Walpole. Walter on the social

level and Walpole on the political level were representative of the image of the false steward. Swift, Gay, Fielding, and Pope all described Walter as a steward who cheated and eventually ruined his masters; moreover, from its very first issue, *The Craftsman* repeatedly portrayed Walpole as the false coachman or steward who misled his master and impoverished his estate.[5]

Pope's note on Ward introduces us to topics that will gain increasing importance as the poem progresses: fraud, the South Sea Company, and Sir John Blunt. These topics are interrelated. In part, understanding why the epistle is addressed to Bathurst, a politician, is difficult because the emphasis on the South Sea Bubble throughout the poem appears to render the work a basically social, rather than pointedly political, satire. References to the bubble or to the fact that Ward "was suspected of joining in a conveyance with Sir John Blunt, to secrete fifty thousand pounds of that Director's Estate, forfeited to the South Sea Company by Act of Parliament"[6] seem at first to be somewhat anachronistic, diffusing the attack by spreading it over time and particularly into the recent past. We usually think of the South Sea Scandal as a concern that ended in the early 1720s; Walpole's proposed Excise Bill is the issue we normally associate with the session of 1733. The absence of references to excise in the *Epistle* tends to make modern readers see the poem as neither topical nor occasional. But to Pope's first readers it probably appeared as both.

The Craftsman returned to the subject of the bubble continuously throughout the 1720s and into the 1730s. We are familiar with the repeated charges that Walpole had "screened" the culprits in order to consolidate his power after the bubble burst in 1720.[7] Contemporaries would have seen his protection of Chartres as another example of a scoundrel "screened" by the prime minister. But the Opposition quickly transformed Walpole from accessory after the fact to one of those originally most responsible for the scandal. Furthermore, they saw him as the prime force behind the other trading monopolies. Thus, in *The Craftsman*, no. 13, "Urbanicus" describes an East India Company director who sounds remarkably like Walpole.

By the parliamentary session of 1732, Walpole was being compared explicitly to the head of the South Sea Company (*The Craftsman*, no. 299), and in what might be called *The Craftsman*'s tour de force of political allegory, Caleb explicates the story of a Hungarian Vampyre, applying it not only to Walpole, but also to past and present directors of both the South Sea Company and the Charitable Corporation. All were seen as vampires sucking the blood of their country. Repeatedly through the session of 1732 the Opposition sought to link the South Sea Company, the Charitable Corporation, and Walpole. Apparently, the Opposition was laying the groundwork for the session of 1733.

A major issue in the Commons during 1732 was the investigation into the conduct of "The Charitable Corporation, for Relief of Industrious Poor, by assisting them with small Sums upon Pledges at legal Interest." As Pope's note to line 102 of the *Epistle* indicates, the outcome of the investigation could be viewed as an Opposition victory over Walpole when "three of the managers, who were members of the house, were expelled."[8] The Opposition sought to draw parallels between the proven mismanagement of the directors and that alleged against Walpole. He was seen to have betrayed his trust to an even greater extent than had the expelled M.P.s. Pope's lines on the scandal reflect the Opposition's point of view: he carefully associates the most notorious scoundrel of the Charitable Corporation, Bond, with the chief villain of the South Sea Bubble, Blunt:

Perhaps you think the Poor might have their part?
Bond damns the Poor, and hates them from his heart:
The grave Sir Gilbert holds it for a rule,
That "every man in want is knave or fool:"
"God cannot love (says Blunt, with tearless eyes)
"The wretch he starves"—and piously denies:
But the good Bishop, with a meeker air,
Admits, and leaves them, Providence's care.   (101–8)

The Craftsman (no. 291) saw the original purpose of the Charitable Corporation as equivalent to that of the South Sea Company, which was also "a very charitable Project, of this Nature, to relieve the Publick from the Burthen of their *Debts*." But in practice the charity of both, according to *The Craftsman*, was like that of a "Great Man"—it begins (and ends) at home. The Opposition was very careful to damn the Charitable Corporation by identifying it with the South Sea Company, "for if there is any such Thing as a Parallel between two Cases, That of the *South Sea Directors*, in the year 1720, and of the Managers of the *Charitable Corporation*, at present, is certainly such" (*The Craftsman*, no. 284).

Thinking that they would be successful in their campaign against the directors of the corporation in 1732, the Opposition strove to prepare their issues for the session of 1733. In its remarks on the last session of Parliament, *The Craftsman* of 1 July 1732 discussed Walpole's role in the inquiry into the Charitable Corporation and predicted that there would be inquiries into the conduct of other companies in the next session. On 25 March 1732, *The Craftsman*, no. 297, produced the vision of

the TREE OF CORRUPTION, which bears a very near Resemblance to the *Tree of Knowledge* in the Garden of Eden. . . . Perched in the Middle of the Tree . . . I spy'd a *round portly Man* [clearly, Walpole], of a swarthy Complexion. . . . He sate enthron'd . . . and, plucking the *golden Apples* on every Side, toss'd them down amongst the Croud beneath Him. . . . As I had a nearer View of *these Apples*, I thought I saw some Words inscrib'd round the Superfices of them . . . and plainly discovered the Words *charitable* Corporation indented in natural Characters upon one of them; on another I read, *forfeited* Estates; on a third, *Army Debentures*; and on a fourth, *Bank Contract*. But there were two Inscriptions, which I could not thoroughly understand. The first was *East India*, . . . The second was *South-Sea*.

In addition to the coverage of the South Sea Scandal in regular issues of *The Craftsman*, at least eleven other publications in 1732 dealt with the scandal and its aftermath.[9] The most ambitious prominwhich pamphlet addressed itself to the exact point that the Opposition was to attack in 1733, the handling of former directors' forfeited estates:

IT CANNOT NOW BE DOUBTED, But every impartial Reader, who judges without Prepossession or Prejudice, is fully convinced by the faithful Account herein given, of the first Formation of the late Scheme of the South-Sea Company, and of the Views upon which it was founded, and of the several Steps taken by the late Directors in the Execution of the Act of Parliament, (which had greatly altered the Original Scheme) together with the Motives which induced the Directors to the executing it in the manner they did; that there was no evil Design in the first preparing this Scheme, nor in the several Proceedings of the Directors: and that tho' they may have committed some Errors, which is common to human Frailty, yet surely none will say that they have been guilty of so black Crimes, as by the popular Cry they were accused of. And consequently they have not deserved the Hardships they have been subjected to.[10]

We see Pope's attack on Blunt in the *Epistle to Bathurst* as especially timely when we recognize that this defense was originally written by Blunt himself in 1722. Howard Erskine-Hill has identified Blunt as the author of *A True State of the South Sea Scheme*, but he does not discuss the republication of the pamphlet at nearly twice its original length less than a year before Pope's poem appeared.[11]

In light of all the evidence, observers of Parliament would have expected the 1733 session to open with an assault on the conduct of past and present South Sea Company directors. These expectations were disappointed by the sudden appearance of the excise issue. Prior to the end of October 1732 there is virtually no reference in *The Craftsman* to the Excise Bill, which quickly became the Opposition's main target in the next session.[12] Even after the Opposition recognized that excise would be the immediate issue, *The Craftsman* (no. 341) reminded its readers, just two days before the publication of Pope's poem, not to forget other important subjects, including the not-yet-resolved Charitable Corporation and the South Sea Company. The South Sea issue was not dropped in 1733; it was simply deferred until after Walpole's opponents had successfully forced him to withdraw the Excise Bill on 11 April in the House of Commons. The Opposition needed an appropriate sponsor to introduce the South Sea topic into the upper chamber. Bathurst, one of the most experienced opponents of the ministry, continued the campaign against the bubble. On 3 May he began the new phase of the assault in the House of Lords when he moved, "That the Directors of the South Sea Company may be required to lay before this house, an Accompt of what Sums of Money, *South Sea* Stock, and *South Sea* Annuities, have been received from the Trustees, for Sale of the Estates of the late Directors and others . . . with all the Orders and Directions of the General Courts of the said Company relating to the Disposition thereof."[13] While Hervey describes the subject of the South Sea Company as one chosen rather suddenly to capitalize in the House of Lords on the Opposition's triumph in the Commons, he also offers additional proof that the subject had shown great political promise in the 1732 session. He reports that even ministerial supporter Lord Scarborough would vote for a motion to investigate the company if it were proposed in the 1733 session.[14]

Pope must have expected the first readers of his *Epistle to Bathurst* to receive the poem as an occasional party piece designed to open the Parliamentary session of 1733. Up until late 1732 there were many indications that the issue Bathurst brought up in May was to be the first line of Opposition attack; only the fortuitous arrival of the Excise Crisis caused it to be postponed. Events soon proved that the Opposition was correct in thinking the South Sea issue a potent one. Even though they eventually lost the war over the issue in the 1733 session, Bathurst and his followers scored an impressive victory with the technical success of a tie vote during the debate.

Neither Bathurst's listeners nor Pope's readers were likely to overlook the connection between the South Sea Scandal and the minister *The Craftsman* (no. 288) called "the Patron of *Stockjobbers, Projectors* and *Bubble-mongers.*" I suggest that Pope knew Bathurst was going to lead the fight over the South Sea directors, and that he emphasizes the corruption and fraud of Ward, Bond, and Blunt, among others, to recapitulate the Opposition triumphs of the previous session as well as to prepare the public for the offensive to come. The stress he places on Chartres's crimes reminds his readers who the "Skreen-master general" is. As the Protest of the Lords at the end of the 1733 session showed, Bathurst attacked the South Sea directors in order to wound their protector, much as Pope uses Chartres to attack Walpole: "Because the Arts made Use of to divert us from our Duty, and defeat this Inquiry, give us Reasons to prosecute it with fresh Vigour; for Impunity of Guilt (if any such there be) is strongest Encouragement to the Repetition of the same practices in future Times, by chalking out a safe Method of committing the most flagitious Frauds under the Protection of some corrupt and all-skreening Minister."[15]

Even the supporters of Walpole recognized the ease with which his opponents could link him with criminals on both the private and the public level. Referring to Bathurst's motion, Hervey admitted that Walpole resisted any parliamentary investigations

> from a fear of making this retrospective manner of inquiry, by the frequency of it, so familiar to Parliament, that at one time or other it might, in any reverse of fortune and by the rage of party, affect himself, his family, and posterity; but by too strict an adherence to this principle he was often smeared with the filth of other people, and gave his enemies occasion to say that whoever had a mind to plunder the public or defraud particulars . . . and let the notoriety of their crimes be never so manifest or the nature of them never so enormous, they would be secure of protection in Parliament whilst Sir Robert Walpole had any power there . . . and his having actually put a stop to this inquiry into the South Sea affairs in the House of Commons, had given but too just grounds for these reflections to be thrown out against him, and left his friends too little room to justify him when his adversaries represented him as the universal encourager of corruption and the sanctuary of the corrupt. (*Memoirs* 1 : 186–87)

As we have seen, Pope opens his poem with references to men who were already associated in the public press and prints with Walpole. The mention of Chartres in particular would have reminded Pope's readers of the minister's reputation as a protector of villainous criminals. By addressing the work to Bathurst, Pope cleverly poses as the righteous satirist who eventually persuades the politican to action. Bathurst first appears in the poem as a cynic who must be convinced that private and public reformation is possible. The poet rehearses for the politician the past triumphs of those opposed to the corruption and fraud Walpole encouraged and protected. Moving from criminals who "defraud particulars" to those who "plunder the public," Pope also introduces to his readers the very issues that Bathurst would be persuaded to investigate in the session of Parliament that was to commence the day after the poem's publication.

In his introduction, Bateson makes the disparaging comment that "Compared with Fielding's contemporary 'dramatic satires,' like *Pasquin* and *The Historical Register*, in this poem Pope too often gives the impression that he doesn't know what he is talking about. Most of his information, for example, about the two great financial scandals of 1732—the misappropriations by the Commissioners for the sale of the Earl of Derwentwater's estates and by the Directors of the Charitable Corporation for the Relief of the Industrious Poor—was derived from the newspapers" (p. xxxiv). To a great extent Bateson is correct in seeing the connection between the poem and contemporary journalism.[16] But rather than marking a weakness, Pope's use of such connections extends his satire from particular objects to an indictment of Walpole's England. To the extent that the *Epistle to Bathurst* was intended as an occasional poem, Pope would have wanted his audience to recall recent accounts of scandals. He would have sought to reinforce and reemphasize the damaging associations between Walpole and publicly recognized criminals like Bond, Ward, Blunt, and Chartres— associations made in contemporary poems, prints, and in newspapers such as *The Craftsman* or *The Grub Street Journal*.

Pope, however, does not simply repeat past charges; while he looks backward to earlier Opposition victories, such as the expulsion from Parliament of the Charitable Corporation directors, he is also concerned with the future Opposition program, particularly in the House of Lords. By balancing his references to individuals with apparently more general satire, Pope skillfully modifies the Opposition maxim of attacking not men but measures. He quickly moves from the personal attack on Ward, Walter, and Chartres in line 20 to the wider social and political implications of the abuse of riches:

> Useful, I grant, it serves what life requires,
> But dreadful too, the dark Assassin hires:
> Trade it may help, Society extend;
> But lures the Pyrate, and corrupts the Friend:
> It raises Armies in a Nation's aid,
> But bribes a Senate, and the Land's betray'd.   (29–34)

Politically alert contemporary readers would have recognized the topicality of the last couplet: Walpole was repeatedly accused of bribing members of Parliament in order to maintain a standing army, which, to the Opposition, was a constant threat to betray the land. Pope manages to strike at Walpole even in the whimsical fantasy of bribery conducted in the days of barter:

> A Stateman's slumbers how this speech would spoil!
> "Sir, Spain has sent a thousand jars of oil;
> "Huge bales of British cloth blockade the door;
> "A hundred oxen at your levee roar."   (43–46)

Presumably, Walpole would still slumber through Spanish depredations on English trade, even if Spain's bribes to get him to do so were as cumbersome as possible. Once again, Pope's readers would be reminded of the South Sea Company, first formed to control trade with the Spanish New World colonies.

The political allusion to the South Sea Company soon leads Pope to a comic discussion of the inconvenience of bulky bribes at the gaming table:

> Shall then Uxorio, if the stakes he sweep,
> Bear home six Whores, and make his Lady weep?
> Or soft Adonis, so perfum'd and fine,
> Drive to St. James's a whole herd of swine?
> Oh filthy check on all industrious skill,
> To spoil the nation's last great trade, Quadrille!   (59–64)

Erskine-Hill points out that this reference to the fashionable card game "seems at once rather an exaggerated and random stroke until one detects . . . the allusion to the Bubble, when the nation ruined itself . . . by attending not to trade or industry but to gambling."[17] He also shows that Pope imitates the rhetoric of Defoe and Blunt when he writes of the South Sea Bubble. But Pope's subject has an even greater influence on the design of his poem than Erskine-Hill suggests.

The metaphor of gambling runs throughout the poem and begins even earlier than in the lines just quoted. Pope's note on Chartres emphasizes his career as a gambler and cheat whose life was one of alternating wins and losses. The vice of gambling soon extends beyond the individual to the whole society, until "all industrious skill" is devoted to "the nation's last great trade, Quadrille!" The greatest gambling in recent English history, Pope soon reminds us, was that done in 1720, and such gambling on the future serves as the model for current social conduct:

> What made Directors cheat in South-sea year?
> To live on Ven'son when it sold so dear.
> Ask you why Phryne the whole Auction buys?
> Phryne foresees a general Excise.
> Why she and Sappho raise that monstrous sum?
> Alas! they fear a man will cost a plum.   (119–24)

Once again, gambling and cheating are seen as inseparable. By its very nature, the gamble of the South Sea Company was one that would cheat first the individuals and finally the whole society who had bet on it. Pope's concern with this connection between cheating, gambling, and the South Sea Bubble should remind us of how often these ideas are associated with each other in prints of the scandal. For example, Hogarth's *The South Sea*

Scheme is full of images of gambling and cheating: the various clergymen playing the game of "pitch and hustle" in the lower-left-hand corner; the women lined up for the marriage lottery; the man in the middle of the print who is apparently dismayed by what he sees while a dwarf picks his pocket; the foxes on the monument, who are conventional emblems of deceit and cheating.

Against such a tradition of seeing the bubble as a game in which the whole nation is cheated, Pope chose Blunt as the recipient of the vision of future gambling, cheating, and corruption in a key passage because he wishes to remind his readers and especially the politician Bathurst that the danger did not end in 1720 and that the implications of the scandal are as politically relevant in 1733 as ever:

> Much injur'd Blunt! why bears he Britain's hate?
> A wizard told him in these words our fate:
> "At length Corruption, like a gen'ral flood,
> "(So long by watchful Ministers withstood)
> "Shall deluge all; and Av'rice creeping on,
> "Spread like a low-born mist, and blot the Sun;
> "Statesman and Patriot ply alike the stocks,
> "Peeress and Butler share alike the Box,
> "And Judges job, and Bishops bite the town,
> "And mighty Dukes pack cards for half a crown.
> "See Britain sunk in lucre's sordid charms,
> "And France reveng'd of ANNE's and EDWARD's arms!"
> No mean Court-badge, great Scriv'ner! fir'd thy brain,
> Nor lordly Luxury, nor City Gain:
> No, 'twas thy righteous end, asham'd to see
> Senates degen'rate, Patriots disagree,
> And nobly wishing Party-rage to cease,
> To buy both sides, and give thy Country peace.   (135–52)

Blunt is probably "Much injur'd" because he now unjustly "bears . . . Britain's hate" for measures he undeniably introduced into English politics and society, but which have been continued by Walpole and his ministerial followers. This passage gives us a good example of the Opposition's rhetorical strategy of attacking measures rather than men. Blunt is personally culpable for his crimes, but to blame him alone is unfair because the measures have been continued and even expanded by others. Pope warns his readers that to punish the former directors is not enough; they must also root out the policies originally introduced by the directors (and, by implication, the men who are currently pursuing these policies). The Opposition frequently argued that present ministerial practices could be traced back to the beginning of Walpole's rule: in *The Craftsman* containing the Dream of the Tree of Corruption we are told that, to write a history of corruption, we must begin at "the famous Aera of 1720."

To the Opposition, the vision given Blunt is true largely because the wizard is probably to be identified with the minister who has been following the same measures for the last ten years. The wizardry of Walpole is already represented by his wand in the vision of the Tree of Corruption, and Pope would again use the image of Walpole as visionary wizard or magician to introduce the final prophecy of *The New Dunciad*.[18] Corruption, according to the Opposition, had been withstood "by watchful Ministers" Robert Harley and Bolingbroke before Walpole's rise to power.[19] By 1733 the wizard's prophecy has already been realized,

> ". . . and Av'rice creeping on,
> "Spread like a low-born mist, and blot[s] the Sun;
> "Statesman and Patriot ply alike the stocks,
> "Peeress and Butler share alike the Box,
> "And Judges job, and Bishops bite the town,
> "And mighty Dukes pack cards for a half a crown."

The terms "job," "bite," and "pack" reinforce the notion that in this new world of universal gambling, cheating is the norm, whether in justice, the church, or personal affairs.

Such cheating and gambling, particularly in the form of financial speculation or usury, lead to social miscegenation: "low-born mist" like Ward or Walter can, through the manipulation of money, upset the proper social balance until "Peeress and Butler share alike the Box." Corruption of the social system was a frequent charge made in prints about the bubble. Pope reproduces a situation depicted in such prints as *The Bubbler Bubbl'd; or, The Devil Take the Hindmost* (B.M. 1625):

> Come all ye mony'd Bites and Culls,
> Dukes Commoners and Nobles,
> Who stray alike from reason's rules,
> To deal in Stocks and Bubbles:
> Here Whig and Tory, Rich and Poor,
> All Languages and Nations,
> Jabber as if at Babels Tow'r.

Through references in the notes to attempts by the "low-born" to defraud the aristocracy of its lands, Pope seeks to prove that the social decay begun by Blunt's measures has continued under Walpole, the minister so often accused of having unjustly risen above his station in life, and whom Pope would soon refer to as "the proud Gamester" (*Sat.* 2:1, l. 107). In 1733

19. *The Bubbler-Bubbl'd; or, The Devil Take the Hindmost* (B.M. 1625)

corruption has become official government policy, and Pope once again alludes to the Opposition charge that Walpole has bribed the representatives of Britain with "lucre's sordid charmes" to follow a dishonorable foreign policy.

At line 146 the vision ends, and Pope returns to his defense of Blunt. The vision describes England both in 1720 and at the present; similarly the defense of Blunt is a two-sided irony attacking both Blunt and Walpole. Pope's readers would recognize that Blunt's principal motivation was the desire for "City Gain" and the "Court-badge" of knighthood he received; so too would they detect the reference to the present minister who had recently been likened to a South Sea director and whose infatuation with his medal and his "lordly Luxury" were often ridiculed in the Opposition press. Blunt and Walpole are equally "righteous" in "nobly wishing Party-rage to cease, / To buy both sides, and give [their] Country peace." Pope warns his readers that all the implications of the bubble are still in existence and that alert politicians must be as ready to oppose the measures of Walpole in government as they had those of Blunt in the economy.

The very structure of the poem with its series of contrasted pairs of portraits is reminiscent of the emphasis on Fortune in South Sea Bubble prints. At the center of Hogarth's *The South Sea Scheme* the wheel of Fortune is transformed into a merry-go-round propelled by directors of the South Sea Company. Just as investors in the scheme experienced rises and falls in their circumstances, Pope's portraits depict the uncertainties of life for those who still put their faith in Fortune. Life is a series of constant changes whose ultimate meaning is unknowable to Man:

> Ask we what makes one keep, and one bestow?
> That Pow'r who bids the Ocean ebb and flow,
> Bids seed-time, harvest, equal course maintain,
> Thro' reconcil'd extremes of drought and rain
> Builds Life on Death, on Change Duration founds,
> And gives th'eternal wheels to know their rounds.   (165–70)

Pope's recurrent allusions to the events of 1720 give the poem a surprisingly medieval tone and help explain why this is perhaps his most overtly Christian work. Contrasting portraits such as those of Cotta and his son serve as exempla in this didactic poem, goading Pope's readers into proper action. The poet reminds Bathurst that the dangers inherent in the original South Sea Scheme will remain as long as men rely on Fortune's gifts. Those who put their faith in Fortune soon find with Turner that Riches can provide no more than "Meat, Cloaths, and Fire" (82), and they become part of an incessant pattern that rises and falls just as surely as does Hogarth's merry-go-round.[20] Thus Old Cotta scrimps and saves only to have his son squander and go bankrupt in a traditional relationship between miser father and spendthrift son that Hogarth would depict in the first plate of *The Rake's Progress*.

Pope's shift earlier in the poem from men to measures is paralleled by his shift from attacking individuals to attacking types. At first the objects of satire are specific, named men, albeit they are names the Opposition had already charged with political implications; then we find increasingly these specific names being replaced by general ones—"Worldly," "Harpax," etc.—though these general names can usually be identified with specific men. When specific names do appear in the latter half of the poem, they are usually representatives of exemplary behavior—Bathurst, Oxford, "The Man of Ross." Such a shift in the tactics of attack allows Pope to make his satire gradually more universal in its applicability. The corruption fomented by the South Sea Scheme is as real now as it was in 1720, and 1720 was only a heightening of the same avaricious drives that had earlier driven Buckingham to his desperate end.

Thus, we need not be able to identify who the models of "Old Cotta" and his son might have been; each is an emblem whose didactic effectiveness is independent of specific individuals. The lines immediately preceding the introduction of the Cottas indicate that in their portraits Pope intends to elaborate an essentially medieval emblem of Avarice:

> Who sees pale Mammon pine amidst his store,
> Sees but a backward steward for the Poor;
> This year a Reservoir, to keep and spare,
> The next a Fountain, spouting thro' his Heir,
> In lavish streams to quench a Country's thirst,
> And men and dogs drink him 'till they burst.   (173–78)

The remedy for the current social and political situation is the fundamentally Christian one of charity on the personal and national levels. Bathurst is the ideal candidate to lead the Opposition attack on the corruption of charity at the national level. And, like Oxford, Bathurst is an exemplum of charity on the social level. Pope must have known that Bathurst had already established the appropriate political credentials in his defense of the poor during the 1732 House of Lords debate on the Salt Tax.[21] Only through charity can the shifts of Fortune be balanced:

> The Sense to value Riches, with the Art
> T' enjoy them, and the Virtue to impart,
> Not meanly, nor ambitiously pursu'd,
> Not sunk by sloth, nor raised by servitude;
> To balance Fortune by a just expence,

Join with Oeconomy, Magnificence;
With Splendour, Charity; with Plenty, Health;
Oh teach us, BATHURST! yet unspoil'd by wealth!
That secret rare, between th' extremes to move
Of mad Good-nature, and of mean Self-love.   (219–28)

Pope, as Wasserman has argued at length, is even more emphatic about the Christian remedy when he describes charity on the purely personal level. "The Man of Ross" is clearly associated with Moses and Christ, while Old Cotta is damned largely because he inverts values that Pope reminds us are not exclusively Christian:

With soups unbought and sallads blest his board.
If Cotta liv'd on pulse, it was no more
Than Bramins, Saints, and Sages did before;
To cram the Rich was prodigal expence,
And who would take the Poor from Providence?
Like some lone Chartreux stands the good old Hall,
Silence without, and Fasts within the wall;   (184–90)

The only blessing in this house is a material one, his fasts dedicated not to God but to Mammon. Old Cotta, like "the good Bishop" of line 107, believes in Providence only insofar as he can use it as an excuse for social irresponsibility. The resemblance of his home to Chartreux is merely physical: the spiritual qualities of the monastery are totally absent from the miser's dwelling.

Pope ends the *Epistle to Bathurst* with the tale of Sir Balaam and thus transforms the poem from one that contains scattered emblems into one that may justly be described as an overall emblem. We are accustomed to emblematic poems that begin with a visual or verbal allegory and then proceed to explain, elaborate, and justify that original fiction. Pope has reversed that structure here as he had done in *Windsor Forest* and as he would do again with the vision of Vice Triumphant in the first dialogue of the *Epilogue to the Satires*, and in the *Fourth Book of the Dunciad*. The themes and images found in the first 340 lines of the poem culminate in the tale; in effect, the meaning and significance of Sir Balaam have already been explained and justified. We see the tale as a parable or exemplum illustrating the social and political accusations the poet makes throughout the poem.

The South Sea Scheme is so important a theme in the *Epistle* that it has affected Pope's representation of the implications of the bursting of the bubble in 1720. Not only does he emphasize many of the ideas found in prints of the 1720s—Fortune, gambling, cheating, etc.—but he also conceives those ideas in ways that seem to be influenced by the ways they had been conceived and represented ten years earlier, when the emblematic tradition was much more apparent. His use of medieval allegorical types, the pattern of rising and falling on Fortune's wheel, the importance of Christian values, the appearance of devils and wizards, and the final emblematic tale of Sir Balaam all strike us as somewhat old-fashioned.

Readers familiar with prints on the bubble would quickly recognize that "Where London's column, pointing at the skies, / Like a tall bully, lifts the head, and lyes" (339–40) is not only a reference to the anti-Catholic Monument, but, more important for this poem, the column signifies Exchange Alley where the growth of the bubble took place. This baleful financial connotation of the column can be seen in Hogarth's *South Sea Scheme* where the monument is actually transformed into one dedicated to the bubble; in verses accompanying the print *The Bubblers Medley; or, A Sketch of the Times: Being Europe's Memorial for the Year 1720* (no. 2) (B.M. 1611), the scene is immediately set by reference to the column in Edward Ward's verses:

In London stands a famous Pile,
And near that Pile an Alley,
Where merry Crowds for Riches toil,
And Wisdom stoops to Folly.

The sinister connotations Pope elicits by allusion to the visual tradition are reinforced by a verbal allusion to lines earlier in the *Epistle*. We begin to suspect Sir Balaam even before we meet him, because we recognize these first two lines of the tale as an echo of lines applied to the "Man of Ross" "who bade the waters flow / Not to the skies in useless columns tost, / Or in proud falls magnificently lost" (254–56). Not only is Sir Balaam's column useless, but also it symbolizes the malevolence of anti-Catholicism and the South Sea Bubble.

We quickly recognize Sir Balaam as a microcosm of the society described and attacked throughout the first 340 lines of the poem: he is uncharitable; he cheats; he recognizes money as his god. The fact that "his word would pass for more than he was worth" links him with the recognized scoundrels like Ward and Walter who were mentioned earlier in the poem, and whose lives Pope in the notes ironically judges in terms of their "*worth*"; even Old Cotta ironically "was not . . . void of wit or worth" (180). Sir Balaam's life illustrates Pope's theme that in modern times wealth corrupts because "Satan now is wiser than of yore, / And tempts by making rich, not making poor" (351–52). Satan's final victory over Sir Balaam's soul is assured when he makes him part of the financial revolution symbolized, for the Opposition, by the bubble:

20. *The Bubblers Medley; or, A Sketch of the Times: Being Europe's Memorial for the Year 1720 (no. 2) (B.M. 1611)*

The Tempter saw his time; the work he ply'd
Stocks and Subscriptions pour on ev'ry side,
'Till all the Daemon makes his full descent,
In one abundant show'r of Cent. per Cent.,
Sinks deep within him, and possesses whole,
Then dubs Director, and secures his soul.   (369–74)

The emblematic shower is just a part of the "gen'ral flood" of corruption the
events of 1720 introduced and Walpole continued.[22]

Sir Balaam's final movement up and then down on the wheel of Fortune
is very similar to that depicted in the pair of South Sea prints *The Bubler's
Mirrour; or, England's Folley, (Joy)* [sic] and *The Bubbler's Mirrour; or, Englands Folly. (Grief)* [sic] (B.M. 1620 and 1621). In the first, we are shown a
successful speculator in the South Sea Scheme who holds a full purse and is
surrounded by representations of the wheel of Fortune. He is "Fortune's
Darling," and like Sir Balaam, who

Ascribes his gettings to his parts and merit,
What late he call'd a Blessing, now was Wit,
And God's good Providence, a lucky Hit.   (376–78)

"Fortune's Darling" exemplifies those

. . . happy Mortals who from Heav'n derive,
Those useful Arts and Means by which they thrive,
Do to themselves Assume, for want of sense,
The praise that's only due to Providence.

The other print shows a less fortunate investor with his empty purse. His
end is very similar to that of Sir Balaam when he

. . . mourns his folly o'er his Empty Bags;
Raves at the tricks a pack of Knaves have playd
And Curses those for whom before he Prayd;
So he that Games and is by Dice undone,
Damns his ill-fortune, when the fault's his own.

Despite critics' attempts to identify a model for Sir Balaam, his function in the poem remains as emblematic as the figures in the pair of
contrasting bubble prints. The most important difference between the
emblem in the poem and the one in the prints is that Pope's is far more
elaborate. Pope's object is to illustrate the Opposition's assertion that "the
Introduction of money'd Companies there [i.e., Rome, but clearly the
parallel with England is to be made] hath, I am afraid, had this Effect, and
converted many an *honest, generous, industrious Merchant into a little, pitiful,*

21. *The Bubler's Mirrour; or, England's Folley, (Joy)* [sic] (B.M. 1620)

22. *The Bubbler's Mirrour; or, Englands Folly. (Grief)* {sic} (B.M. 1621)

pilfering Stockjobber" (*The Craftsman*, no. 329). Although Sir Balaam does not start out as honest and generous as he might have been, his end is pathetic because Pope presents us with a type who is more victim than malefactor. He has been victimized by the financial revolution symbolized in the bubble of 1720, whose implications must still be resisted by politicians like Bathurst.

The South Sea Bubble and its aftermath remained in the English consciousness long after 1720. The scandal was a perfect target for satirists suspicious of the new economic order the events of 1720 apparently represented. The South Sea Company, created in 1711 by a Tory administration and consequently overseen by Whigs, offered a nonpartisan subject for critical examination. Furthermore, the bubble was considered only the English manifestation of a European financial phenomenon, as expressed by the anonymous author of *Majesty Misled; or, The Overthrow of Evil Ministers. A Tragedy, as intended to be acted at one of the Theatres, but was refus'd for Certain Reasons* (London, 1734):

> *THUS* the directors of the *South-sea* scheme,
> Entail'd upon themselves perpetual shame;
> While the contagion reach'd, from hence to *France*,
> And led whole families a *cushion-dance*;
> Statesmen polluted were, scarce one was free,
> The *taint* infected the *NOBILITY*.
> Then *South-sea* lost its name by dextrous art,
> And *Mississippi* was the second part.   (P. 25)

Distrust of the bubble and all it represented was not limited to Pope and those who shared his political and economic beliefs. The evil stockjobber, an English villain since the late 1600s, is associated with the devil and treason by Defoe in *The Villainy of Stock-Jobbers Detected* (London, 1701). Defoe returned to the subject of the evil stockjobber in *The Anatomy of Exchange Alley* (1719), in which he warns of the dangers that lie ahead for England because of its gambling fever. So widespread was the infection that Gay mocks himself along with the profiteers in his South Sea poem, *A Panegyrical Epistle To Mr. Thomas Snow* (London, 1720).

When Pope's *Epistle to Bathurst* appeared in January 1733, neither its major subject, the South Sea Bubble, nor its visual allusions in the emblematic tale of Balaam should have struck the poem's readers as novel. Pope's decision to end the epistle with such a tale may have been influenced by Gay, who ends his *Epistle* the same way: "If to instruct thee all my Reasons fail, / Yet be diverted by this Moral Tale" (ll. 38–39). An even more likely influence on Pope was Swift's *The Bubble* (London, 1720), a poem Pope edited for the 1727 *Miscellanies*. Swift's satire is essentially a string of emblems drawn from Biblical, classical, Aesopian, proverbial, and folkloric sources. Images of magic, disease, and wizardry appear in a poem which also associates the bubble with the devil: "A narrow Sound, though deep as Hell, / CHANGE-ALLY is the dreadful Name" (ll. 139–40). Pope's reference in the Balaam tale to "two rich ship-wrecks [which] bless the lucky shore" (356) may well have been inspired by a stanza Pope edited out of the *Bubble* in 1727, when he changed the title of Swift's poem to "The South-Sea. 1721":

> Mean time secure on GARR'WAY Clifts
> A savage Race by Shripwrecks fed,
> Ly waiting for the foundred Skiffs,
> And strip the Bodyes of the Dead.   (ll. 153–56)

Because Pope was familiar with Swift's satire, he may have known that ten of its stanzas appear on the print *The Bubblers Medley; or, A Sketch of the Times: Being Europe's Memorial for the Year* 1720 (no. 1) (B.M. 1610), an engraving completely distinct from *The Bubblers Medley . . .* (no. 2), mentioned earlier. *The Bubblers Medley . . .* (no. 1) is like Pope's *Epistle to Bathurst* in the prominence it gives to "Old Nick, the first Projector." The devil is one of the most common figures in bubble prints. He appears in Hogarth's *South Sea Scheme*. In Pope's tale of Balaam, he links economic, moral, and political corruption, drawing Balaam into Walpole's service: "In Britain's Senate he a seat obtains, / And one more Pensioner St. Stephen gains" (393–94). Similarly, visual satirists transferred the devil from the economic context of the bubble prints to the political setting of the anti-Walpole engravings, and, like Pope, without losing the earlier associations. We noted the devil in the second frontispiece of *Robin's Reign*. Satan reappears in two Excise prints of 1733, *Britannia Excisa* and *The Scheme Disappointed A Fruitless Sacrifice* (B.M. 1928). In the latter, the devil, an ally of Cardinal Fleury, leads Walpole to the "Great Man's" expected execution. Later examples of the devil in political engravings include the 1738 *The Lyon in Love; or, The Political Farmer* (B.M. 2347), in which he prompts Walpole, and the 1740 *The State Pack-Horse* (B.M. 2420), in which he oversees Walpole's political landscape.

Closely allied to the image of the devil in Pope's epistle and in contemporary prints is the allusion to Judas in the Balaam emblem.[23] Balaam betrays his country and master for money, for which he "hangs," "curses God and dies" (396–402). Judas, prototype of the traitor, appears in the anonymous *Mr. Taste's Tour From the Island of Politeness, to that of Dulness and Scandal* (London, 1733): "Money first tempted *Judas* to betray, / 'Tis the

23. *The Bubblers Medley; or, A Sketch of the Times: Being Europe's Memorial for the Year 1720 (no. 1) (B.M. 1610)*

THE
Lyon in Love.
OR THE
POLITICAL FARMER.
An Æsopian Tale,
Applicable to the present Times.

A Lyon, once to Love inclin'd,
Thus to a Farmer broke his Mind:
Your Daughter, Sir, then fetch'd a Sigh—
Give me your Daughter, or I die.
Hob stood aghast, then made a Pause—
But weighing well his Length of Claws,
And the huge Fangs between his Jaws,
Consented to his mad Petition;
But notwithstanding on Condition.
Poll, Sir, you know, is young & tender:—

Those Grinders may perhaps offend her,
Let them be Drawn, & spare your Nails.
The Bargain's struck; Hang him if fails.
Overjoy'd the Amorous Fool complies,
And, like a whining Coxcomb, cries,
Polly's the Only Thing I prize.
The Job perform'd, & all things safe,
Hob, & all round him grin, and laugh:
Fearless, grow monstrously uncivil,
And send him packing to the D—l.

THE
APPLICATION.

Call Home your Fleet, cries Artful SPAIN,
And BRITAIN shall no more complain:—
But should we be such Fools—What then?
We should be Slaves,—be drubb'd again.—

24. *The Lyon in Love; or, The Political Farmer* (B.M. 2347)

25. *The State Pack-Horse* (B.M. 2420)

false Guide that *leads Mankind astray*" (p. 16). The political application of the Judas-type available to Pope is clear in the fourth frontispiece of *Robin's Reign*:

> See R[ober]t[,] O[rator]'s[,] L[ord]'s[,] and B[ishop]'s buy
> Speak then Spectator, —is Corruption high.
> Mark well the Visage of each slavish Tool,
> The Blockhead, Hyprocrite, and gawdy Fool,
> Tis' these Great Men, who give our Wealth away,
> Borrow in P[e]n[sion]'s, but in V[ote]'s they Pay,
> Like Judas thus, for Gold betray the State
> His Crimes they share, and may they share his Fate!

The question that initiated this chapter has compelled us to reinvestigate the *Epistle to Bathurst* in its political context. The *Epistle* achieves literary stature because Pope succeeds in combining the particular with the general to create a poem that is both occasional and timeless. Pope writes as the virtuous satirist who tries to convince the politician, Bathurst, that England's present political and financial corruption may be traced back to "the famous Aera of 1720" when Walpole rose to power. To make his point, he uses the older patterns of imagery that were employed in the earlier satires of the South Sea Bubble. He also emphasizes the sense of continuity and timelessness through the structure of the poem: the pattern of rising and falling as on the wheel of Fortune renders the poem essentially static. Unlike the final vision in the cyclically organized *Windsor Forest*, which moves outward in time and space, the emblematic tale of Sir Balaam merely recapitulates what has preceded it. He too is on the wheel, and we feel that it will simply keep turning unless the public and private vices that propel it are controlled by men of action, like Bathurst, who can "balance Fortune."

CHAPTER IV

"The Snarling Muse": Pope's *Imitations of Horace* and Political Satire in the 1730s

parcere personis, dicere de vitiis
   —Martial 10.23.10

A hundred smart in *Timon* and in *Balaam*:
The fewer still you name, you wound the more;
Bond is but one, but *Harpax* is a Score.
   —*Imitations of Horace*

The *Epistle to Bathurst*, with its combination of visual traditions drawn from classical, Biblical, and popular sources, illustrates the range of rhetorical means a verse satirist could use against the "Great Man." *Bathurst* is also an example of the fact that satirists in verse were often more willing than satirists in prints to make personal attacks on named targets. In this chapter we shall consider the variety of tactics satirists, particularly in poetry, employed in the 1730s. Authors could choose between taking what might be called the high road of principle and historical precedent—the one Pope and Johnson traveled—or the lower road of personality and caricature— the one Swift and Walpole's defenders took. But, as we shall see, the roads often crossed, as in Pope's Sporus portrait.

    Truly nonpartisan political satires did exist during Walpole's rule, though they were rare. One such is the print *Ready Mony* {sic] *the Prevailing Candidate; or, The Humours of an Election* (B.M. 1798), a 1727 attack on campaigning methods used by all candidates. In the middle of the street of a country village stands the voter, saying "No Bribery but Pockets are free" to the two candidates who are filling some of his many pockets. One of the candidates hypocritically advises the voter, "Sell not your Country." Next to him, another candidate asks a voter who grovels for money on the ground to "Accept this small acknowledgment." Together they strike a pornographic pose, whose suggestion of sexual irregularity is reflected in the image on the right, of the tavern keeper, who wears the horns of the cuckold and shouts, "He kist my Wife, he has my Vote." Other illustrations of the theme of corruption include the classical philosopher in the right-hand corner of the foreground. His hand behind him, he takes a bribe while looking at the scene before him and saying, "Let not thy right hand know what thy left does." On the left side of the street is a statue of Justice with empty scales, ignored by all except one man who advises a companion to "Regard Justice." The companion replies, "We fell out, I lost money [sic] by her." Opposite Justice, Folly sprinkles gold on a worshipper who prays, "Help me Folly or my Cause is lost," as a butcher looks on approvingly. *Ready Mony* displays the structure of an emblem with its title, epigraph, and explanatory verse. The epigraph—"O Cives! Cives! quaranda Pecunia primum est / Virtus post nummos."—is from Horace, *Epistle* 1.1.50–51, a source Pope would later use for a far more partisan purpose.

Horace is again the source for an essentially nonpartisan political satire in *Risum Teneatis Amici?* (B.M. 1833), frontispiece to James Bramston's *The Art of Politicks* (London, 1729), an imitation of the *Ars Poetica*. The print illustrates the poem's first eight lines, on the present confusion of formerly distinct parties:

> If to a Human Face Sir *James* [Thornhill] should draw
> A Gelding's Mane, and Feathers of Maccaw,
> A Lady's Bosom, and a Tail of Cod,
> Who could help laughing at a Sight so odd?
> Just such a Monster, Sirs, pray think before ye,
> When you behold one Man both *Whig* and *Tory*.
> Not more extravagant are Drunkard's Dreams,
> Than *Low-Church* Politicks with *High-Church* Schemes.   (Pp. 1–2)

At a time when politicians "Begin like Patriots, and like Courtiers end" (p. 2), Bramston advises, "But you, from what e'er Side you take your Name, / Like *Anna's Motto*, always be the same" (p. 3).

The poem contains many references to specific people, including Addison, Carteret, Cibber, Congreve, Curll, Caleb D'Anvers, Defoe, Dryden, Durfey, Eusden, Gay, George II, Heidegger, Mist, Mother Needham, Otway, Pope, Pulteney, Ridpath, Roper, Swift, Walpole, Woolston, and others. Praise and blame are distributed equally among the ministry's supporters and opponents in this analysis of contemporary political rhetoric. Seventeenth-century typological political satire is referred to:

26. *Ready Mony* [sic] *the Prevailing Candidate; or, The Humours of an Election*
(B.M. 1798)

> Not long since *Parish-Clerks*, with saucy airs,
> Apply'd *King David's Psalms* to *State-Affairs*.
> Some certain *Tunes* to Politicks belong,
> On both Sides Drunkards love a Party-Song.   (P. 9)

But now the typology has changed:

> Some *Rufus*, some the *Conqueror* bring in,
> And some from Julius Caesar's days begin.
> A cunning Speaker can command his chaps,
> And when the *House* is not in humour, stops;
> In Falsehood Probability imploys,
> Nor his old Lies with newer Lies destroys.   (P. 16)

And successful partisan poets must learn how to use the past:

Dramatick Poets that expect the Bays,
Should cull our Histories for Party Plays;
Wickfort's Embassador should fill their head,
And the *State-Tryals* carefully be read:
For what is *Dryden's* Muse and *Otway's* Plots
To th' *Earl of Essex* or the *Queen of Scots?*   (P. 32)

Bramston's *Art of Politicks*, like Pope's *Epistle to Bathurst*, ends with an emblematic tale. The general political satire of *Ready Mony* appears again in the story of "Sir *Harry Clodpole*," one of the "unwary Knights" infected by the "Itch" of "*Parliamenteering.*" He has gone through "Two good Estates," and "he'd spend a third" for votes because

"Dearly the free-born neighborhood is bought,
They never leave him while he's worth a groat:
So Leeches stick, nor quit the bleeding wound,
Till off they drop with Skinfuls to the ground."   (Pp. 44–45)

When Pope turned to Horace for inspiration, however, the Roman satirist was enlisted in a distinctly partisan cause.

Two weeks after the publication of the *Epistle to Bathurst*, Pope wrote John Caryll, "I find the last I made had some good effect, and yet the preacher less railed at than usually those are who will be declaiming against popular or national vices. I shall redouble my blow very speedily."[1] The result of this threat would be Pope's *Imitation of the First Satire of the Second Book of Horace*, a poem that quickly "made the town too hot to hold him."[2] It began the series of poems we usually refer to as Pope's *Imitations of Horace*, a group that includes the *Epistle to Dr. Arbuthnot*, the *Satires of Dr. Donne*, and the *Epilogue to the Satires*. Although John Butt has said, "In the earliest *Imitations of Horace* there is little reflection of these [political] struggles," Pope's comment to Caryll suggests that even the first *Imitation* was intended as a continuation of the political attacks found in the *Epistle to Bathurst*.[3]

Pope explained to Spence the genesis of the first *Imitation*:

When I had a fever one winter in town [probably January 1733] that confined me to my room for five or six days, Lord Bolingbroke came to see me, happened to take up a Horace that lay on the table, and in turning it over dipped on the First Satire of the Second Book. He observed how well that would hit my case, if I were to imitate it in English. After he was gone, I read it over, translated it in a morning or two, and sent it to the press in a week or fortnight after. And this was the occasion of my imitating some other of the Satires and Epistles afterwards.[4]

For Pope, adapting Horatian satire to modern circumstances offered an excellent means to attempt again to strike the blow that had been earlier deflected by events. The unexpected appearance of the issue of excise had diminished the immediate political impact of Pope's *Epistle to Bathurst*. The often brief *Imitations* enabled Pope to produce topical and occasional poetry quickly. And the Horatian pose was one Pope at first felt comfortable in.[5]

Pope's political interests coincided with the polemical practices of Bolingbroke and his allies. In December 1729 the correspondent "Phil-Horatius" called on Caleb D'Anvers to "expose the prevailing *Madness* of the present Age, as Horace did That of ancient Rome[.] . . . there is ample Matter for a fine Dissertation on this Subject, if you think the Times are not too tender and generally infected to bear it; especially, if you might be allowed to trace the Marks of *State-Lunacy* (as you formerly did Those of a *wicked Minister*)" (*Craftsman*, no. 182). How much more effective for the Opposition to have the greatest poet of the age play the role!

By distorting the historical Horace, Bolingbroke was able to adapt the Roman poet to an eighteenth-century ideology based on the assertion that the only real political divisions in the nation were those between Court and Country. Bolingbroke and his supporters contended that their disapproval of the current ministry was based on those measures that would be anti-patriotic at any time and in any nation. Horace was available to them as a satirist who had attacked the very same Court methods of corruption and favoritism centuries earlier. Moreover, he had done so with the tactics the Opposition currently used. "Phil-Horatius" describes how Horace was able to attack the Court and escape punishment "by concealing his courtly Satire in *ironical Panegyrick*; or by dressing it up in *Allegories* and *Parallels*; or veiling it under the Fable of a *Country Mouse* and a *City Mouse*; or putting it into the Mouth of *Damasippus*, or any other Adversary." This passage could just as easily be applied to the poetic practice of Pope in the 1730s. With the publication of *The First Satire of the Second Book of Horace* in February 1733, the Opposition found their poet laureate and their modern Horace.

This first in the series of *Imitations* constitutes a defense of the poet's position. With the Latin original published alongside his *Imitation*, Pope exploits the authority and precedent of Horace to justify playing a similar "role of poet-sage, cultivator of a Muse, a garden, and himself, whose daily life of old-fashioned friendships and simplicity, with a grotto at its center could be felt to differ pointedly from the sick hurry and divided aims of the madding world."[6] He also shows how skillfully he can adapt Horace to the current situation. Pope adopts the dialogue form from Horace to present a conversation between a supposedly apolitical satirist who is morally opposed to the current political realities and a friend who seeks to reconcile him with those very forces he opposes.

Fittingly, the interlocutor is Pope's friend, the lawyer William Fortescue, who had earlier served as an intermediary in a series of meetings
between Pope and Walpole.[7] Formerly Walpole's private secretary, Fortescue was now a loyal parliamentary supporter of the ministry. As friend to
both poet and minister, Fortescue was the appropriate recipient of the poem
intended to "redouble the blow" of Pope's now public opposition to Walpole.[8] The man who had introduced them to each other would be the ideal
means to dissolve the relationship between satirist and statesman.

As a lawyer, Fortescue was a fitting interlocutor in a poem that discusses the problem of legal censorship in the 1720s and 1730s. The "Advertisement" Pope added to the collected *Imitations* in 1735 makes clear his
intention to reinforce the attack on actions rather than individuals by
appealing to the supposed traditions of classical and English poets who had
criticized earlier courts. This tactic, Pope hopes, will protect him from the
charge of libel:

> The Occasion of publishing these *Imitations* was the Clamour raised on
> some of my *Epistles*. An Answer from *Horace* was both more full, and of
> more Dignity, than any I cou'd have made in my own person; and the
> Example of much greater Freedom in so eminent a Divine as Dr. *Donne*,
> seem'd a proof with what Indignation and Contempt a Christian may
> treat Vice or Folly, in ever so low, or ever so high, a Station. Both these
> Authors were acceptable to Princes and Ministers under whom they
> lived: The Satires of Dr. *Donne* I versify'd at the Desire of the Earl of
> Oxford while he was Lord Treasurer, and the Duke of Shrewsbury who
> had been Secretary of State; neither of whom look'd upon a Satire on
> Vicious Courts as any Reflection on those they serv'd in. And indeed
> there is not in the world a greater Error, than that which Fools are so apt
> to fall into, and Knaves with good reason to incourage, the mistaking a
> *Satyrist* for Libeller; whereas to a *true Satyrist* nothing is so odious as a
> *Libeller*, for the same reason as to a man *truly Virtuous* nothing is so
> hateful as a *Hypocrite*.[9]

Within the poem itself, Pope adds Boileau and Dryden as authorities who
help establish the precedent for his satire:

> Could pension'd *Boileau* lash in honest Strain
> Flatt'rers and bigots ev'n in *Louis'* Reign?
> Could Laureate *Dryden* Pimp and Fry'r engage,
> Yet neither *Charles* nor *James* be in a Rage?   (111–14)

Like the poem it defends, Pope's preface emphasizes that his is only the
latest in a historical series of satires attacking earlier courtly follies and
vices.

However, if we consider all the *Imitations*, we quickly realize that Pope is disingenuous in denying that he libels his targets. As a group, these poems mark a notable shift toward the personal attack. If we think of the print *A Tryal of Skill* as representing the spectrum of satiric imagery ranging from the emblematic Hercules to the expressive Fox, the Horatian imitations certainly indicate a shift toward more personal, caricatured attacks. We have not left the emblematic world entirely behind, but personalities have become very prominent in the political verse of Pope.

"The Clamour raised on some of [his] Epistles" was the effect of Pope's increasingly personal attacks in the 1730s. The opening lines of *Sat.* 2 : 1 are intended to remind his enemies of his new method:

> *P.* There are (I scarce can think it, but am told)
> There are to whom my Satire seems too bold,
> Scarce to wise *Peter* complaisant enough,
> And something said of *Chartres* much too rough.
> The Lines are weak, another's pleas'd to say,
> Lord *Fanny* spins a thousand such a Day.   (1–6)

Here we have two people specifically named. A third, Lord Hervey, appears in the guise of Lord Fanny, whom Pope's readers could probably have identified. In the corresponding lines of Horace, no one is named. This is the first example of Pope's being specific where Horace is only general. Pope quickly develops this method of adaptation into a pattern he returns to throughout the series of poems. But, as we shall see later, Pope never loses his ability to generalize from specific examples.

The names in these opening lines are just as suggestive here as they had been at the beginning of the *Epistle to Bathurst*. In the previous chapter we discussed the associations Pope's readers could have made between the criminal gambler, Chartres, and his ministerial master, Walpole, or between the private false steward, Walter, and the public one. The names of Chartres and Walter would have alerted readers to the possibility that this might well be a very political *Imitation* of Horace. We should not be surprised that a poem that opens with references to surrogates for Walpole closes with the name of "Sir Robert" himself.

In this most playful of his political satires, Pope begins by doing the very thing that first raised the "Clamour" against him—he names names. Just in case any of his readers should fail to recognize where his tongue is placed, Pope describes himself as he was known to no one: "Tim'rous by Nature, of the Rich in awe, / I come to Council learned in the Law" (7–8). Beneath the whimsical language lie the serious subjects of libel law and press censorship. Naturally, freedom of the press was a subject that much concerned the leading Opposition journal. The second number of *The*

Craftsman contains a negative definition of press freedom, a definition that describes the kind of charges Pope is supposed to be defending himself against in *Sat.* 2 : 1:

> By the Liberty of the Press, we are not to understand any licentious Freedom to revile our lawful Governors and Magistrates; to traduce the establish'd Laws and Religion of our Country; or any Attempts to weaken and subvert, by opprobrious Writings, that sacred Respect and Veneration, which ought always to be maintained for Authority and Persons in Authority. Neither ought the *Press* to be made an Engine to destroy the Reputation of our Neighbours, or to prejudice any private Subject, by insulting his personal Frailties, Misfortunes, or Defects; or by exposing the Secrets of his Family to publick Laughter and Ridicule; for as these are Things only of a private Nature, which do not affect the Publick, so the Publick has no Right to the Knowledge of them; and indeed the *Law* has provided . . . wholsome Remedies against all these Enormities, both of *publick* and *private Scandal.*

Although Pope claims to be defending himself against charges such as these, in the poem he seems to try to earn as many of the accusations as possible. For example, the "Reputation of our Neighbour" Lady Mary Wortley Montagu is not enhanced by these lines: "From furious *Sappho* scarce a milder Fate, / P——x'd by her Love, or libell'd by her Hate" (83–84).[10] And "personal Frailties, Misfortunes, or Defects" seem to be the subjects in this passage:

> *P.* Each Mortal has his Pleasure: None deny
> *Scarsdale* his Bottle, *Darty* his Ham-Pye;
> *Ridotta* sips and dances, till she see
> The doubling Lustres dance as fast as she;
> F{ox} loves the Senate, *Hockley-Hole* his Brother
> Like in all else, as one Egg to another. (45–50)

The king himself receives ridicule for his well-known desire for martial glory—a desire that would not be realized, thanks to Walpole's pacific policy, until the Battle of Dettingen—in one of many passages found in the *Imitations* and *The Dunciad* where the sin of bad poetry is compounded by that of bad politics:

> *P.* What? like Sir *Richard*, rumbling, rough and fierce,
> With ARMS, and GEORGE, and BRUNSWICK crowd the Verse?
> Rend with tremendous Sound your ears asunder,
> With Gun, Drum, Trumpet, Blunderbus & Thunder?
> Or nobly wild, with *Budgell's* Fire and Force,
> Paint Angels trembling round his *falling Horse*? (23–28)

The addition of "Angels trembling" creates a ridiculous history painting inspired by Budgell's absurd verse.

Pope might here be following the instructions for writing ironic heroic verse found in James Miller's *Harlequin-Horace; or, The Art of Modern Poetry* (London, 1731):

> The Way to write of Heroes, and of Kings,
> And sing in *wond'rous* Numbers, *wond'rous* Things;
> Of mighty Matters done in bloody Battle,
> How Arms meet Arms, Swords clash, and Cannons rattle,
> How such strange Toils, and Turmoils to rehearse,
> Is learnt from *Bl{ackmor}e*'s everlasting Verse.   (P. 11)

So much for "that sacred Respect and Veneration, which ought always to be maintained for Authority and Persons in Authority." What begins as mockery soon takes a more serious turn.

By the end of the poem, Walpole has replaced the ridiculous George II as ruler of Britain. After Fortescue warns Pope of the specific laws and penalties he is liable to, the poet denies that he attacks only individuals:

> P. *Libels* and *Satires!* Lawless Things indeed!
> But grave *Epistles*, bringing Vice to light,
> Such as a *King* might read, a *Bishop* write,
> Such as Sir *Robert* would approve—
>   F. Indeed?
> The Case is alter'd—you may then proceed.
> In such a Cause the Plaintiff will be hiss'd,
> My Lords the Judges laugh, and you're dismiss'd.   (150–56)

As the presence of the Horatian original emphasizes, Pope has translated "Sir Robert" for Horace's "CAESARE," thus replacing the supreme ruler of Rome with the minister of Britain. Pope in these lines is playing with an accusation that gets increasingly more serious treatment in Opposition prints, prose, and verse: Bolingbroke charged that Walpole, as the modern Colossus of the land, "govern'd Church and State" (*Craftsman*, no. 363). But in 1733, when Opposition hopes were high in the midst of the Excise Crisis, Pope could be light-hearted about this particular threat to the "ancient Constitution."

Pope's ridicule of George II in *Sat.* 2:1 consists mainly of nose-thumbing. The poet observes the letter if not the spirit of the maxim "the King can do no wrong," and, at least in the final passage of the *Imitation*, he follows the Horatian precedent of "putting [the satire] into the Mouth of *Damasippus*, or any other Adversary." Fortescue implies that Walpole is a greater authority than the king. But the irony in Fortescue's lines does not result simply from the fact that he has replaced a master with a man. We often mistakenly assume that writers in the early eighteenth century uncritically saw Caesar Augustus as a good man and ruler.[11] Pope, in the last lines of his poem, is counting on his readers' recognition of one of Caesar's more flagrant faults—he practiced censorship:

> We are informed by *Tacitus*, that *Augustus* was the first Person in *Rome*, who took Cognizance of *scandalous Libels*, under colour, and by a forced contruction of the *Lex Majestatis*; being provoked to this Method of Proceeding by the licentious Behavior of *Cassius Severus*, who had traduced several illustrious Persons, of both Sexes, in his satirical Writings; and that afterwards *Tiberius* fell into the same Practices; exasperated, in like manner, by some Lampoons, which were published against his *Pride* and *Cruelty*, by unknown Authors.
>
> From hence we may perceive the evil Consequences of bad *Precedents*, and the Danger of departing, in any Degree, from the original Intention of *Penal* Statutes; for this Procedure of *Augustus*, in straining a Law, which was design'd only against *Actions*, to the Punishment even of the *worst Kind of Writings*, paved the way for his next Successor to prosecute the most innocent Books, and destroy entirely that *just Liberty*, which is the greatest Blessing of a free People. (*Craftsman*, no. 4)

Thus, Pope's lines are ironic not only because the original Latin allows us to see that Fortescue has unwittingly transferred authority from an emperor to a minister; irony results as well from the fact that Caesar Augustus set the precedent for the censorship currently practiced in Britain. Even if Fortescue had translated George for Caesar, his lines would remain satiric. As lines 145–49 make clear, Pope must avoid breaking the English *Lex Majestatis*:

> It stands on record, that in *Richard's* Times
> A Man was hang'd for very honest Rhymes.
> Consult the Statute: *quart*. I think it is,
> *Edward Sext.* or *prim.* & *quint. Eliz:*
> See *Libels, Satires*—here you have it—read.

The topic of press censorship had been much discussed since the conviction in December 1731 of Richard Francklin, printer of *The Craftsman*.[12] In November 1729 he had been acquitted on a charge of libel. The ministerial prosecution failed because Opposition sentiment was so high in London that the Tory Lord Mayor, John Barber, was able to pack the jury with men favorable to *The Craftsman's* cause. The government responded with the Juries Act of 1730, which permitted judges to appoint special juries with higher property qualifications for cases tried at Westminster. Consequently, the ministry gained a much firmer control of the composition of the juries, and Francklin was convicted in 1731 for having published the "Hague Letter" (*Craftsman*, no. 235). Thereafter, Pope and his readers were well aware of the truth in Fortescue's warning: "Your Plea is good. But still I say, beware! / Laws are explain'd by Men—so have a care" (143–44). And they were unlikely to have forgotten the importance placed on a free press in the third engraving of *Robin's Reign; or, Seven's the Main*, whose accompanying verses read:

> Hail Typographic Art!—what Blessings flow
> Peace, Plenty, Justice, to thy Aid we owe!
> Sacred and Civil Rights unmask'd we see,
> From All the Tricks of Priests & Statesmen free.
> Their various Arts thy Noble page explains,
> And Reason only unresisted Reigns.
> Tis thou Alone canst awe the Guilty Great.
> Thy Press is the Palladium of the State.

Fortunately for the Opposition, the ministry was unable to control totally the satirical assaults. Perhaps the explanation is found in James Bramston's *The Man of Taste* (London, 1733): "Can Statutes keep the *British Press* in awe, / When that sells best, that's most against the Law?" (p. 8). Pope's recognition of governmental impotence may help explain his light-hearted treatment, in 1733, of such a serious theme. Or the tone of Pope's First Horation *Imitation* may reflect the high hopes the Opposition had in early 1733 of defeating Walpole on excise, hopes whose fulfillment is recognized in *The Scheme Disappointed A Fruitless Sacrifice* (B.M. 1928), artistically one of the best of the excise prints. Let us, for the moment, concentrate on the design on the left side of the print, *The Scheme Disappointed*. The descriptive text identifies many of the emblematic and heraldic images:

> Fig. 1. *BRITTAIN* intent on Magna Charta, repulsing Fig. 2. [Sir Robert Walpole] Offering her the Excise Scheme. Fig. 3. *SCOTLAND* [identifiable by the heraldic thistle on her shield]. Fig. 4. The Empire [of Germany] directing. Fig. 5. A naked Boy with a pointless Sword (the Princes of the Empire) to look up to Brittain. Fig. 6. A Bull dog [with "RW," i.e., Robert Walpole, on his collar] licking and overturning an Imperial Crown, the Map of Naples & Sicily lying before. Fig. 7. Rome [a nun] ready to seize Brittain if she accepts the Scheme.

Throughout *Sat*. 2:1, Pope writes as one whose cause is imminently triumphant and whose satiric utterances are irrepressible. His first justification for writing satire is that it is an involuntary, biological need:

27. *The Scheme Disappointed A Fruitless Sacrifice* (B.M. 1928)

> *P.* Not write? but then I *think*,
> And for my Soul I cannot sleep a wink.
> I nod in Company, I wake at Night,
> Fools rush into my Head, and so I write.   (11–14)

Soon, however, he talks of himself as the conscious satirist:

> Satire's my Weapon, but I'm too discreet
> To run a Muck, and tilt at all I meet;
> I only wear it in a Land of Hectors,
> Thieves, Supercargoes, Sharpers, and Directors.
> Save but our *Army!* and let *Jove* incrust
> Swords, Pikes, and Guns, with everlasting Rust!
> Peace is my dear Delight—not *Fleury's* more:
> But touch me, and no Minister so sore.
> Who-e'er offends, at some unlucky Time
> Slides into Verse, and hitches in a Rhyme,

Sacred to Ridicule! his whole Life long,
And the sad Burthen of some merry Song.   (69–80)

Pope's language keeps the passage humorous rather than allowing it to
rise to the heroic level. Words such as "a Muck," "tilt," with its suggestion
of a dwarfish Don Quixote, "sore," "hitches," and "merry" maintain the
playful tone.[13] His reference to discretion reminds us of the accusations
about libel and of the need to attack measures rather than men in a country
populated by "Hectors, / Thieves, Supercargoes, Sharpers, and Directors"—the men who swarm in the *Epistle to Bathurst*. But once again Pope
pointedly attacks both men and measures when he goes out of his way to be
specific and particular where the Horatian original is not. Horace's words
are neither:

> . . . O Pater & Rex
> Jupiter! ut pereat positum rubigine telum,
> Nec quisquam noceat cupido mihi pacis! at ille,
> Qui me commorit (melius non tangere clamo)
> Flebit, & insignis tota cantabitur urbe.   (42–46)

Pope's imitation turns Horace's request that his lance-pen of satire be eaten
by rust into an ironic attack on the ministerial measure of supporting
standing armies in peacetime:

> Save but our *Army!* and let *Jove* incrust
> Swords, Pikes, and Guns, with everlasting Rust!
> Peace is my dear Delight—not *Fleury's* more:
> But touch me, and no Minister so sore.   (73–76)

References to Fleury and to the "Minister" particularize the original by
making the satire more specific. The Opposition frequently charged that
Cardinal Fleury, foreign minister to France, could afford to be peaceful
because Walpole's pacific foreign policy served French interests (e.g.,
Craftsman, no. 26). And *The Craftsman* had previously counseled Walpole
about controlling his violent temper (no. 23).

The significance of Pope's reference to Fleury becomes clearer if we
glance once again at *A Fruitless Sacrifice* but this time consider the design on
the right and its explanatory text:

Fig. 1. The Sacrificer [Sir Robert Walpole] on his knees pushing [*sic*] a
Torch to Magna Charta, etc. [Free Electio, Liberty of Europ], but the
fire not kindl'd, the Sacrifice directed to, Fig. 2. The Devil holding out
with one hand the Excise Scheme, the other holds a Rope, & Fig. 3. A
Cardinal [Fleury] with one hand holding out a bag to the Sacrificer,
with the other grasping at a Globe in the Clouds [the emblem of the

fleur-de-lis represents France's alleged plan to establish universal monarchy]. Fig. 4. The Altar a Pile of Books founded on a heap of Gold with proper Inscriptions [Treaty of Hanover, Account of ye Sinking funds, Treaty of Seville and Vienna . . . Stock jobbing, Bank Contract . . . Clodious and Cicero . . . Bastimentos a Tragedy . . .]. Fig. 5. The Statue of Brittain on a Column held by an Almighty hand. Fig. 6. The British Fleet in Port. Fig. 7. The French Fleet under Sail.

Pope portrays Horace as a satirist who clearly enjoys his work. Horace describes himself as a relatively passive opponent who keeps his sword sheathed until provoked to use it:

Sed hic stylus haud petit ultro
Quenquam animantem; & me veluti custodiet ensis
Vagina tectus, quem cur distringere coner,
Tutus ab infestis latronibus?   (39–42)

Pope, however, sounds as if he rambles about the countryside on his Rosinante, despite his assertion of discretion.

Toward the end of the poem, in lines one recent critic sees as the object of the whole poem, Pope moves beyond comical defense of his satire:[14]

P. What? arm'd for Virtue when I point the Pen,
Brand the bold Front of shameless, guilty Men,
Dash the proud Gamester in his gilded Car,
Bare the mean Heart that lurks beneath a Star;
Can there be wanting to defend Her Cause,
Lights of the Church, or Guardians of the Laws?
Could pension'd Boileau lash in honest Strain
Flatt'rers and Bigots ev'n in Louis' Reign?
Could Laureate Dryden Pimp and Fry'r engage,
Yet neither Charles nor James be in a Rage?
And I not strip the Gilding off a Knave,
Un-plac'd, un-pension'd, no Man's Heir, or Slave?
I will, or perish in the gen'rous Cause.
Hear this, and tremble! you, who 'scape the Laws.
Yes, while I live, no rich or noble knave
Shall walk the World, in credit, to his grave.   (105–20)

There is no gaiety here. The seriousness of this passage is at odds with the light-hearted tone of the rest of the poem and is more appropriate to the later, increasingly serious Imitations—particularly the Juvenalian Epilogue to the Satires. Paradoxically, because of its discordant tone, this, the best passage in the poem, causes a flawed Imitation.

What we have in lines 105–20 is a variation of the poet's structural device of moving from particulars to a pictorial closing passage. Although the "arm'd for *Virtue*" passage does not conclude the poem, it strikes most readers as the emotional and literary zenith of the poem. The very power of these lines renders the remainder of the *Imitation* somewhat anticlimactic, a falling off from high seriousness back to the comic level. Like the emblematic Balaam episode at the end of the *Epistle to Bathurst*, the "arm'd for Virtue" passage is intended to summarize and justify what has preceded it in the poem. In previous lines Pope has reminded us of the crimes and sins of his contemporaries. In the lines that introduce the passage under discussion, Fortescue reiterates the charge that Pope attacks individuals and warns him that his life is endangered as a result: "Plums, and Directors, *Shylock* and his Wife, / Will club their Testers, now, to take your Life!" (103–4).

In his response, Pope appropriates to himself a traditional emblematic representation of Virtue.[15] He may have hoped that his readers would recognize in the image of the virtuous poet tilting at Vice an allusion to the emblem of "Force of Virtue," number 320 in Caesar Ripa's *Iconologia; or, Moral Emblems* (London, 1709): " 'Tis a very handsom [*sic*] young Man, call'd *Bellerophon*, mounted upon *Pegasus*, who with a Dart kills a Chimera; which allegorically signifies a certain multiform Variety of *Vices*, which *Bellerophon* kills; the Etymology of his Name denotes a *Killer* of Vice."

Just as Hogarth had adapted traditional emblems to the contemporary situation depicted in the *South Sea Scheme*, or as graphic artists emphasized the continuous dangers of Walpolean measures by presenting the minister in the pose of a colossus, Pope seeks to rise above the present and particular by wrapping himself in traditional imagery. He is not simply libeling insignificant sinners, criminals, and fools; our dwarfish Don Quixote has transformed himself into the embodiment of Virtue herself. While readers would probably identify the phrases "shameless, guilty Men," "the proud Gamester," and "the mean Heart that lurks beneath a Star" with Walpole,[16] all the references are certainly general enough that they are applicable to others as well. Pope's satirical motivation is no longer revenge for attacks on himself. In lines 69–80 he has already indicated his willingness to seek out opponents. Now, in the "arm'd for *Virtue*" passage, he aggressively attacks evildoers in a world where "there be wanting to defend Her Cause, / Lights of the Church, or Guardians of the Laws." His appeal to the historical precedents of Dryden and Boileau reinforces the idea that the satirist has become a force rather than merely an individual. And the implication that the crimes he attacks are those that also deserved attack in another time and another land supports the contention of Walpole's adversaries that they were more interested in principles than in men. In lines 105–20, Pope does with the emblem of Virtue what the graphic artist does with the image of Hercules in *A Tryal of Skill*. Recognition by the reader or viewer of the emblematic context immediately renders the depiction general as well as particular in application. In both the verbal and visual representations, the importance of the poet transcends his identity as Alexander Pope. He is linked with all former and future defenders of Virtue and Eloquence. This desire to associate himself with "the gen'rous Cause" of Virtue impels him to appropriate Horace's description of Lucilius—"TO VIRTUE ONLY and HER FRIENDS, A FRIEND" (121)—to himself.

In addition to portraying himself in the literary satiric tradition, Pope joins the political Opposition to Walpole by the satiric pose he strikes. He writes as a man of moderation or neutrality in matters artistic, religious, and political:

> My Head and Heart thus flowing thro' my Quill,
> Verse-man or Prose-man, term me which you will,
> Papist or Protestant, or both between,
> Like good *Erasmus* in an honest Mean,
> In Moderation placing all my Glory,
> While Tories call me Whig, and Whigs a Tory.   (63–68)

Pope's life may well have been an *imitatio Horatii*. But from a political perspective, his satiric existence is an *imitatio* of Caleb D'Anvers, the principal persona of *The Craftsman*. Pope's assertion of political neutrality and his disregard for political labels indicate his affinities with the group surrounding Bolingbroke and Pulteney. In the Dedication to the volumes of *The Craftsman* collected in 1731, Caleb makes a similar claim, though he is more explicit about its political implications:

> We have very cautiously avoided . . . to give Offence to any Party, or to confine our selves to the narrow Views of any Party; though We have always pass'd under the Denomination of *Whigs*, and argued upon the Principles, which *that Party* hath formerly attributed to Themselves; but We have lately seen those noble Principles so scandalously prostituted by *some Persons*, who are pleas'd to call Themselves *Whigs*, and so strenuously asserted by *many others*, who have been reputed *Tories*, that We are ashamed to value our selves upon such an idle Distinction of *Names* any longer.

Caleb's supposed disinterest is illustrated in the last engraving of *Robin's Reign; or, Seven's the Main* where Virtue encourages Caleb at his desk while another divinity hands him a pen. Before him is a paper marked, "The Spirit of Liberty." The supplementary verses link him with his classical type:

In Contemplation deep is D'Anvers seen,
And Tully's Eloquence directs his Pen.
Bids him his wonted Energy retain,
And still the Cause of Liberty maintain.
While Virtue thus,—since for my sake engaged,
Thou a just War, hast with Corruption waged.
Thy full Reward, in Glory then receive,
And Long as Cic'ro, let the Craftsman Live.

Against the background of Bolingbroke's continuous objections to the use of party labels, whenever we find someone mocking the validity of such labels, we can be fairly certain of Opposition sympathies. Pope becomes more explicit about the meaninglessness of "Whig" and "Tory" in *The Epistle to Augustus*:

Now Whig, now Tory, what we lov'd we hate;
Now all for Pleasure, now for Church and State;
Now for Prerogative, and now for Laws;
Effects unhappy! from a Noble Cause.   (157–60)

Similarly, Pope's boast that he is "Un-plac'd, un-pension'd, no Man's Heir, or Slave" and his readiness to "perish in the gen'rous Cause" of Virtue would have sounded to his readers very much like the language and sentiments of the anonymous author of *The British Patriot; or, A Timely Caveat against Giving into the Measures of any Evil and Corrupt Minister* (London, 1731):

What led me into these Thoughts is the present Cavils and Bickerings that exist between the authors of the *Craftsman* . . . and their Opponents. I profess myself to be a Neuter in their Disputes; that I am no Party-man, no Hireling, or mercenary Person; that I have no Employment or Pension, nor expect any; that I have no sinister Ends in view; but I do frankly own, I am one who has his Country so much at heart, that I would not only use my utmost Endeavors, but sacrifice even my Life, to promote the Good and Welfare of my Fellow Subjects. (P. 11)

For Pope and the pamphleteer, "the gen'rous Cause" of Virtue is identified with the Opposition, who "promote the Good and Welfare" of Britain.

Pope's political independence and integrity are based on his assertion of personal integrity, though his praise of the Jacobite William Shippen indicates that the poet's allegiance cannot be with Walpole:

I love to pour out all myself, as plain
As downright *Shippen*, or as old *Montagne*.
In them, as certain to be lov'd as seen,
The Soul stood forth, nor kept a Thought within;

In me what Spots (for Spots I have) appear,
Will prove at least the Medium must be clear.
In this impartial Glass, my Muse intends
Fair to expose myself, my Foes, my Friends.   (51–58)

"To be a great satirist, a man must have . . . a place to stand, an angle
of vision. For Pope . . . the garden and the grotto supplied this."[17] Besides
the literary and biographical justifications for Pope's "place to stand," the
poet exploits the political tradition of using the Country as a perspective
from which to attack the Court.[18] The virtually automatic opposition between Court and Country that arose in the early seventeenth century continued into the eighteenth, and Bolingbroke clearly saw the skeptical,
basically apolitical backbenchers in Parliament as an essential constituency
for any effective Opposition party. The importance of the Country interest
was not lost on Walpole, who carefully emphasized his own rustic origins
and who sought, whenever possible, to placate this group by lowering the
Land Tax. Bolingbroke knew that the Country interest was originally
identified with Whig opposition to the Tory Courts of the Stuarts; if he
could succeed in linking the present Opposition with the tradition of
Country opposition, he would strengthen his assertion that Walpole's antagonists were the true inheritors of Whig principles. Such a distinction
between Court and Country would also remove the party labels of Whig and
Tory: "I think nothing more demonstrable, than that the *Court-Whigs* of
this Age are exactly the same Kind of Creatures with the *Court-Tories* before
the *Revolution*; that, *vice versa*, the Body of the present Tories have adopted
the Spirit of the *old Whigs*; and by acting in Conjunction with the *independent Whigs* of our Times, who adhere to their ancient Principles, have
in a great Measure abolish'd those *silly Appelations*, and made COURT
and COUNTRY the only prevailing Distinction amongst us" (*Craftsman*,
no. 379).

The Opposition introduced Caleb D'Anvers to the world on 15 July
1726. His appearance in *The Country Gentleman* established his identity as
an independent country gentleman, and the allegorical story about his
untrustworthy coachman, Robin (Walpole), indicated his political allegiance. Bolingbroke's desire to appeal to the Country interest is further
reflected by the fact that the official title of *The Craftsman* became, in no.
45, *The Country Journal*, a name that never quite caught on. Through the
course of *The Craftsman*, we learn that Caleb was born in 1660 (no. 1), a
descendant of William the Conqueror, and that his family included a
seventeenth-century regicide (no. 461). Caleb had a Tory education (no. 1),
but his political creed was and still is that of a "Old Whig" (no. 368). With
his conservative ways exemplified by his old-fashioned clothes (no. 480),

Caleb is now retired to his small but comfortable home outside London, from whence he periodically makes short trips (no. 1). Caleb is obviously intended to be a political English Everyman. Surely if Caleb opposes ministerial measures, every virtuous Briton ought to.

The anonymous *A Collection of State Flowers* (London, 1734) concludes with a description of Caleb D'Anvers as a figure of Pope-like virtue and independence:

> Oh! glorious *D'Anvers*, born of noble Race,
> Who beg'st no *Pension*, and who scorn'st *all Place*.
> *Titles* and *Honours* are but *empty Things*,
> *Helpless Rewards* confer'd by gracious Kings;
> Gay, gaudy Names, that set off humble Birth,
> But add no *Lustre* to *intrinsick Worth*:
> *These*, with a *native Greatness*, *You* decline,
> For *Gold* still brings its *Value* from the *Mine*.

As a satirist of the Court, Caleb too needs "a place to stand," and his is much like that of Pope:

> As it is frequently observed, that those Persons *think most, who speak least*; so perhaps it will hold equally true, that They form the soundest Judgment of what passes in the World, who live most retired from the Bustle of it. As to myself, however inconsiderable I may have been thought for the greatest Part of my Life, I hope to convince the World that I am . . . as warmly affected with the Interest of my Country, as any Man in it; and look with equal Concern upon the manifold Vices and Corruptions; upon that general Prostitution of Principles and Degeneracy of Manners, which have by degrees over-run the whole Kingdom, and put Virtue and Honesty almost quite out of Countenance. (*Craftsman*, no. 1)

Pope, too, turned to retirement as a means to judge his age. Twenty years earlier, in *Windsor Forest*, he had worn the guise of a retired philosopher-historian to praise Anne. He realized that the pose would work at least as well for a satirist in the 1730s. As a Roman Catholic, he could not be accused of having personal political ambitions, and his retirement might at first suggest his neutrality in state affairs:

> Know, all the distant Din the World can keep
> Rolls o'er my *Grotto*, and but sooths my Sleep.
> There, my Retreat the best Companions grace,
> Chiefs, out of War, and Statesmen, out of Place.

There *St. John* mingles with my friendly Bowl,
The Feast of Reason and the Flow of Soul:
And He, whose Lightning pierc'd th' *Iberian* Lines,
Now, forms my Quincunx, and now ranks my Vines,
Or tames the Genius of the stubborn Plain,
Almost as quickly, as he conquer'd *Spain*.   (123–32)

References to Bolingbroke and Peterborough, however, render the passage partisan. They were "out of Place" and "out of War" as a result of the Hanoverian succession. Bolingbroke fled the country in 1715 rather than stand trial, and Peterborough retired from the army at the accession of George I. In addition, Pope's pointed praise of Peterborough's Spanish conquests stand in contrast to Walpole's present pacific strategy and to the Spanish insults the Opposition feels the English have suffered. Pope implies that the current government may be judged against the capable and glorious men it has forced into inactivity.

As the introduction to the *Imitations, The First Satire of the Second Book* deals with many of the subjects and employs most of the tactics found in the later poems. Moving from men to measures, from the particular to the general, Pope discusses the themes of censorship, standing armies, Walpole's unconstitutional position, and his own relationship to contemporary evils and establishes himself as an essentially comical political satirist imitating *The Craftsman*'s Caleb D'Anvers and a modernized Horace. His satiric pose also establishes him as the spokesman for the Opposition in their rhetorical strategy of asserting themselves as the true inheritors of seventeenth-century Whig Country party political tradition.

In Pope's next published poem, *The Impertinent; or, A Visit to the Court, A Satyr, By an Eminent Hand* (November 1733), he is even more explicit about the antagonism between Court and Country.[19] We may speculate that he was encouraged to be so by the simultaneous publication of Bolingbroke's *Dissertation upon Parties* in issues of *The Craftsman*. Bolingbroke's *Dissertation* argues at great length and with a heavy reliance on historical evidence that "nothing can be more reasonable than to admit the nominal division of constitutionists and anti-constitutionists, or of a court and a country-party, at this time, when an avowed difference of principles makes this distinction real." Pope's poem, an imitation of *The Fourth Satire of Dr. John Donne*, dramatizes the conflict between the two political groups. Imitating Donne enabled Pope to set his satire in an earlier historical context, thereby illustrating the Opposition tactic of emphasizing their ties with the past and particularly with the legacy of Whig tradition. The same impulse to associate the antiministerial cause with that of earlier "Country" writers encouraged *The Craftsman* to cite Andrew Marvell as an authority on issues including excise (no. 217), Court favorites (no. 449), and the evils of a slavishly political Bench of Bishops in the House of Lords (no. 482).

In *The Impertinent*, the poet serves time in "Purgatory" on earth when he must go to Court, despite his own disinclination to do so:

> With foolish *Pride* my Heart was never fir'd,
> Nor the vain Itch *t'admire*, or be *admir'd*;
> I hop'd for no *Commission* from his Grace;
> I bought no *Benefice*, I begg'd no *Place*;
> Had no *new Verses*, or *new Suit* to show;
> Yet went to COURT!—the Dev'l wou'd have it so.   (9–14)

There the poet encounters the monstrous "Impertinent," a courtier of outlandish dress, speech, and manners. During the dialogue that ensues between the Country and Court representatives, Pope again uses the Horatian satiric device of "putting [his satire] into the Mouth of *Damasippus*, or any other *Adversary*," just as he had in *Sat.* 2:1. The "Impertinent" himself, supposedly a ministerial supporter, affirms some of the more frequent charges the Opposition leveled against "the *Great Man*," Walpole:

> Then as a licens'd Spy, whom nothing can
> Silence, or hurt, he libels the *Great Man*;
> Swears every *Place entail'd* for Years to come,
> In *sure Succession* to the Day of Doom:
> He names the *Price* for ev'ry *Office* paid,
> And says our *Wars thrive ill*, because *delay'd*;
> Nay hints, 'tis by Connivance of the Court,
> That *Spain* robs on, and *Dunkirk's* still a Port.   (158–65)

Not even the ministerial lackey, in his moments of candor, is able to support the shameful policies of Walpole's administration, policies that allegedly include the treasonous complicity by the Court (including the king?) in Spanish crimes. Walpole's government is further undercut by the servility, hypocrisy, and ingratitude the "Impertinent" displays when

> Away he flies. He bows, and bows again;
> And close as *Umbra* joins the dirty Train.
> Not *Fannius* self more impudently near,
> When half his Nose is in his Patron's Ear.   (176–79)

Bolingbroke and Peterborough had been cast out so that men of this caliber might serve. Self-interest is the only motivation of ministerial supporters, for they have ties to neither measures nor to other men.

Shocked and frightened by what he has heard and seen, the poet flees the Court to seek "the place to stand" of political satirists like Pope and Caleb:

Bear me, some God! oh quickly bear me hence
To wholesome Solitude, the Nurse of Sense:
Where Contemplation prunes her ruffled Wings,
And the free Soul looks down to pity Kings.   (184–87)

Now that he is back in the Country, the poet can turn to his imagination to transform his experience into fiction. In the now familiar pattern, Pope transcends the particular with the use of emblematic and allegorical generalization to end the poem. As if following the advice of "Phil-Horatius," Pope employs an allegory, or vision, much like those so commonly found in *The Craftsman*:

There sober Thought pursu'd th'amusing theme
Till Fancy color'd it, and form'd a Dream.
A *Vision* Hermits can to Hell transport,
And force ev'n me to see the Damn'd at Court.
Not *Dante* dreaming all th'Infernal State,
Beheld such Scenes of *Envy, Sin*, and *Hate*.   (188–93)

The poet discovers that all is illusion, with roles being played by those he had previously taken seriously:

And why not Players strut in Courtiers Cloaths?
For these are Actors too, as well as those:
Wants reach all States; they beg but better drest,
And all is *splendid Poverty* at best.   (222–25)

The oxymoron "splendid Poverty" probably refers to another often lamented contrast between the Court and the Country. The current economic situation was an issue contested by the Opposition and the ministry. Supporters of Walpole argued that his policies brought England unprecedented prosperity; Bolingbroke, on the other hand, maintained that the prosperity was superficial and illusory, and that the British were, paradoxically, "*a luxurious impoverish'd* People" (*Craftsman*, no. 464). To the Opposition, all the luxury was concentrated in the corruption of the Court, whose external splendor only masked the poor nation supporting the extravagance. Thus, Pope's courtiers can only *act* as if they were wealthy; their true condition is one of poverty, because Walpole's policies have weakened the English economy. Not even the king is what he appears; his clothes alone distinguish him from a more easily recognizable actor, and even they can mask him for little more than a week:

"That's *Velvet* for a *King!*" the Flattr'er swears;
'Tis true, for ten days hence 'twill be *King Lear's*.
Our Court may justly to our Stage give Rules,
That helps it both to *Fool's-Coats* and to *Fools*.   (218–21)

The poet's "*Vision*" enables him to see beyond the illusions of particular men and to expose the reality that is the Court. The imagery of lines 218–21 is taken from perhaps the most important visual source available to satirists—the theater—where words and pictures are interdependent. In this passage, Pope animates the earlier, static, "*Court in Wax*" (206):

Such painted Puppets, such a varnish'd Race
Of hollow Gewgaws, only Dress and Face,
Such waxen Noses, stately, staring things,
No wonder some Folks bow, and think them *Kings*.   (208–11)

The performance the satirist sees is directed by "the *Great Man*" (159), represented as the "Harlequin of State" in the second frontispiece of *Robin's Reign; or, Seven's the Main*. Walpole is represented as "Punch" in a satiric playbill of 1735 (B.M. 2140). Pope returns to the visual image of the stage in *Epistle* 2 : 1 : 318–19 to satirize how different the present times are from those of Edward III: "to complete the jest, / Old Edward's Armour beams on Cibber's breast!"

The apparent splendor of the presence-chamber—"The *Presence* seems, with things so richly odd, / The Mosque of *Mahound*, or some Queer *Pa-god* (238–39)—is quickly undercut by the entrance of "the Captain," presumably George II:

But here's the *Captain*, that will plague them [the Fops] both,
Whose Air cries Arm! whose very Look's an Oath:
Tho' his Soul's Bullet, and his Body Buff!
Damn him, he's honest, Sir,—and that's enuff.
He spits fore-right; his haughty Chest before,
Like batt'ring Rams, beats open ev'ry Door;
And with a Face as red, and as awry,
As *Herod's* Hang-dogs in old Tapestry,
Scarecrow to Boys, the breeding Woman's curse;
Has yet a strange Ambition to *look worse*:
Confounds the Civil, keeps the Rude in awe,
Jests like a licens'd Fool, commands like Law.   (260–71)

Jacobites often referred to George II as the "captain,"[20] and the "*Captain*" of the "*Pyrates*" (228) has many of the attributes the Opposition ascribed to the king, including his martial desires, his haughtiness, his quickness to anger, and his notable lack of civility. The king, too, "Confounds the Civil, keeps the Rude in awe" because he often rudely turned his back on people at his levée as an indication of disfavor. After he turned his back on Lord Falmouth, twenty-seven peers who had shared this treatment formed "The Liberty or Rumpsteak Club" in 1734.[21]

With his "Face as red, and as awry, / As *Herod's* Hang-dogs in old Tapestry" the Captain-King is transformed from an individual into an emblem of frightening Anger that causes the terrified poet to reenact his earlier flight from Court. The Captain-King immediately becomes the first of a series of pictures on tapestries:

> Frighted, I quit the Room, but leave it so,
> As Men from Jayls to Execution go;
> For hung with *Deadly Sins* I see the Wall,
> And lin'd with *Giants*, deadlier than 'em all:
> Each Man an *Ascapart*, of Strength to toss
> For Quoits, both *Temple-Bar* and *Charing-Cross*.   (272–77)

Pope mocks the kind of history painting one would expect to find at Court. The "Impertinent" himself had earlier indicated the perversion of the didactic purposes of art that are accepted by this reign:

> "No Lessons now are taught the *Spartan* way:
> Tho' in his Pictures Lust be full display'd,
> Few are the Converts *Aretine* has made;
> And tho' the Court show *Vice* exceeding clear,
> None shou'd, by my Advice, learn *Virtue* there."   (93–97)

The more conventional way of showing a monarch's proper relation to the Vices appears in the print *Le Couronement Du Roy George De La Grande Bretagne* . . . (B.M. 1590), published in late 1714 or early 1715 to celebrate the accession of George I. George is on his throne and the Vices of Envy, Error, Fraud, and Discord are subdued by Hercules and Mercury, representing Virtue and Eloquence.

By moving from the particular to the emblematic in this way, the poet can justifiably maintain that his motive for satire is more religious than political. Just as he earlier saw the actors beneath their costumes, he now sees individuals not only as particular political figures but also as the various sins they exemplify. His *"Vision"* has allowed him to see the truth beneath appearances; he sees and understands the universal and emblematic implications of the corruption underlying the court of George II. The poet seeks to avoid the label of partisan political satirist; by placing the current Court within the context of a medieval tapestry depicting the Seven Deadly Sins he succeeds in presenting himself as a religious satirist assailing sinners

L. Cheron. In. del.   C. Dubosc. Sculp.

Le Couronement Du Roy George · · · · Roy De la Grande Bretagne

Estant assis Sur Son Trone, Et Couronné par
proche Sont Les Armes d'Angleterre et La
Prince, et La Princesse, parlants avec
comme le Modelle de la Sagesse, et de la
Globe du monde, qui fait connoitre, Sa
qui Luy offre L'Angleterre, Laquelle luy
est L'Abondance du Pays; plus, bas est,
animé Contre Les vices, qui Sont L'Envie
tems decouvre toutes les machinations
Vertu Et L'Eloquence Representées par Hercule et

La Renommée, et Les Genies des Peuples;
Religion; à coste de Sa Majesté est Le
Minerve, laquelle leur montre Le Roy,
Prudence; Sous Sa main gauche, est Le
Domination. A Sa droite est La Justice
met Le Sceptre en main; et pres d'Elle
le Lion attribué L'Angleterre, qui est
L'erreur, La Fraude, et La Discorde, dont le
renversées Sous les pieds de Sa Majesté, par La
Mercure. Presente à Sa Majeste par Son tres humble
et tres obeissant Serviteur Et fidel Suj et C. Dubosc.

28. *Le Couronement Du Roy George De La Grande Bretagne . . .* (B.M. 1590)

who just happen to be at Court. But he modestly (and ironically) admits
that his powers are not quite up to the job.

> *Courts* are too much for Wits so weak as mine;
> Charge them with Heav'n's Artill'ry, bold *Divine!*
> From such alone the Great Rebukes endure,
> Whose *Satyr's sacred*, and whose Rage *secure.*
> 'Tis mine to wash a few slight Stains; but theirs
> To deluge Sin, and drown a Court in Tears.
> Howe'er, what's now *Apocrypha*, my Wit,
> In time to come, may pass for *Holy Writ.*   (280–87)

Like the figure of Colossus-Walpole, the emblem of George II—"Herod's
Hang-dogs"—allows the poet to oppose measures and men by developing
the general implications that may be drawn from the behavior of particular
politicians.

This same process of moving from the particular to the general, from
men to measures, may be seen in the Sporus passage of *An Epistle to Dr.
Arbuthnot* (1735). Thus, Hervey is at first satirized in his personal capacity:

> Let *Sporus* tremble—"What? that Thing of silk,
> "*Sporus*, that mere white Curd of Ass's milk?
> "Satire or Sense alas! can *Sporus* feel?
> "Who breaks a Butterfly upon a Wheel?"
> Yet let me flap this Bug with gilded wings,
> This painted Child of Dirt that stinks and stings
>
> . . . .
>
> So well-bred Spaniels civilly delight
> In mumbling of the Game they dare not bite.
> Eternal Smiles his Emptiness betray,
> As shallow streams run dimpling all the way.   (305–10 313–16)

In the initial interchange of this passage between Pope and Arbuthnot,
the latter objects that Pope is, in effect, attacking only an individual, and
not a particularly significant one at that. Even in his reply, Pope acknowledges that Hervey is innocuous, cowardly, and essentially passive. We are
struck most of all by "his Emptiness." Why indeed break this "Butterfly
upon a Wheel?" The answer comes in the rest of the passage, as Pope moves
beyond the man to the policies he embraces or facilitates:

> Whether in florid Impotence he speaks,
> And, as the Prompter breathes, the Puppet squeaks;
> Or at the Ear of *Eve*, familiar Toad,
> Half Froth, half Venom, spits himself abroad,

In Puns, or Politicks, or Tales, or Lyes,
Or Spite, or Smut, or Rymes, or Blasphemies

.   .   .   .

Amphibious Thing! that acting either Part,
The trifling Head, or the corrupted Heart!
Fop at the Toilet, Flatt'rer at the Board,
Now trips a Lady, and now struts a Lord.
Eve's Tempter thus the Rabbins have exprest,
A Cherub's face, a Reptile all the rest;
Beauty that shocks you, Parts that none will trust,
Wit that can creep, and Pride that licks the dust.

(317–22, 326–33)

Hervey's passivity is only apparently innocuous. Like the Courtiers in *The Impertinent*, his true condition is revealed to be that of a "Puppet" or actor, whose "Prompter" is presumably Hervey's political master, Walpole. Pope denies Hervey's status as a human being; now his very breath must come from the "Prompter." His existence is dictated by the measures his master imposes on him, and Hervey is transformed into a surrogate for Walpole. Once we realize that Hervey as a man is inconsequential—in fact, almost nonexistent—we recognize that his actions are not his own. His satanic posture "at the Ear of *Eve*" would almost certainly have reminded Pope's readers of the frequent Opposition charge that Walpole secretly influenced the queen, and through her, the king (e.g., *Craftsman*, nos. 376, 387, 456, 499, 503). Pope wittily suggests that both Caroline and George are as much puppets of the "Prompter" as is Hervey. Walpole is ultimately in control if through his puppet he can rule the whole Court, and "what can be more ignominious than for a *great King* to become the TOOL *of his* MINIS-TER, and in a Manner change Stations with Him?" (*Craftsman*, no. 498). The satanic implications of betrayal and usurpation are more appropriate to Walpole than to his puppet; readers of *The Craftsman*, for example, were well-instructed in the notion that Walpole posed a threat to the throne itself (e.g., no. 489). The image of Walpole as "Prompter," or "Puppet-master," was one shared by verbal and visual satirists, as can be seen in the 1742 print *The Screen. A Simile* (B.M. 2540), where Walpole is both "*Punch*" and "The *Puppet Man*,—behind the *Screen*." A visual reference to Walpole's alleged satanic deception and usurpation is found in the side panel on the left of *The Scheme Disappointed A Fruitless Sacrifice*, where a snake entwines a throne, on which only a crown sits, perhaps a comment on George II's frequent absences from England.

The references in Pope's Sporus portrait to "Eve's Tempter" extend the satire beyond the world of politics into that of religion, a tactic we have seen

Pope turn to in earlier poems. As the passage progresses, Hervey is gradually almost lost sight of; Pope nearly eradicates the man in order to stress the measures the poet opposes. As with Sir Balaam in the *Epistle to Bathurst*, the actual model for "Sporus" is not as important as is the reader's recognition of the actions and attributes that render this "Amphibious Thing" an emblem for courtly corruption, both personally and politically.

Pope uses animal, insect, and inanimate imagery to satirize followers of the Court, and particularly Hervey. From the implicit spider image of "Lord *Fanny* spins a thousand such a Day" (*Sat.* 2:1:6) to the monstrous "Impertinent" (perhaps intended for Hervey, as well), "A Thing which *Adam* had been pos'd to name" (25), to the great Sporus passage, Pope shows how well he can dehumanize and diminish his political targets. But, like the visual satirists, Pope enhances rather than reduces the figure of Walpole, for the rhetorical reasons discussed in chapter 2. Walpole is always in control, above the others, manipulating them. Similarly, in Paul Whitehead's *Manners: A Satire* (London, 1739) a careful distinction is made between Walpole himself—"some great Leviathan of Pow'r" (p. 13)—and his minion "*Fanny*," who crawls, "an Ear-wig on the King" (p. 15). Except for prints whose subject is foreign affairs, where artists had to simplify complex relationships for the domestic audience, animal prints are quite rare. One such is the frontispiece to *The Court Monkies. Inscrib'd to Mr. Pope* (London, 1734) (B.M. 2026), in which ministerial monkeys forge fetters for their masters in a smith's workshop. Walpole is shown as one of the three gentlemen who oversee the operation.

A genre that demanded the skills of both verbal and visual satirists was the illustrated Aesopian fable, often used for political ends. An early example is the 1720 South Sea print *Bombario Actionist En De Geest Van Esopus*, ("Bombarios the Share Jobber, and the Ghost of Aesop," B.M. 1663). *The Tale of the Robbin, and the Tom-titt, Who All the Birds in the Air Have Bitt* (1729?) (B.M. 1839) combines a crude woodcut with a poem about the degeneration of political institutions. *The Lyon in Love; or, The Political Farmer, An Aesopian Tale, Applicable to the Present Times* (1738) (B.M. 2347) is an anti-Walpole satire on England's relationship with Spain. Each of these prints illustrates the definition Samuel Johnson gives of *fable* in his "Life of Gay":

> A *Fable*, or Apologue, . . . seems to be, in its genuine state, a narrative in which beings irrational, and sometimes inanimate, *arbores loquantur, non tantum ferae*, are, for the purpose of moral instruction, feigned to act and speak with human interests and passions.[22]

What a recent critic says of Swift's poetry is even truer if applied to Gay's:

29. *The Court Monkies. Inscrib'd to Mr. Pope* (B.M. 2026)

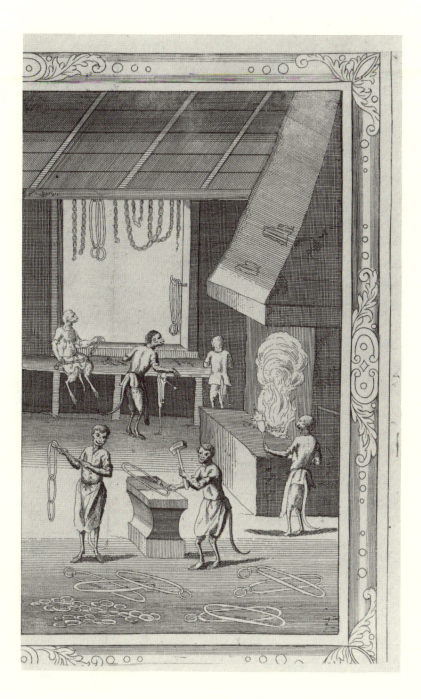

An approach to Swift's allusions must not be patterned on the methods critics have developed for the poems of Alexander Pope. . . . Swift was rarely subtle about including allusions. . . . To a great extent . . . the important thing in a study of Swift's poetry is not the *discovery* of allusions, but the consideration of their *use* in the poems.[23]

Both series of Gay's *Fables* demonstrate how easily the rhetorical strategy of the *Craftsman* could be adapted to a wider audience, including children. For example, in a passage from *Fables* 2 : 2 (one of those whose "Morals . . . are of the political kind")[24] we easily recognize images and themes familiar in Opposition prints and poems, yet general enough to still be applicable to the essential nature of political power:

> I've heard of times, (pray God defend us,
> We're not so good but he can mend us)
> When wicked ministers have trod
> On kings and people, law and God;
> With arrogance they girt the throne,   35
> And knew no int'rest but their own.
> Then virtue, from preferment barr'd,
> Gets nothing but its own reward.
> A gang of petty knaves attend 'em.
> With proper parts to recommend 'em   40
> Then, if his patron burn with lust,
> The first in favour's pimp the first.
> His doors are never clos'd to spies,
> Who chear his heart with double lyes;
> They flatter him, his foes defame,   45
> So lull the pangs of guilt and shame.
> If schemes of lucre haunt his brain,
> Projectors swell his greedy train;
> Vile brokers ply his private ear
> With jobs of plunder for the year.   50
> All consciences must bend and ply;
> You must vote on, and not know why:
> Through thick and thin you must go on;
> One scruple, and your place is gone. $(31-54)$[25]

We note the tactic of placing the satire in the past $(31-34)$; the association of irreligion and bad politics (reminiscent of Pope's *The Impertinent* and the Vision of Vice Triumphant, which concludes Dialogue 1 of Pope's *Epilogue to the Satires*); the similarity of the image in line 35 to the snake-entwined throne of *The Scheme Disappointed A Fruitless Sacrifice*; and the opposition between Virtue and the Court seen in Pope's *Sat.* 2 : 1 and *The Impertinent*. The "gang" of line 39 recalls the central metaphor of *The Beggar's Opera* as well as the comparison of Walpole ("Appius") to Jonathan Wild in *The State Dunces, Inscribed to Mr. Pope. Part II* (London, 1733). The reference to pimping in line 42 reminds us of the picture of Walpole as pimp, prompted by the devil, in *The Lyon in Love*. Gay's passage concludes with reminders of *The Impertinent* and the *Epistle to Bathurst*, which also satirize flattery, bribery, and corruption.

Although Gay's poetry does not have the kind of allusive complexity found in the work of Pope or other poets who use classical and historical precedents in their political satire, we should not underestimate the sophistication of Gay's art. Consider briefly the visual tradition suggested by the description of "Yon minister so gay and proud" (l. 100) in *Fables* 2 : 7:

> See him, mad and drunk with power,
> Stand tott'ring on ambition's tower:
> Sometimes, in speeches vain and proud,
> His boasts insult the nether crowd;
> Now, seiz'd with giddiness and fear,
> He trembles lest his fall is near.   (115–20)

Contemporary readers of Gay's *Fable* who followed his command to "See" the image given them might well have recalled "Scene VIII" of *R——B——N's Progress in Eight Scenes; From his first Coming up from Oxford to London to his present Situation* (ca. 1733) (B.M. 1938). Walpole stands on the point of a pyramid ("ambition's tower") and is supplicated by kneeling and bowing courtiers to whom he drops gold and paper money. Walpole says, "This is my last Step & I wish I were safe-down." His future is anticipated by the bonfire beneath his effigy hanging behind him. In "Scene VI" Walpole's Genius warns him that his "progress" parallels dangerously that of an earlier evil minister: "remember Woolsey & tremble."

Gay's readers were even more likely to recall the sixth frontispiece of *Robin's Reign; or, Seven's The Main*, in which Walpole, within a frame of four columns, stands on the pinnacles of rocks to grasp Minerva's hand. He offers a bag of money as he looks hopefully at the ducal coronet she holds over his head. On the top of the coronet is a zany's head. Walpole is mocked by a female figure with a staff, mask, and snakes. The verses interpret the scene:

> Blinded with Pride, and mad with vain Desires,
> Thus to a Coronet the wretch Aspires.
> Heedless of Dangers, tho' encompass'd stands,
> With Insolence, his fawning slaves Commands,
> Thinks by his Mony [*sic*], all Things may be Done,

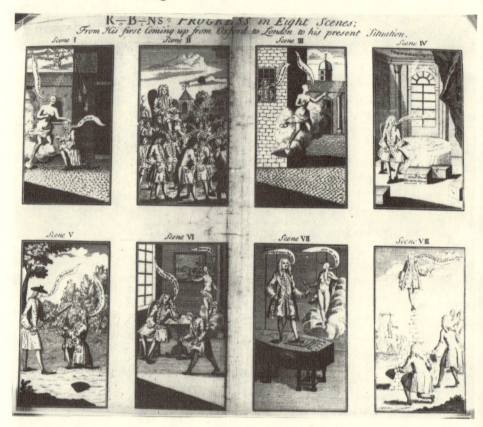

30. *R——B——N's Progress in Eight Scenes; From his first Coming up from Oxford to London to His present Situation* (B.M. 1938)

> And upwards o're the Rocks he Blunders on,
> Till by one Slip, from the steep Summit thrown.
> His Mangled Corps, is as a Warning shown.

The prose tract of *Robin's Game* elaborates on the picture, linking it to other associations of Walpole and Sejanus, such as one in the poem *The Duchess's Epistle to Her Son Don Pedro; occasion'd by his late Promotion at Court* (London, 1734),[26] and another in the print *The Downfall of Sejanus* (ca. 1733) (B.M. 1939): "I must not pass by in Silence the Manner by which this Dignity [the ducal coronet] is obtained; Monsieur Ruperto [Walpole] urges his usual Argument, a long B[riber]y; and by help of that, seeks to ascend the steepy *Pinnacle* of Honour; but as the Rock under him appears sharp and craggy,

31. *The Downfall of Sejanus* (B.M. 1939)

and the Divinity is in a doze that guides him, 'tis not impossible, that spight of all his Money, his Steps may be slippery, and one short Trip send him headlong to the Bottom, like a Predecessor of *Sejanus's*" (p. 17). Clearly, then, Gay's emblem of "ambition's tower" can be linked to other types of overweening pride and transient greatness like Wolsey, Sejanus, and the colossus figures discussed in chapter 2.

Not all Opposition writers chose to enhance rather than diminish their principal target. Many of the street ballads, for example, use the contemptuously familiar "Bob" when referring to Walpole. But of the major authors attacking the ministry, Swift is the one who most often departs from the rhetorical strategy discussed earlier. To Swift, Walpole is "Sir *Robert Brass*" (*Epistle to a Lady*, l. 252) or "*Bob*, the Poet's Foe" (*To Mr. Gay on his being Steward to the Duke of Queensberry*, l. 4). In the latter poem, we have a good example of poetic caricature applied to Walpole, which attacks him more as a person than as a politician. Even the figure of the ostrich, emblem of insatiable and indiscriminate appetite (as it appears at the bottom of the print *The Scheme Disappointed A Fruitless Sacrifice*) is directed more at the man than the minister:

> And first: To make my Observation right,
> I place a ST[ATESM]AN full before my Sight.
> A bloated *M{iniste}r* in all his Geer,
> With shameless Visage, and perfidious Leer,
> Two Rows of Teeth arm each devouring Jaw;
> And, *Ostrich*-like, his all-digesting Maw.
> My Fancy drags this Monster to my View,
> To show the World his chief Reverse in you.

When Swift writes a beast fable, as in *On Mr. P{ultene}y being put out of the Council. Written in the Year 1731*, he is likely to point the application: "Thus was the Hare pursu'd, tho' free from Guilt; / Thus *B{ob}* shal't thou be mawl'd, fly where thou wil't" (37–38). Where Pope reserves animal imagery for Walpole's supporters, Swift uses it on the minister himself, giving him "dirty Paws" in *To Mr. Gay* (l. 157). Nothing could be more satirically reductive than the final image of this poem: "Thus, when a greedy Sloven once has thrown / His *Snot* into the *Mess*; *'tis all his own*." When Swift increases the stature of Walpole in *On Poetry: A Rapsody* (1733), he does so ironically:

> Now sing the *Minister* of *State*.
> Who shines alone, without a Mate.
> Observe with what majestick Port
> This *Atlas* stands to prop the Court.   (441–44)

Perhaps the most effective way to appreciate how Swift's rhetorical tactics differ from those of other Opposition satirists is to compare his treatment of Pulteney's dismissal on 1 July 1731 from the Privy Council with the ways an anonymous print designer and Gay handle the same subject. Swift's *On Mr. P{ultene}y being put out of the Council* verbally reduces "Sir R——" of line 1 to "*Bob*" in line 4. Swift warns Walpole that even if

32. *Three Courtiers (Honest, Thriving, Slighted)* (B.M. 1870)

the minister should "Produce at last thy dormant Ducal Patent" (10), whose supposed existence is the subject of frontispiece six of *Robin's Reign*, "Yet still I fear your Work is done but Half; / For while he [Pulteney] keeps his Pen, you are not safe" (13–14). Like Pope and Gay, Swift next offers his emblem or fable, but unlike his fellow satirists, Swift goes on to make the application.

The designer of the 1731 engraving *Three Courtiers (Honest, Thriving, Slighted)* (B.M. 1870) leaves the application to the viewer. This print originally appeared as the untitled frontispiece to the satirical poem *An Epistle from a Merchant's Clerk to his Master, on his being discharg'd the Compting-House. . . .* . Under a canopy of state sits a king on his throne. Before him stands "The Thriving Courtier" (Walpole), who apparently accuses "The Slighted Courtier" (Pulteney) of authoring a copy of the *Craftsman*, which "Thriving" holds. "The Honest Courtier," Frederick George Stephens suggests, may be ironically intended for Lord Hervey, Pulteney's recent dueling opponent. Although the proper application is easily made, the design of the print and the poem itself indicate that here the focus of the satire moves from the specific people involved to the situation or relationship as the artist and poet generalize the event.

Even more general is what I believe to be Gay's rendering of Pulteney's expulsion—*Fables* 2:10, "The Degenerate Bees." Addressed "To the Reverend Dr. Swift, Dean of St. Patrick's," the prologue depicts Gay, Swift, and Pope as virtuous outsiders, members of a moral minority:

> All dunces too in church and state
> In frothy nonsense show their hate,
> With all the petty scribbling crew,
> (And those pert sots are not a few)
> 'Gainst you and Pope their envy spurt.   (17–21)

The fable proper reflects both the visual (e.g., in Hogarth's *The Lottery* and commonly in emblem books) and the verbal (e.g., Virgil's *Aeneid*, bk. 1, and Mandeville's *Fable of the Bees*) traditions of the beehive as an emblem of industry. In Gay's hive, however, a very Walpolean bee presides:

> A Bee, of cunning, not of parts,
> Luxurious, negligent of arts,
> Rapacious, arrogant and vain,
> Greedy of pow'r, but more of gain,
> Curruption sow'd throughout the hive.
> By petty rogues the great ones thrive.   (37–42)

"From his cell dismiss'd" is the one bee, analogue to Pulteney, who protests the way the hive is run. If I am correct in suggesting that the occasion of

"The Degenerate Bees" was Pulteney's dismissal from Court, Gay has succeeded in shifting Swift's emphasis on men to an emphasis on actions.

Swift acknowledges in *An Epistle to a Lady* that his rhetorical tactics differ from those of the *Craftsman*:

> If I can but fill my Nitch,
> I attempt no higher Pitch.
> Leave to D'ANVERS and his Mate,
> Maxims wise, to rule the State.
> POULTNEY deep, accomplish'd ST. JOHNS,
> Scourge the Villains with a Vengeance.
> Let me, tho' the Smell be Noisom,
> Strip their Bums; let CALEB hoyse 'em;
> Then, apply ALECTO'S Whip,
> Till they wriggle, howl, and skip.   (175–84)

Ironically, the writers most like Swift in the use of personal caricature and reductive satire before the fall of Walpole from power were on Walpole's side. One example is the notorious closing image of Lady Mary Wortley Montagu and John Lord Hervey's *Verses Address'd to the Imitator of the First Satire of the Second Book of Horace. By a Lady* (London, 1733): "And with the Emblem of thy crooked Mind, / Mark'd on thy Back, like *Cain*, by God's own Hand; / Wander like him, accursed through the Land."

When Walpole's supporters tried to use Opposition tactics for their own satire, they were generally not very successful. As we saw earlier, the Opposition easily turned the panegyric engraving *To the Glory of the R'. Honble. S'. Robert Walpole* (B.M. 1842) into the satiric *To the Glory of Colonel Don Francisco, upon his Delivery out of Goal* [sic] (B.M. 1841). An even more direct parody of the pro-Walpole original is the sixth frontispiece of *Robin's Reign* discussed above. Although the ministerial artists were outwitted in their attempt to praise Walpole through the iconography of classical myth, they were rhetorically more successful in associating the "Great Man" with the visual tradition of the English fairy tale *Jack and the Beanstalk* in the 1739 engraving *Fee Fau Fum* (B.M. 2434). Walpole is portrayed as Jack the defeater of Giants (Spain; France; France-Spain; France, Spain, and Sweden) in this print supporting his foreign policy. Even the Sinking Fund gets positive treatment since it is the quicksand which entraps the Giant of Spain in the first design.[27]

A ministry satirist used a combination of images drawn from exemplar history, classical myth, uniformitarianism, and allegorical history painting in the illustration accompanying the widely circulated 1740 broadside *The Patriot-Statesman* (B.M. 2459). The panegyrical nature of the iconography of this engraving is expressed in the verse appended to it:

33. *Fee Fau Fum* (B.M. 2434)

> See virtuous WALPOLE to FAME'S *Temple* goes,
> Where the known Entrance mightly BURLEIGH shows.
> *Pallas*, to every *Hero's* Cause inclin'd,
> Keeps Envy's meagre *Offspring* far behind.

Walpole is "Like *Burleigh*, shining with victorious Rays."

But a pro-Walpole print such as this is very rare compared to the number of prints like the frontispiece to *The Life And Death Of Pierce Gaveston, Earl of Cornwal; Grand Favorite, And Prime Minister To that Unfortunate Prince, Edward II, King of England, With Political Remarks, by way of Caution to All Crowned Heads and Evil Ministers. By a True Patriot* (London, 1740) (B.M. 2462). Through the use of parallel history in the print and text, Walpole's condign punishment is clearly suggested.

Proministerial verse, like that of the anonymous patronage-seeking *The Muse in Distress: A Poem. Occasion'd by the Present State of Poetry* (London, 1733), was usually answered by refutation or parody. A poem that devotes three pages to attacking Pope's ties to the Opposition, *The Muse in Distress* praises Walpole as a new Maecenas and asks:

> Shall *Britain's* better CAESAR [i.e., George II] then remain
> Unsung in any, but his Laureat's Strain?
> Must all *his* Labours for *her* Peace be curst
> With a *Bathyllus* duller than the first?
> Whilst firm for Europe's Liberty he stands,
> Her *Ballance* holding in his steady Hands;
> And whilst he guards his Subjects from their Foes;
> *Himself* refusing for *their* sake Repose:
> *Why* sleeps the *British Muse* with unstrung Lyre?   (P. 6)

Paul Whitehead, in *Manners: A Satire*, will have none of this sort of ministerial panegyric:

> I cannot truckle to a Slave in State,
> And praise a Blockhead's Wit, because he's great;
> Down, down, ye hungry Garretteers, descend,
> Call W{alpol}e Burleigh, call him *Britain's* Friend.   (P. 15)

The author of *The Muse in Distress* gets a very different response, however, when, looking at Pope, he asks:

> "*Where* is the *Poet*, whose aspiring Strains,
> Anticipating the Historian's Pains,
> To Ages yet to come shall nobly dare
> AUGUSTUS's heroick Worth declare?"   (P. 15)

The answer comes directly from Pope. With *The First Epistle of the Second Book of Horace* (1737), he returns to the historical satire he earlier practiced in *Windsor Forest*.[28] The later poem opens with several ironic references to contemporary events:

> While You, great Patron of Mankind, sustain
> The balanc'd World, and open all the Main;
> Your Country, chief, in Arms abroad defend,
> At home, with Morals, Arts, and Laws amend;
> How shall the Muse from such a Monarch, steal
> An hour, and not defraud the Publick Weal?   (1–6)

Pope's irony is underscored by the subtitle—"To Augustus"—first found in advertisements of the poem. George II had the misfortune to be also christened Augustus, and even the Courtier Hervey recognized the contrast between the present king and his namesake:

Not that there was any similitude between the two princes who presided in the Roman and English Augustan ages besides their names, for George Augustus neither loved learning nor encouraged men of letters, nor were there any Maecenases about him. There was another very material difference too between these two Augustuses. For as personal courage was the only quality necessary to form a great prince which the one was suspected to want, so I fear it was the only one the other was ever thought to possess.[29]

Pope immediately mocks the king's military ambitions, as he had in *Sat.* 2 : 1, because the only "Arms abroad" George was involved with were those of his German mistress, Lady Walmoden. Contemporary readers would also have recognized that these opening lines illustrate the "*ironical Panegyrick*" of "Phil-Horatius," because the Opposition repeatedly charged the ministry with having allowed Spanish depredations to close all the Main. Similarly, the phrase "balanc'd World" had become a loaded one. In prints, pamphlets, poems, and journals, the Opposition frequently tarred Robert Walpole and his brother Horace with the label of "Ballance-Master," to stress their concern about the precarious nature of a pacific foreign policy that, they believed, relied heavily on the faith of Fortune. This image of the precarious balance can be more effectively rendered visually than verbally as demonstrated in the fifth frontispiece of *Robin's Reign*, where the strutting cock of France triumphs over the slumbering British lion:

> In this famed Ballance, —mark the heavier Scale,
> And see how Wisdom, —does o're fraud Prevail,
> Soul saving Fleury, view profoundly Wise,
> By reach of Thought, Defect of Power Supplies.
> The Scale in steady form, his Conduct keeps,
> While W{alpo}le vainly, Reams of Treaties heaps.
> What Briton sighs not, at the Guilty Scene,
> Whence Blenheim's Rebus thus revers'd has been.

Pope's irony continues with the mention of "Morals, Arts, and Laws." The "Morals" of George were notorious, and the Opposition constantly accused the king and his minister of breaking the "Laws" by extending the royal prerogative. But in a poem imitating Horace's compliments to Caesar on the ruler's literary interests, the ironic praise of George's concern for the "Arts" is especially delightful. Pope probably intended George II himself as "th'affected fool / At Court, who hates whate'er he read at School" (105–6). The king's reputed stupidity was often noted by his opponents, and Hervey's testimony lends the charge support: "The King used often to brag of the contempt he had for books and letters; to say how much he hated all that stuff from his infancy; and that he remembered when he was a child he did not hate reading and learning merely as other children do upon account of the confinement, but because he despised it and felt as if he was doing something mean and below him.[30]

The next twenty-five lines of the poem illustrate the tactic of "dressing [satire] up in Allegories and Parallels" mentioned by "Phil-Horatius." Here we recognize the assumptions of uniformitarianism, exemplar history, the immemorial constitution, and "the Norman Yoke" we saw earlier in *Windsor Forest*:

> Edward and Henry, now the Boast of Fame,
> And virtuous Alfred, a more sacred Name,
> After a Life of gen'rous Toils endur'd,
> The Gaul subdu'd, or Property secur'd,
> Ambition humbled, mighty Cities storm'd
> Or laws establish'd, and the World reform'd.   (7–12)

In *London: A Poem* (1738), Samuel Johnson uses many of the same tactics, invoking "Eliza" (23) and "Illustrious Edward" (99) to "call Britannia's Glories back to view" (26) so that his "snarling Muse" (161) can contrast the degenerate present with "Alfred's golden Reign" (248).[31]

However, a significant change had taken place in historiography between 1713 and the late 1730s.[32] When Pope wrote *Windsor Forest* he could be certain that virtually all of his readers would agree with his assumptions about history, even if they disagreed with how he applied them. But in 1737 his allusions to beliefs in the immemorial constitution (by references to "Property secur'd" or "Laws establish'd," for example) would clearly have indicated to his readers his political allegiance.

In 1713, almost everyone accepted the idea first promoted by Whiggish opponents of the Stuart Courts that, until the Glorious Revolution, seventeenth-century English monarchs sought to overturn a constitutional balance of powers that had existed since time immemorial. They argued that the Stuart kings were aberrations in the long history of English "LIBERTY" (*Epistle* 2:1:25). Brief, though important, opposition to this Whig view of history arose in the seventeenth century. The royalist Tory Dr. Robert Brady, agreeing with the more accurate historical interpretations of Sir Henry Spelman and Sir William Dugdale, contended that because William I had indeed been a conqueror who successfully imposed feudal government on England the Stuart monarchs ruled as they should have been expected to. Furthermore, Brady argued, the real aberration in English history was the one proposed by the Whigs, which resulted in the events of 1688.

Recognizing how sound a strategy the Opposition had chosen, Walpole's supporters eventually surrendered to his enemies the legacy of Whig history prior to 1688. Gradually, ministerial writers began to embrace Brady's view of early English history in their attempts to identify adherents of the present government as the only true Whigs. According to them, there was no liberty until 1688 and progress in "LIBERTY" had been made only since that date. Consequently, to the ministry, the present rule of George II and Walpole was undeniably preferable to the past so nostalgically and inaccurately longed for by Bolingbroke and his friends.

The dispute over history between the Opposition and ministerial writers was discussed at length in *The Craftsman*: "The only Difference between *Us* [the Opposition], and the ministerial Writers, consists in This; that *They* date all our *real Liberty* from the REVOLUTION, as its original Aera, and set us forth as a *Nation of Slaves, by Law establish'd*, before that Time; whereas We look upon it only as a *Renewal of our ancient Constitution*, or a Superstructure built on the same *Foundations of Liberty*" (no. 478). Pope's use of the same constitutional theories he had first employed in *Windsor Forest* illustrates his alliance with the Opposition against "a *Set of Men*, who call Themselves the *Advocates of a Whig Ministry*, defending these *Prerogative Principles*, and licking up the Spittle of such slavish Writers as *Brady* and his Followers" (*Craftsman*, no. 456). For Pope, English glory and liberty reside in the past; it is the poet's misfortune to live in an age where "to complete the jest, / Old Edward's Armour beams on Cibber's breast" (318–19). The greatest achievement of George II's reign was its unintentional encouragement of satire. Pope echoes earlier ironic praise found in *The Craftsman*, no. 20, for an age that brought forth a Swift who, though "The Rights a Court attack'd, a Poet sav'd" (224).

In the *Epistle to Augustus*, Pope balances attacks on measures with attacks on men much as he had earlier in the *Imitations*. The personal faults of George II are referred to in the later poems almost as often as are his political and constitutional failings. What is striking about this fact is that such personal attacks on the king were rare enough to be exceptional. The doctrine that "the King can do no wrong" gets a lot of stretching in Pope's last poems.

Samuel Johnson goes even further than Pope in mocking the king. He refers to George II's trips to his Hanoverian mistress, Amalie von Walmoden, in the poem *London*—"Lest ropes be wanting in the tempting spring / To rig another convoy for the k{in}g" (ll. 246–47)—as well as in *Marmor Norfolciense*—"While he lies melting in a lewd embrace."[33] To some degree at least, Lord Hervey is justified in charging that when the Opposition realized that they would not succeed in getting the king to remove Walpole, they sought to remove the minister by first changing kings.[34] There was a detectable shift toward attacks on the king after 1737, when popular dissatisfaction was growing over his fondness for his foreign mistress and over English inaction toward Spain.

But in comparison to attacks on Walpole, the number of satiric references to George II remained small. In prints of the late 1730s we find several attacks on the king's person. For example, *Aeneas in a Storm* (B.M. 2326) mocks the king's habit of kicking during temper tantrums, while *The Festival of the Golden Rump* (B.M. 2327) attacks that habit and makes the serious charge that George II is worshipped as an idol whose high priestess is the queen. Walpole is depicted as a wizard officiating at the rites of worship. *Solomon in his Glory* (B.M. 2348) satirizes George's dalliance with Madame Walmoden when he should be in mourning for Caroline.[35] Attacks on the king's habit of bad-tempered kicking and on his sexual misconduct reappear in the 1740 engraving *The C{our}t Shittle Cock* (B.M. 2451), which refers to the 30 April 1740 resignation of John, Duke of Argyll, from all his ministerial employments. In a game of shuttlecock played by George II and Walpole, the shuttlecock is the duke of Argyll. The king, whose right foot is identified as "The K{ic}k{in}g Foot," is embraced by "Madame Wallmoden, now Countess of Yarmouth." She assures the king, "Your cockey my Love mounts rarely."

Throughout the *Imitations*, Pope tries to maintain a balance between attacking persons and assailing general evils. He is rhetorically most effective, as in the "Sporus" passage, when he succeeds in extending his satire from men to measures. In the two *Dialogues* that compose the *Epilogue to the Satires*, "Pope's chief point . . . is the dilemma of the satirist, forced to choose between the advantages and disadvantages of writing personal particulars or abstract generalizations."[36] Pope had earlier raised this subject in *Sat.* 2:1: "A hundred smart in *Timon* and in *Balaam*: / A fewer still you name, you wound the more; / *Bond* is but one, but *Harpax* is a score" (42–44), as well as in the *Epistle to Dr. Arbuthnot*: "'No names—be calm—learn Prudence of a Friend'" (102). The theme is probably best expressed in the famous letter from Pope to Arbuthnot (2 August 1734).

But General Satire in Times of General Vice has no force, & is no Punishment: People have ceas'd to be ashamed of it when so many are joind with them; and tis only by hunting One or two from the Herd that any Examples can be made. If a man writ all his Life against the Collective Body of the Banditti, or against Lawyers, would it do the least Good, or lesson the Body? But if some are hung up, or pilloryed, it may prevent others. And in my low Station, with no other Power than this, I hope to deter, if not to reform.[37]

34. *The C(our)t Shittle Cock* (B.M. 2451)

The tension between the particular and the general, between politicians and principles, remains in the *Epilogue*. At the outset of Dialogue 1, Pope carefully distinguishes between Walpole the man and Walpole the minister:

Seen him [Sir Robert] I have, but in his happier hour
Of Social Pleasure, ill-exchang'd for Pow'r;
Seen him, uncumber'd with the Venal tribe,
Smile without Art, and win without a Bribe.   (29–32)

Like previous political poems we have discussed, each Dialogue rises from specific individuals to an essentially emblematic conclusion. The final lines of Dialogue 1 are among Pope's most powerful verses:

Vice is undone, if she forgets her Birth,
And stoops from Angels to the Dregs of Earth:
But 'tis the Fall degrades her to a Whore;
Let *Greatness* own her, and she's mean no more:
Her Birth, Her Beauty, Crowds and Courts confess,
Chaste Matrons praise her, and grave Bishops bless:
In golden Chains the willing World she draws,
And hers the Gospel is, and hers the Laws:
Mounts the Tribunal, lifts her scarlet head,
And sees pale Virtue carted in her stead!
Lo! at the Wheels of her Triumphal Car,
Old *England's* Genius, rough with many a Scar,
Dragg'd in the Dust! his Arms hang idly round,
His Flag inverted trails along the ground!
Our Youth, all liv'ry'd o'er with foreign Gold,
Before her dance; behind her crawl the Old!
See thronging Millions to the Pagod run,
And offer Country, Parent, Wife, or Son!
Hear her black Trumpet thro' the Land proclaim,
That "Not to be corrupted is the Shame."
In Soldier, Churchman, Patriot, Man in Pow'r,
'Tis Av'rice all, Ambition is no more!
See, all our Nobles begging to be Slaves!
See, all our Fools aspiring to be Knaves!
The Wit of Cheats, the Courage of a Whore,
Are what ten thousand envy and adore.
All, all look up, with reverential Awe,
On Crimes that scape, or triumph o'er the Law:
While Truth, Worth, Wisdom, daily they decry—

"Nothing is Sacred now but Villany."
    Yet may this Verse (if such a Verse remain)
Show there was one who held it in disdain.   (142–72)

Critics have long recognized that "in the course of the *Epilogue* Pope manages to rise from the occasion with its personalities to the most general and most eloquent affirmation of the value of satire and to a vision of Vice triumphant that is anything but local."[38] In light of the fact that, as Pope stresses in the *Epistle to Bathurst*, the Opposition often traced the history of modern economic, social, and political corruption back to "the famous Aera of 1720," we should not be surprised to discover that Pope's allegory of Vice in "her Triumphal Car" bears a striking resemblance to a South Sea Bubble print. *A Monument Dedicated to Posterity in Commemoration of ye Incredible Folly Transacted in the Year 1720* (B.M. 1629) is the English imitation of the original engraving "*B. Picart fecit*" satirizing the French stock scandal, with verses and description in French and Dutch.[39] The popularity of the print design is attested to by the existence of two different states of the foreign original, in addition to the English adaptation and parodies. The text engraved beneath the print gives some idea of the similarities between the engraving and the later poetic vision:

> Here is represented, Fortune conducted by Folly. . . . The Chair is drawn by the Principal Company's, who began this pernicious Trade, as ye Mississippi, with a Wooden Leg. [The] South Sea [Company is depicted] with a Sore-Leg, and Ligament upon ye other. . . . On ye spokes of ye Wheel are seen ye names of several Companys, some up and some down, according as ye Wheel turns, with Books of Merchandise crushed and torn beneath ye Wheels of ye Chariot, representing ye destruction of Trade and Commerce; you likewise see a great throng of People of all conditions and Sexes, running after Fortune.

In the print, Folly, blessed by Fortune, is riding in the chariot; in the poem it is the more malevolent but equally alluring Vice who rides in triumph, as if the devil, Folly, and Fortune in the engraving were combined to form the single allegorical Vice in the poem. In print and poem there is an emblematic figure crushed or "Dragg'd in the Dust" by the chariot's wheel. In both representations, this figure illustrates an aspect of "Old *England*" destroyed by overpowering corruption. In each depiction, the image of Fame's trumpet appears to proclaim "thro' the Land" "That not to be corrupted is the Shame."

Although the Vision of Vice Triumphant seems to be general satire, there are several recognizable personal allusions within the allegory. References to Theodora and to Walpole's former mistress and new wife, Molly

Skerrett, have been identified.[40] Maynard Mack has shown that readers of the poem would probably have identified "the Pagod" with George II, because the king had appeared a year earlier in that role in an issue of *Common Sense* which explicated the engraving of the *Festival of the Golden Rump*.[41] Also Pope had associated the image of "some queer *Pa-god*" with George II in 1733 when he wrote "*The Presence* [presence-chamber] seems, with things so richly odd, / The Mosque of *Mahound*, or some queer *Pa-god*" (*Donne* 4:238–39).

I think that these references in prose, engraving, and poem may in turn be traced back to a source not mentioned by Mack, found in Letter 19 of Bolingbroke's *Remarks on the History of England*, first published in *The Craftsman* (1730–31). During a discussion of the unconstitutional actions of James I, which led to his unpopularity, Humphrey Oldcastle (Bolingbroke) notes the similarities between the English king and Oriental despots: "Some will be respected, like eastern monarchs, unseen within the shrine of their court. Others grow fond of public triumphs; delight in noisy acclamations; and are pleased to drive, like Indian pagods, over a prostrate crowd."[42]

Several of the details in Bolingbroke's image clearly anticipate the imagery of Pope's Vision. Vice, the allegorical representation of George II, is worshipped as "the Pagod" because the king and his minister rule just as despotically as do "eastern monarchs" and as did James I. Consequently, Pope implies that Vice triumphs after she has overcome the constitutional legacy of "Old England's Genius." Like the "prostrate crowd" in Bolingbroke's description or the figure in the bubble engraving, the emblem of "Old England" is beneath the wheels of the ruler's car amidst the "thronging Millions" noisily acclaiming the public triumph of Vice and George II. Even if Pope were unaware of the existence of this particular bubble print, the similar emblematic expressions of the financial and political manifestations of corruption exemplify the remarkably strong pictorial tradition the satirist inherited.

But the victory of Vice is not yet irreversible, as it would become in *The New Dunciad*. The rhetorical effect of Pope's final couplet in Dialogue 1 is perfect. In just two lines he defies the powerful vision he has given us. With Dialogue 2 we are back in the company of the aggressive satirist, albeit without the comedy, of the earlier *Imitations*.

Like Dialogue 1, Dialogue 2 is full of thematic, visual, and verbal echoes of preceding *Imitations*. For example, "Vice with such Giant-strides comes on amain" (6) apparently alludes to the vision that ends *The Impertinent*. Thus, Dialogue 2 starts off as if it were intended to be a continuation of the earlier satire on courtiers, and that is indeed what the poem becomes as it rises to an emblem in the Westphaly Hogs simile, which, Purvis E.

Boyette has pointed out, "functions as the ethical center" of the poem. "It is
the structural climax of the poem and thus strategically placed integrates
theme, tone, and image with perfect precision."[43]

> [P.] Let Courtly Wits to Wits afford supply,
> As Hog to Hog in Huts of *Westphaly*;
> If one, thro' Nature's Bounty or his Lord's,
> Has what the frugal, dirty soil affords,
> From him the next receives it, thick or thin,
> As pure a Mess almost as it came in;
> The blessed Benefit, not there confin'd,
> Drops to the third who nuzzles close behind;
> From tail to mouth, they feed, and they carouse;
> The last, full fairly gives it to the *House*.
>   *Fr.* This filthy Simile, this beastly Line,
> Quite turns my Stomach—*P.* So does Flatt'ry mine;
> And all your Courtly Civet-Cats can vent,
> Perfume to you, to me is Excrement.   (171–84)

The pictorial quality of this passage is emphasized when Pope identifies
it as a scatalogical representation of the same courtly corruption and flattery
he had assailed in the "Impertinent" and "Sporus" portraits. The emblem
here is part of the debate over men versus measures begun by *Fr.*'s admoni-
tion that *P.* "Spare then the Person, and expose the Vice" (12). In the
Westphaly Hogs passage Pope combines the person and the vice by showing
that, Circe-like, evil measures have turned courtiers into swine. Much as a
seventeenth-century emblem book would, Pope moves from the illustration (the simile itself) to its meaning (Flattery) and then concludes with an
application intended to justify his choice of image:

> But hear me further. —*Japhet*, 'tis agreed,
> Writ not, and *Chartres* scarce could write or read,
> In all the Courts of *Pindus* guiltless quite;
> But Pens can forge, my Friend, that cannot write.   (185–88)

Dialogue 2 concludes as Pope seeks to extend his political satire by
giving it theological sanction as a "sacred Weapon" (212), and in so doing
his self-portrayal reminds us of the *vir politicus*, "arm'd for *Virtue*," who
began the series of *Imitations*. The two Dialogues are a fitting close to the
political satires initiated by Bolingbroke, with many of the themes and
structural devices found in the earlier poems still being employed in the
later ones. The most important of these themes is that of balancing
measures and men. Although the *Epilogue* contains some of the most effec-

tive personal and general satire to be found in the series, Pope apparently renounces satire of both politicians and their policies in his final footnote to Dialogue 2:

> This was the last poem of the kind printed by our author, with a resolution to publish no more; but to enter thus, in the most plain and solemn manner he could, a sort of PROTEST against that insuperable corruption and depravity of manners, which he had been so unhappy as to live to see. Could he have hoped to have amended any, he had continued those attacks; but bad men were grown so shameless and so powerful, that Ridicule was become as unsafe as it was ineffectual. The Poem raised him, as he knew it would, some enemies; but he had reason to be satisfied with the approbation of good men, and the testimony of his own conscience.

Within a few years, however, Pope returned to political satire and produced his greatest work, *The New Dunciad* (1742), and then *The Dunciad, in Four Books* (1743), in which measures, distinct from the men who enact them, again play a prominent role.

CHAPTER V

The Politics of Education in *Dunciad* 4

Pedantry, as the Spectator formerly observed, is not confined to Learning only, though it is commonly understood in that sense. . . . But of all Sorts of *Pedantry* there is one, which, in my Opinion, far transcends the rest, both as to the Absurdities it leads Men into, and the pernicious Effects it often produces. I mean the *Pedantry of Politicks*. . . . This Spirit of *political Pedantry* hath been carried to an extravagent Height in *former Reigns*; and, to speak very moderately, seems to have lost no Ground amongst us, of late.
—*The Craftsman*, no. 319

What think you of the *School* of W[alpol]e, whom you formerly for many Years opposed with so much Eloquence and Applause? Does it not still exist in his *Disciples*, Men greatly inferior to him in Abilities, and yet without any Principles but what they derived from him?
—*An Expostulatory Letter to a Certain Right Honourable Person upon His Late Promotion*, 1747

The *Dunciad, in Four Books* (October 1743) has recently been described aptly as "Pope's transcendent revitalizing of anti-Walpole commonplaces."[1] In the *Imitations of Horace* we detected a shift from an emphasis on measures to an emphasis on men. Earlier we saw Pope frequently rise from a discussion of particular men to an emblematic conclusion, as if to illustrate the supposedly inductive logic underlying his attacks on the ministry. This same process of transformation from the particular to the emblematic, from the specific to the symbolic, and from the literal to the allegorical reappears in the 1743 *Dunciad*. Book 4 of the *Dunciad* (originally published as the *New Dunciad* in March 1742) is to the previous three books what the emblematic tale of Balaam is to the earlier part of the *Epistle to Bathurst*. Book 4 is the judgment, expressed emblematically, derived from the particular evidence found in the first three quarters of this "anti-epic."[2] The character of Dulness, however, changes in the course of the four books, even as revised by Pope between March 1742 and October 1743. The primarily literary satire of the *Dunciad Variorum* (1729), with its jauntily witty tone, is supplemented by the almost tragic tone of the profoundly political last book.[3] I believe that Pope refers to this political aspect of book 4 in his first footnote to the *New Dunciad*: "This Book may properly be distinguished from the former, by the Name of the GREATER DUNCIAD, not so indeed in Size, but in Subject."[4] The true subject of the *New Dunciad* is not the spread of literary corruption; the true subject is the *translatio* of political tyranny—over the mind, soul, and body—which finally overwhelms the world at the end of book 4. That tyranny and Dulness become synonymous in the last book can be demonstrated by an examination of Pope's notes to his verses and a comparison of the poem to earlier "dissident Whig panegyrics"[5] on the spread of liberty, including Pope's own *Essay on Man* (1733–34) and James Thomson's *Liberty: A Poem* (1735–36). Viewing the *New Dunciad* from a political perspective will enable us to recognize that Pope sees contemporary education as serving the political ends of Dulness.

The political satire of the fourth book encompasses far more than an attack on a specific administration or its particular members. Maynard Mack is surely correct in describing Colley Cibber as, at different times, a surrogate for Walpole as well as for George II, "just as Queen Dulness blurs into Queen Caroline."[6] Caroline had died in 1737, and Sir Robert Walpole resigned during the first week of February 1742. As a reward for past services and as a defense against future prosecution, he was created earl of Orford a few days later, several weeks before the 20 March publication of the *New Dunciad*. Pope's interest in the poem is not nearly so much in the individuals Caroline or Walpole as it is in the present and future affected by the actions of the former queen and first minister, the operatives of Dulness. In the final footnote to Dialogue 2 of the *Epilogue to the Satires*, Pope had promised "to publish no more" because "bad men were grown so shameless and so powerful, that Ridicule was become as unsafe as it was ineffectual." Publication of the *New Dunciad* broke that promise, if we understand Pope to have forsworn any political satire whatsoever, but perhaps by calling Dialogue 2 "the last poem of the kind printed by our author" Pope was speaking of satire aimed at particular men. The emblematic and allegorical nature of the *New Dunciad* expresses Pope's shift back to a greater emphasis on practices rather than men. Particular men are not totally absent from the new poem, but the ones named are usually objects of praise, not blame: Chesterfield, Wyndham, Talbot, Murray, and Pulteney.

To understand the reasons for Pope's attack on practices rather than men in a poem seemingly written in response to the long-anticipated occasion of Walpole's fall, we must keep in mind that "what the poet sets out to describe is no longer the manner in which one dunce succeeded another on the throne of Dulness, but the activities of the 'Mighty Mother' herself (together with those of her son)."[7] William Warburton is explicit about this change in subject matter from that of earlier versions of the *Dunciad*:

> The Reader ought here to be cautioned, that the *Mother*, and not the *Son*, is the principal Agent of this Poem; the latter of them is only chosen as her Collegue (as was anciently the custom in Rome before some great Expedition) the main action of the Poem being by no means the Coronation of the Laureate, which is performed in the very first book, but the Restoration of the Empire of Dulness in Britain, which is not accomplished 'till the last.[8]

Readers of the 1728 *Dunciad*, published just after the succession of George II, had no difficulty in finding a political application for Pope's question: "Say from what cause, in vain decry'd and curst, / Still Dunce the second reigns like Dunce the first?" (A: 1 : 5 – 6). Pope turned his attention in the 1743 *Dunciad* from succession to restoration. Its occasion may have been not the fall of one minister but the struggle for power by Walpole's successors. The nature of the succession to Walpole prompted Pope to treat Dulness as the heroine of his new poem. The force of Tyranny, or Dulness, is consequential, not the often unwitting actions of her human agents. In 1743, like Walpole, who had been elevated to the House of Lords,

> Great Cibber sate: The proud Parnassian sneer,
> The conscious simper, and the jealous leer,
> Mix on his look: All eyes direct their rays
> On him, and crowds turn Coxcombs as they gaze.
> His Peers shine round him with reflected grace,
> New edge their dulness, and new bronze their face.   (2 : 5 – 10)

Cibber and Walpole, his master, are equally passive among their "Peers." Even by the time of the *New Dunciad*, Walpole, the man, has ceased to be a worthy opponent for Pope. But Walpolean measures outlive the personal power of the former minister. The process begun in *The Craftsman* and *Sat.* 2 : 1 of asserting that George II is king but not ruler of England is completed in the *Dunciad* when Dulness "unmistakably 'mounts' a political throne":[9]

> She mounts the Throne: her head a Cloud conceal'd,
> In broad Effulgence all below reveal'd,
> ('Tis thus aspiring Dulness ever shines)
> Soft on her lap her Laureat son reclines.   (4 : 17 – 20)

Pope's note to these lines makes the analogy between Cibber's passivity and that of George II:

> With great judgment it is imagined by the Poet, that such a Collegue as Dulness had elected, should sleep on the Throne, and have very little share in the Action of the Poem. Accordingly he hath done little or nothing from the day of his Anointing; having past through the second book without taking part in any thing that was transacted about him, and thro' the third in profound Sleep. Nor ought this, well considered, to seem strange in our days, when so many *King-consorts* have done the like.

Dulness reigns, not her earthly representatives in literature or politics.

Pope notes that "To blot out Order, and extinguish Light" (4 : 14) are "The two great Ends of her Mission; the one in quality of Daughter of *Chaos*, the other as Daughter of *Night*. *Order* here is to be understood extensively, both as Civil and Moral, the distinctions between high and low in Society, and true and false in Individuals: *Light*, as Intellectual only, Wit, Science, Arts." The perversion of Order inaugurated by Dulness once she is enthroned is represented by a demonic image taken from contemporary physico-theology: [10]

> The young, the old, who feel her inward sway,
> One instinct seizes, and transports away.
> None need a guide, by sure Attraction led,
> And strong impulsive gravity of Head;
> None want a place, for all their Centre found,
> Hung to the Goddess, and coher'd around.
> Not closer, orb in orb, conglob'd are seen
> The buzzing Bees about their dusky Queen.   (4:73–80)

As if ironically following the advice of his ministerial interlocutor in Dialogue 2 of the *Epilogue to the Satires* to "write next winter more *Essays on Man*" (l. 255), Pope parodies the proper Order described in Epistle 3 of the *Essay on Man*:

> Look round our World; behold the chain of Love
> Combining all below and all above.
> See plastic Nature working to this end,
> The single atoms each to other tend,
> Attract, attracted to, the next in place
> Form'd and impell'd its neighbour to embrace.
> See Matter next, with various life endu'd,
> Press to one centre still, the gen'ral Good.   (Epistle 3 : 7 – 14)

Epistle 3 of the *Essay on Man* is concerned with "the Nature and State of Man with respect to Society" and, like *Dunciad* 4, is a poem of political restoration, expressed in images of light and music, images Dulness darkens and discords:

> 'Twas then, the studious head or gen'rous mind,
> Follow'r of God or friend of human-kind,
> Poet or Patriot, rose but to restore
> The Faith and Moral, Nature gave before;
> Re-lum'd her ancient light, not kindled new;
>
> .   .   .   .
>
> Taught Pow'r's due use to People and to Kings,
> Taught nor to slack, nor strain its tender strings,
>
> .   .   .   .
>
> 'Till jarring int'rests of themselves create
> Th' according music of a well-mix'd State.
> Such is the World's great harmony, that springs
> From Order, Union, full Consent of things!   (Epistle 3:283–96)

In these lines Pope describes the effects of restoring the political system, temporarily disrupted by the loss of Liberty, to the rule of Natural Law under which "Self-love and Social be the same" (Epistle 3:318). How different from the rule of Dulness, who teaches her citizens to "Find Virtue local, all Relation scorn, / See all in *Self*, and but for self be born" (*Dunciad* 4:479–80)—precisely the kind of behavior that leads to Tyranny in the *Essay on Man!*

Dulness's reign seeks to "extinguish Light" (4:14) and is accompanied by the dissonant sounds of opera, as *Dunciad* 3:299–302 had predicted:

> 'Till rais'd from booths, to Theatre, to Court,
> Her seat imperial Dulness shall transport.
> Already Opera prepares the way,
> The sure fore-runner of her gentle sway.

Dulness can arrive at the place of power in Court once the foreign and effeminate Opera has overcome the Muses. As Pope's note to *Dunciad* 4:43 makes clear, the failure of Chesterfield's admirable political effort to defeat the 1737 Licensing Act prepared the way for the theatrical supremacy of Opera:

> When lo! a Harlot form soft sliding by,
> With mincing step, small voice, and languid eye;
> Foreign her air, her robe's discordant pride
> In patch-work flutt'ring, and her head aside.   (4:45–48)

The musical harmony that accompanies the well-ordered state of the *Essay on Man* is parodied by the dissonant strains that introduce the reign of "imperial Dulness":

> "O *Cara! Cara!* silence all that train:
> Joy to great Chaos! let Division reign:
> Chromatic tortures soon shall drive them hence,
> Break all their nerves, and fritter all their sense."   (4:53–56)

As early as 17 March 1727 *The Craftsman*, no. 29, had warned that the encouragement of foreign Opera was a means for initiating tyranny:

> Operas and Masquerades, with all the politer Elegancies of a wanton Age, are much less to be regarded for their Expence (great as it is) than for the Tendency, which they have to deprave our Manners. MUSICK has something so peculiar in it, that it exerts a willing Tyranny over the Mind, and forms the ductil Soul into whatever Shape the Melody directs. Wise Nations have observed its Influence, and have therefore kept it under proper Regulations. [11]

The Craftsman gives some brief historical examples of the power of music, mentions the opinion of "the divine Plato . . . that the *Musick* of a Country cannot be changed, and the *publick Laws* remain unaffected," and observes that

> A noble manly Musick will place Virtue in its most beautiful Light, and be the most engaging Incentive to it. A well wrought Story, attended with its prevailing Charms, will transport the Soul out of itself; fire it with glorious Emulation; and lift the Man into a Hero; but the soft *Italian* Musick relaxes and unnerves the Soul, and sinks it into Weakness; so that while we receive their *Musick*, we at the same Time are adopting their *Manners*.

The Craftsman concludes, "He is the Statesman formed for Ruin and Destruction, whose wily Head knows how to disguise the fatal Hook with Baits of Pleasure, which his artful Ambition dispenses with a lavish Hand, and makes himself popular in undoing. . . . This is the finish'd Politician; the darling Son of Tacitus and Machiavel." The politically didactic implications of Opera make the "Harlot form" the fitting harbinger of the reign of Dulness. The populace must be softened in preparation for tyranny. Accordingly, the influence of Tragedy, whose didactic virtues Pope praises in his "Prologues" to Addison's *Cato* and Thomson's *Sophonisba*, must be restrained—"There to her heart sad Tragedy addrest / The dagger wont to pierce the Tyrant's breast" (*Dunciad* 4:37–38). Similarly, Handel, whose music, Opera warns Dulness, would provoke "Rebellion" against the new order, must be banished:

> "But soon, ah soon Rebellion will commence,
> If Music meanly borrows aid from Sense:
> Strong in new Arms, lo! Giant Handel stands,
> Like bold Briareus, with a hundred hands;
> To stir, to rouze, to shake the Soul he comes,
> And Jove's own Thunders follow Man's Drums.
> Arrest him, Empress; or you sleep no more"—
> She heard, and drove him to th' Hibernian shore.   (4:63–70)

Handel is seen here as serving the cause of Liberty in opposition to the tyranny of Dulness.

The theme of miseducation as the necessary prelude to the political tyranny of Dulness, which we have traced thus far, becomes explicit in Dulness's most important Speech from the Throne:[12]

> "Oh (cry'd the Goddess) for some pedant Reign!
> Some gentle JAMES, to bless the land again;
> To stick the Doctor's Chair into the Throne,
> Give law to Words, or war with Words alone,
> Senates and Courts with Greek and Latin rule,
> And turn the Council to a Grammar School!
> For sure, if Dulness sees a grateful Day,
> 'Tis in the shade of Arbitrary Sway.
> O! if my sons may learn one earthly thing,
> Teach but that one, sufficient for a King;
> That which my Priests, and mine alone, maintain,
> Which as it dies, or lives, we fall, or reign:
> May you, may Cam, and Isis preach it long!
> 'The RIGHT DIVINE of Kings to govern wrong.'"   (4:175–88)

Warburton's note to line 175 underscores the relationship between education and statecraft generally accepted by Pope and his readers:

Nothing can be juster than the observation here insinuated, that no branch of Learning thrives well under Arbitrary government but *Verbal*. The reasons are evident. It is unsafe under such Governments to cultivate the study of things of importance. Besides, when men have lost their public virtue, they naturally delight in trifles, if their private morals secure them from being vicious. Hence so great a Cloud of

Scholiasts and Grammarians so soon overspread the Learning of Greece and Rome, when once those famous Communities had lost their Liberties.

Pope himself, in the *Essay on Criticism* (1711), had drawn the same parallel between the loss of Learning and the rise of Tyranny:

And the same Age saw *Learning* fall, and *Rome*.
With *Tyranny*, then *Superstition* join'd,
As that the *Body*, this enslav'd the *Mind*;
Much was Believ'd, but little understood,
And to be *dull* was constru'd to be *good*.   (686–90)

Pope makes clear in Dulness's lines on "some pedant Reign" that the miseducation of the people is the necessary precondition for the establishment of political tyranny so essential to her reign. The satire on education in this speech and throughout *Dunciad* 4 is aimed at attacking the unconstitutional ideas allegedly espoused, practiced, and taught under the reign of Walpole and George II. Pope's note to line 176, with its reference to Bolingbroke's *Dissertation upon Parties*, emphasizes the Opposition view that James I virtually invented the notions of divine right, passive obedience, and nonresistance—notions (with the exception of divine right) the Opposition for twenty years had been charging George II and Walpole with trying to reinstitute. Pope's note to lines 181 and 182 is convincing evidence that Dulness's speech was aimed at the present king and the previous ministry.

> 181, 182. *if Dulness sees, etc.*] And fateful it is in Dulness to make this confession. I will not say she alludes to that celebrated verse of Claudian [*De Consulatu Stilichonis*, iii 113],
>
> —*nunquam* Libertas *gratior extat*
> *Quam sub* Rege pio—
>
> But this I will say, that the words *Liberty* and *Monarchy* have been frequently confounded and mistaken one for the other by the gravest authors. I should therefore conjecture, that the genuine reading of the forecited verse was thus,
>
> —*nunquam* Libertas *gratior exstat*
> *Quam sub* Lege pia—
>
> and that *Rege* was the reading only of Dulness herself: And therefore she might allude to it. SCRIBL.
>
> I judge quite otherwise of this passage: The genuine reading is *Libertas*, and *Rege*: So Claudian gave it. But the error lies in the first verse: It should be *Exit*, not *Exstat*, and then the meaning will be, that

Liberty was never *lost*, or *went away* with so good a grace, as under a good King: it being without doubt a tenfold shame to lose it under a bad one [Bentley].

To be sure, the notes of Scriblerus and Bentley offer conflicting interpretations, but either one reflects badly on the current monarch, whose legitimacy and piety were often questioned. Pope probably expected his reader to recall or check the context of "the celebrated verse of Claudian" he cites. Were the reader to do so he would discover not only that Scriblerus's version is indeed the correct one, but that the lines that immediately follow translate as: "Those he himself [i.e., "a good king"] appoints to rule he in turn brings before the judgment-seat of people and senate, and gladly yields whether they claim reward for merit or seek for punishment. Now the purple lays aside its pride and disdains not to have judgement passed upon itself" (115–19).[13] How many readers of the *Dunciad* would not have been tempted to apply these omitted verses to the current political climate produced from parliamentary demands for an investigation into Walpole's stewardship of the government?

I think that we would be mistaken, however, to argue that Pope seeks to identify James I exclusively with George II in Dulness's speech. All sides agreed that the concept of divine right was evil, and no one would have contended seriously that George II was trying to resurrect the idea. Pope has, I believe, a more fundamentally political intent than merely to mock George II. In this speech and in its accompanying notes the poet reminds his readers that—as he had warned them in the verses and notes of the *Essay on Man*, Epistle 3—even the best form of government is liable to abuse. The "Mixt Government"—to use Addison's phrase—of England contained in its form the inherent tension between the force of monarchy and that of liberty. Recognition of this tension prompted Pope's continuation of his note to *Dunciad* 4:181, 182, in which he emends a couplet from his *Essay on Criticism*:

> This farther leads me to animadvert upon a most grievous piece of nonsense to be found in all the Editions of the Author of the *Dunciad* himself. A most capital one it is, and owing to the confusion above mentioned by Scriblerus, of the two words Liberty and Monarchy. Essay on Crit. [90–91].
> *Nature, like* Monarchy, *is but restrain'd*
> *By the same Laws herself at first ordain'd.*
> Who sees not, it should be, *Nature like* Liberty? Correct it therefore *repugnantibus omnibus* (even tho' the Author himself should oppugn) in all the impressions which have been, or shall be, made of his Works. BENTL. P. W.

From 1711 until 1743 the couplet in the *Essay on Criticism* had read: *Nature, like Monarchy, is but restrain'd / By the same Laws which first herself ordain'd."* The substitution of *"Liberty"* for *"Monarchy"* is significant because the original version recognized more power vested in the prerogative of the throne than Pope (and the Opposition) thought wise to concede by 1743. Pope's concern about balancing the demands of *"Liberty"* with those of *"Monarchy"* reflect Bolingbroke's warning in Letter 17 of his *Remarks on the History of England* (1730–31):

> There may be conspiracies against liberty, as well as against prerogative. Private interest may screen or defend a bad administration, as well as attack or undermine a good one. In short, conspiring against any one part of the constitution in favor of another, or perverting, to the support of national grievances, the very means which were instituted to redress them, are destructive of the whole frame of such a government, and are the proper characteristics of faction.[14]

Thus, George II's screening of Walpole from parliamentary investigation conspires against *"Liberty"* and consequently weakens "the whole frame of . . . government." Another "teacher" like "gentle JAMES" could appear "to stick the Doctor's Chair into the Throne" and miseducate the populace into accepting the political tyranny of Dulness.

Pope elaborates the idea of James I as consciously teaching the doctrines associated with absolute monarchy. The poet's emphasis on the king's miseducating his people to accept tyranny and on the political significance of James I's pedantry does not find much support in the two historians most likely to have influenced him: Bolingbroke and Paul de Rapin Thoyras.[15] In Letter 17 of his *Remarks*, Bolingbroke follows quite closely the account of James I's pedantry he would have found in Rapin, whom Hervey called "the Craftsman's own political Evangelist."[16] Rapin had remarked that "If some take care to extol his knowledge in Philosophy, Divinity, History, polite Learning, others affirm, it was but real Pedantry, and that from all his acquired knowledge he learnt only to talk very impertinently on every subject, instead of framing solid and sure rules for the government of his Dominions."[17] For Bolingbroke and Rapin, the pedantry of James I served mainly to divert him from the affairs of statecraft he should have learned. If Pope had a precedent for his metaphor of James I as teacher of tyranny in *Dunciad* 4:175–88, he probably found it in a passage of Thomson's *Liberty: A Poem*, which anticipated as well Pope's attack on "metaphysic" and "wordy war":

> That rancour, he [James I] began; while lawless sway
> He, with his slavish doctors, tried to rear

> On metaphysic, on enchanted ground,
> And all the mazy quibbles of the schools:
> As if for one, and sometimes for the worst,
> Heaven had mankind in vengeance only made.
> Vain the pretence! not so the dire effect,
> The fierce, the foolish discord thence derived,
> That tears the country still, by party rage
> And ministerial clamour kept alive.
> In action weak, and for the wordy war
> Best fitted, faint this prince pursued his claim—
> Content to teach the subject herd, how great,
> How sacred he! how despicable they!   (4:968–81)

Thomson's passage is perhaps the lowest point in his "dissident Whig panegyric," a political progress poem tracing the rise and triumph of liberty in England; Pope's similar passage marks a high point, from the perspective of Dulness, in the regression of liberty in England.

Perhaps both Thomson and Pope were attracted by the metaphor of teaching because, according to the Whig myth of constitutional development, tyranny is a form of government that is unnatural to England and that must be imposed, or taught, from without. Thomson and Pope have replaced with the human agent of the educator James I the allegorical force of the teacher Superstition fround in Epistle 3 of *Essay on Man*:

> Who first taught souls enslav'd, and realms undone,
> Th' enormous faith of many made for one;
> That proud exception to all Nature's laws,
> T' invert the world, and counter-work its Cause?
> Force first made Conquest, and that conquest, Law;
> 'Till Superstition taught the tyrant awe,
> Then shar'd the Tyranny, then lent it aid,
> And Gods of Conqu'rors, Slaves of Subjects made:
>
> . . . .
>
> She taught the weak to bend, the proud to pray,
> To Pow'r unseen, and mightier far than they.   (241–52)

In the *Dunciad*, however, James I is more accurately described as the well-trained student of his teacher Dulness, who, like her predecessor "Superstition" in *Essay on Man*, "taught the tyrant awe" that she might share "the Tyranny" and lend it aid. Much of the fantastic and unnatural qualities critics have noticed in "this new world of Dulness" (Pope's note to *Dunciad* 4:76–101) expresses the political tyranny which is "That proud exception to all Nature's laws."[18]

Once we recognize the relationship between education and political tyranny in *Dunciad* 4, we can appreciate the significance of Pope's statement to Spence, "What was first designed for an Epistle on Education as part of my essay-scheme is now inserted in the fourth book of the *Dunciad*." [19] Pope attacks education as it is misused, consciously or not, to instill the principles of political tyranny. The attack is not restricted to lines 149–336; rather, the attack pervades the satirist's most fundamentally political poem, describing the politically inspired perversion of humanistic education from "The pale Boy-Senator" (4:147) of grammar school to "Palinurus" (4:614) himself.

In *Dunciad* 4 the pedagogical use of fear, so essential to the spread of "Superstition" and "Tyranny" in *Essay on Man*, is first practiced by the "Spectre" of Dr. Busby, "whose index-hand / Held forth the Virtue of the dreadful wand" (139–40) to frighten "The pale Boy-Senator" and "Westminster's bold race" (145). The "Spectre" introduces his students to Pope's version of Thomson's "wordy war": "'Since Man from beast by Words is known, / Words are Man's province, Words we teach alone" (149–50). The education he gives them is one of restriction and confinement:

> When Reason doubtful, like the Samian letter,
> Points him two ways, the narrower is the better.
>
> . . . .
>
> Whate'er the talents, or howe'er design'd,
> We hang one jingling padlock on the mind.   (151–62)

The reference to "the Samian," (i.e., Pythagoras) may itself be political because "the Samian sage" appears in Thomson's *Liberty* (3:32–70) as an opponent of Tyranny who helps spread liberty by teaching men to open their minds to reason. The "Spectre's" speech becomes overtly political by its end:

> "A Poet the first day, he dips his quill;
> And what the last? a very Poet still.
> Pity! the charm works only in our wall,
> Lost, lost too soon in yonder House or Hall.
> There truant WYNDHAM ev'ry Muse gave o'er,
> There TALBOT sunk, and was a Wit no more!
> How sweet an Ovid, MURRAY was our boast!
> How many Martials were in PULT'NEY lost!
> Else sure some Bard, to our eternal praise,
> In twice ten thousand rhyming nights and days,
> Had reach'd the Work, the All that mortal can;
> And South beheld that Master-piece of Man."   (163–74)

The "Spectre's" concept of the poet is the antithesis of the figure Pope presented to us in his *Imitations of Horace*. To the "Spectre," ersatz classical poets need no training and can be mass-produced so that they can write epigrams (South's "Master-piece of Man"). For the "Spectre," satire (if it exists at all for him) is hardly Pope's "sacred Weapon" of the *Epilogue to the Satires*, and the "Poet or Patriot" who restores liberty in *Essay on Man* is not desired. The "Spectre" contrasts his school with "yonder House [the House of Commons] or Hall [Westminister Hall]" where the "truant" members of the Opposition have gone. He and Dulness regret that they have not become poetasters of the most impotent kind.

The "Spectre's" reference to Westminster Hall, combined with the name and location of his own school, might have recalled to the minds of Pope's readers an advertisement in *The Craftsman*, no. 42 (1 May 1727), of another academy at Westminister:

> This is to give Notice.
> To all Noblemen with large Families and small Estates, decayed Gentlemen, Gamesters, and others, that, in the great *School* in *Westminster*, Boys are thoroughly instructed in all Parts of useful Learning. The said School is furnished with a *Master*, and one *Usher*, who does all the Business himself, and keeps his Scholars in such order, that the *Master* never attends but upon some great *Occasion*. This school is of a more excellent Foundation than any that were ever yet known; for the Scholars, instead of paying for their Learning, are *rewarded* for every Lesson the *Usher* gives them; provided they are *perfect* in it, and have it ready at their Fingers Ends.
> N.B. This is no Free School.

Like Pope in *Dunciad* 4, *The Craftsman* had used the metaphor of education to satirize the political system of England. *The Craftsman*'s "Master" (George I), like Queen Dulness, is a monarch who needs make only occasional appearances because his "*School*" is so well conducted by its "*Usher*" Walpole. The "*Usher*" teaches his students the arts of corruption, thereby rewarding and enslaving them at the same time. The school is not free because the students must give up their liberty if they want to receive such "useful Learning." As *The Craftsman* said repeatedly, the political stability of Walpole's ministry was bought at the price of English freedom. *The Craftsman*'s is a kind of political finishing school; the "Spectre's" prepares its students for the education to come. The Opposition members Pope mentions simply have not learned their lessons well.

With Dulness's pronouncement of "'The RIGHT DIVINE of Kings to govern wrong'" the next stage of education for "the pale Boy-Senator" begins: "Prompt at the call, around the Goddess roll / Broad hats, and hoods, and caps, a sable shoal [i.e., school]" (189–90). Part 5 of Thomson's *Liberty* details the vision of what must occur before political liberty can be restored and maintained:

> . . . see the young mind
> Not fed impure by chance, by flattery fooled,
> Or by scholastic jargon bloated proud,
> But filled and nourished by the light of truth,
>
> . . . .
>
> Till moral, public, graceful action crowns
> The whole.
>
> . . . .
>
> . . . Instead of barren heads,
> Barbarian pedants, wrangling sons of pride,
> And truth-perplexing metaphysic wits,
> Men, patriots, chiefs, and citizens are formed.   (599–611)

In the "sable shoal" of Dulness, the "Fragments, not a Meal" (230) of knowledge do not fill or nourish the students "by the light of truth"; the bits and pieces of Dulness's "barbarian pedants" are "chewed by blind old Scholiasts o'er and o'er" (232). Dulness's "shoal" avoids the sort of political education by which "Men, patriots, chiefs, and citizens are formed":

> "See! still thy own, the heavy Canon roll,
> And Metaphysic smokes involve the Pole.
> For thee we dim the eyes, and stuff the head
> With all such reading as was never read:"   (*Dunciad* 4:247–50)

The "wordy war" Thomson sees as a threat to liberty is practiced by Dulness's votaries, who "Plague with Dispute, or persecute with Rhyme" (260) because "on Words is still our whole debate" (219). The purpose of education in *Dunciad* 4 is to destroy the liberty Thomson celebrates and to undermine the well-ordered State of the *Essay on Man*, which is based on Man's recognition that

> Nothing is foreign: Parts relate to whole;
> One all-extending, all-preserving Soul
> Connects each being, greatest with the least;
>
> . . . .
>
> All serv'd, all serving! nothing stands alone;
> The chain holds on, and where it ends, unknown.   (3:21–26)

Dulness's "shoal" seeks to fragment this ethical foundation of government:

> The critic Eye, that microscope of Wit,
> Sees hairs and pores, examines bit by bit:
> How parts relate to parts, or they to whole,
> The body's harmony, the beaming soul,
> Are things which Kuster, Burman, Wasse shall see,
> When Man's whole frame is obvious to a *Flea*.   (4:233–38)

His sojourn in the "shoal" completed, "the pale Boy-Senator" takes his next educational step on the Grand Tour, and *Dunciad* 4:275–336 shows us what he has learned. A political context is suggested almost immediately by the fact that the "Pupil" acts "As if he saw St. James's and the Queen" (280). We must not forget that one of the principal ends of the Grand Tour was supposed to be a political education in which the student learned how liberty had been lost by other nations. Thomson's poem *Liberty* was prompted by his experience as touring companion of Charles Talbot. Many would have agreed with Robert Molesworth's judgment: "Thus 'tis a great, yet rare advantage to learn rightly how to prize *Health* without the expence of being sick, but one may easily and cheaply grow sensible of the true value of *Liberty* by travelling into such Countries for a season as do not enjoy it."[20] Addison's travels, recounted in *A Letter from Italy* (1703), impressed him with the paradox of an Italy blessed with beauty yet cursed with tyranny, an Italy he contrasts with his homeland where " 'Tis liberty that crowns Britannia's isle, / And makes her barren rocks and her bleak mountains smile."[21] When George Lyttelton wrote his *Epistle to Pope* (1730) from Italy, he encouraged the poet to celebrate English liberty, to "sing the Land, which now alone can boast / That Liberty unhappy Rome has lost."[22]

What political edification has the "Pupil" of *Dunciad* 4 had? His "lac'd Governor" tells Dulness that the student has been "Thine from birth" and that

> "Europe he saw, and Europe saw him too,
> There all thy gifts and graces we display,
> Thou, only thou, directing all our way!
> To where the Seine, obsequious as she runs,
> Pours at great Bourbon's feet her silken sons;
> Or Tyber, now no longer Roman, rolls,
> Vain of Italian Arts, Italian Souls:
>
> .   .   .   .
>
> To lands of singing, or of dancing slaves,
>
> .   .   .   .
>
> But chief her shrine where naked Venus keeps,
> And Cupids ride the Lyon of the Deeps;

Where, eas'd of Fleets, the Adriatic main
Wafts the smooth Eunuch and enamour'd swain.

. . . .

Saw ev'ry Court, heard ev'ry King declare
His royal Sense, of Op'ra's or the Fair."   (4:294–314)

Pope's note to the lines on Venice reminds us of how much the former power
of that republic has degenerated in modern times. The "Pupil," however,
learns only Dulness's lesson from his travels: "if a Borough chuse him, [he
is] not undone" (328) because he seeks to imitate the obsequious and servile
citizens of continental tyrannies. He has learned all he needs to know to be
able to "Prop thine, O Empress! like each neighbour Throne" (333).

The next two hundred lines of *Dunciad* 4 (337–436), describing "a
lazy, lolling sort, / Unseen at Church, at Senate, or at Court" (336–37), are
probably the least specifically political verses in the poem.[23] "Annius,"
"Mummius," the gardener, and the lepidopterist I take to be representatives of that "class" of Dulness's "state" (Pope's note to 4:76–101) which
includes, "Not those alone who passive own her laws, / But who, weak
rebels, more advance her cause" (85–86). The political lesson of *Essay on
Man* is reversed by these passive compliers with Queen Dulness's command
that reason be misused:

"O! would the Sons of Men once think their Eyes
And Reason giv'n them but to study *Flies!*
See Nature in some partial narrow shape,
And let the Author of the Whole escape:
Learn but to trifle; or, who most observe:
To wonder at their Maker, not to serve."   (453–58)

Pope notes that Dulness's speech "completes the whole of what she had to
give in instruction on this important occasion, concerning Learning, Civil
Society, and Religion." Her instructions, like the antiempirical episte-
mology of her "gloomy Clerk" (459–92), replace the bases for the well-
ordered State of *Essay on Man*, Epistle 3. "Silenus" reiterates the close
connection between the satire on education and the establishment of political tyranny in *Dunciad* 4:

. . . "From Priest-craft happily set free,
Lo! ev'ry finish'd Son returns to thee:
First slave to Words, then vassal to a Name,
Then dupe to Party; child and man the same;
Bounded by Nature, narrow'd still by Art,
A trifling head, and a contracted heart."   (499–504)

The "pale Boy-Senator" has undergone an education whose principles are antithetical to those of *Essay on Man*. He has progressed from Thomson's "wordy war" to "party rage" and the results for liberty should be obvious. Lest his readers miss his point about the role of education in the establishment of Dulness's essentially political tyranny, Pope adds a lengthy note to "Silenus's" lines:

> A Recapitulation of the whole Course of Modern Education describ'd in this book, which confines Youth to the study of *Words* only in Schools, subjects them to the authority of *Systems* in the Universities, and deludes them with the names of *Party-distinctions* in the World. All equally concurring to narrow the Understanding, and establish Slavery and Error in Literature, Philosophy, and Politics. The whole finished in modern Free-thinking; the completion of whatever is vain, wrong, and destructive to the happiness of mankind, as it establishes *Self-love* for the sole Principle of Action.

Pope's allegorical representations of Dulness's officiating "WIZARD OLD" (517), who rewards those who forsake principles for "Homage to a King" (524), and the descent of darkness upon the land may have been inspired by the metaphors Bolingbroke uses in *A Dissertation upon Parties* to describe what would happen if factional party distinctions were to replace the proper opposition of Country to Court: "That day [of proper distinctions], which our fathers wished to see, and did not see, is now breaking upon us. Shall we suffer this light to be turned again into party-darkness by the incantations of those who would not have passed for conjurors, even in the days of superstition and ignorance."[24] The optimism Bolingbroke expressed in 1733 has been replaced by Pope's analysis of the political reality following the fall of Walpole. As Dulness's "WIZARD OLD," Walpole has so successfully corrupted his countrymen that his methods are embraced by his erstwhile opponents. To Pope's eyes, Walpole's iniquitous incantations have conjured forth the spirit of "party-darkness," which is more powerful than any individual. The general satire of *Dunciad* 4 reflects what Pope saw as the final triumph of measures over men. The wizard's prediction to Blunt in the *Epistle to Bathurst* (135–52) has come true. Corruption has become so acceptable that even the former "Cashier of the South-Sea Company, who fled England in 1720," (Pope's note), has been pardoned and prospers: "Knight lifts the head, for what are crowds undone / To three essential Partriges in one?" (561–62).

The metaphor of political education continues both as "The Queen confers her *Titles* and *Degrees*" (566) on those who have helped bring about the political transformation of England, and in her last commands:

> Then blessing all, "Go Children of my care!
> To Practice now from Theory repair.
> All my commands are easy, short, and full.
> My Sons! be proud, be selfish, and be dull.
> Guard my Prerogative, assert my Throne:
>
> .   .   .   .
>
> Others import yet nobler arts from France,
> Teach Kings to fiddle, and make Senates dance."   (579-96)

The conclusion of Dulness's final speech is often said to refer to Walpole:

> "Perhaps more high some daring son may soar,
> Proud to my list to add one Monarch more;
> And nobly conscious, Princes are but things
> Born for First Ministers, as Slaves for Kings,
> Tyrant supreme! shall three Estates command,
> And MAKE ONE MIGHTY DUNCIAD OF THE LAND!"
>   (597-604)

But if Walpole is the primary referent, the lines are anticlimactic because he had already fallen from power when the poem first appeared. Certainly the Opposition had long charged that he was the effective ruler of England, but in keeping with the general tone of *Dunciad* 4, Pope is more likely inveighing here against the allegedly tyrannical system developed by Walpole. In a "Persian Letter" to *The Craftsman* (no. 172, 18 October 1729) Usbeck describes, to Rustan, Walpole's political system as the "*Robinarchy* or *Robinocracy*," which is "compounded of a *Monarchy*, an *Aristocracy* and a *Democracy*." The proper form of "Mixt Government" has been corrupted, however, by "the *Robinarch*, or Chief Ruler . . . nominally a *Minister* only and Creature of the Prince; but in Reality a Sovereign; as despotick, arbitrary a *Sovereign* as this Part of the World affords." William Pitt was probably more perceptive than he could have known when in the House of Commons he charged Walpole's successor, Carteret, with being "an execrable, sole minister, who had renounced the British nation and seemed to have drunk of the potion described in poetic fictions, which made men neglect their country."[25] In "1740" (which Pope never completed and did not publish until 1797) Pope had applied an earlier version of *Dunciad* 4:602-3 to Carteret:

> C[arteret], his own proud dupe, thinks Monarchs things
> Made just for him, as other fools for Kings;
> Controls, decides, insults thee [Britain] every hour,
> And antedates the hatred due to Pow'r.   (5-8)

Trained in the school of Walpole, Carteret becomes only one of those who inherit the *"Robinocracy"* from the fallen minister. Pope's lines express a charge made repeatedly after Walpole's loss of office: that politicians "stormed the closet" and forced unwanted ministers on George II. The accusation is more explicitly made in Hervey's "The Patriots Are Come; or, A Doctor for a Crazy Constitution. A New Ballad":

> Oh! E[n]g[lan]d attend while thy Fate I deplore,
> Rehearsing the Schemes and the Conduct of Pow'r;
> And since only of those who have Power, I sing;
> I'm sure none can think I hint at the [king]
> From the time his S[o]n made him Old *Robin* depose,
> All the Power of a [king] he was known to lose;
> But of all, but the Name and the Badges bereft,
> Like Old Women his Paraphonalia [*sic*] are left.
> To tell how he shook in St. J[ame]s's for fear,
> When first these New M[iniste]rs bully'd him there,
> Makes my blood boil with Rage to reflect what a Thing
> They made of a Man we obey as a [king].

We should note, however, that as Pitt's own career demonstrates, forcing new personnel on George II usually had little if any effect on ministerial policy. No one particular minister is the sole object of attack in *Dunciad* 4. Thus in lines 611–18 even "Lost was the Nation's Sense" (identified in Pope's note as the House of Commons) and "Ev'n Palinurus [Walpole] nodded at the Helm" (presumably just before he fell) during Dulness's yawn. Walpole himself is merely an agent of Dulness.

Pope's implications that the methods of Walpole outlive his personal power reflect the growing disillusionment of Pope and others with the political integrity of members of the Opposition. In Dialogue 1 of the *Epilogue to the Satires* Pope had acknowledged that the "Patriots" in the Opposition were not necessarily motivated by virtue: "In Soldier, Churchman, Patriot, Man in Pow'r, / 'Tis Av'rice all, Ambition is no more!" (161–62). In the fragmentary "1740," Pope's disgust with the Opposition becomes explicit in light of their actions after the death of William Wyndham, Bolingbroke's spokesman:

> O wretched B[ritain], jealous now of all,
> What God, what mortal, shall prevent thy fall?
> Turn, turn thy eyes from wicked men in place,
> And see what succour from the Patriot Race.   (1–4)

Carteret seeks only to replace Walpole, not to change his measures; Pulteney's sole motivations are a peerage and greed:

Thro' Clouds of Passion P[ulteney]'s views are clear,
He foams a Patriot to subside a Peer;
Impatient sees his country bought and sold,
And damns the market where he takes no gold.   (9–12)[26]

Pope's letters reveal a similar disgust and despair over the political and consequently the moral situation in England, feelings exacerbated by his own physical sickness. On 27 March 1739 he wrote Fortescue, "My own health is breaking more ways than one; and I began to be so great a fool, as to be concerned for the Publick weal, which I think breaking too," and he "lamented not any of his fortune here, but that of living to see an Age, when the Virtue of his Country seem'd to be at a period."[27] In a letter to the Earl of Marchmont, Pope refers to the English as "the most dirty, rascally Race on Earth," and he feels that "our Great Men & Patriots . . . hate Honour openly, & pray devoutly for the Removal of all Virtue."[28]

Events seemed to prove Pope's judgments correct. The fall of Walpole in 1742 brought little change in the corrupt system he had built, and most members of the Opposition simply took whatever places they could get. Nothing symbolized the continuity of corruption better than the retention of Newcastle as overseer of the vast patronage network that Pope thought was what kept it all going. Bolingbroke had warned in the "Introduction" to *The Idea of a Patriot King* what would happen if the crimes of kings and ministers were not checked:

> The iniquity of all the principal men in any community, of kings and ministers especially, does not consist alone in the crimes they commit, and in the immediate consequences of these crimes: and therefore their guilt is not to be measured by these alone. Such men sin against posterity, as well as against their own age: and when the consequences of their crimes are over, the consequences of their example remain . . . if the history of this administration descends to blacken our annals, . . . the greatest iniquity of the minister [Walpole], on whom the whole iniquity ought to be charged, is the constant endeavor he has employed to corrupt the morals of men.[29]

Pope's belief that the forces of corruption and immorality are triumphant underlies the whole dark vision of the 1743 *Dunciad* and especially the description of the Wizard near its end. The measures have outlived the man. The playful Dulness of bad writing in the first three books has been changed into a Dulness of vice, slavery, and ultimately death—the death of England Pope said he was awaiting.[30] England's former political liberty has been replaced by the tyranny of Dulness.

It would be inaccurate to say that *Dunciad* 4 is alone either a satire on education or a satire on politics. The satire on education has a political purpose. From the harbinger of tyranny, Opera, to Dulness's awarding of "*Titles* and *Degrees*," the didactic side of the poem complements Pope's vision of Tyranny replacing Liberty in England. Dulness is the heroine of the poem much as "Liberty" is the heroine of Thomson's "dissident Whig panegyric." Pope reverses the progress of political freedom celebrated in *Liberty* and in his own *Essay on Man*. Admittedly, Dulness's ascension would be made even easier by the conscious aid of "Some gentle JAMES" or of "some daring son," but her success seems irresistible. The abuses of education that foster tyranny in *Dunciad* 4 are not truly understood by most of the abusers themselves; Dulness is served by many who know not what they do:

> The gath'ring number, as it moves along,
> Involves a vast involuntary throng,
> Who gently drawn, and struggling less and less,
> Roll in her Vortex, and her pow'r confess.
> Not those alone who passive own her laws,
> But who, weak rebels, more advance her cause.   (4:81–86)

Pope is not concerned with detailing a conscious conspiracy: to him the threat to English liberty is more invidious and subtle than that. England lies threatened by her educational and governmental systems themselves, which seem naturally to promote the tyranny of Dulness.

In a letter of 25 March 1736 Pope describes to Swift his plan for a new project:

> The subject is large, and will divide into four Epistles, which naturally follow the Essay on Man, *viz*, 1. Of the Extent and Limits of Human Reason, and Science, 2. A View of the useful and therefore attainable, and of the un-useful and therefore un-attainable, Arts. 3. Of the nature, ends, application, and the use of different Capacities. 4. Of the use of *Learning*, of the *Science* of the *World*, and of *Wit*. It will conclude with a Satire against the misapplication of all these, exemplify'd by pictures, characters, and examples.[31]

The final result of this project, I believe, was *The New Dunciad* of 1742, a kind of ironic *Essay on Man*, particularly Epistle 3, "Of the Nature and State of Man, with respect to Society." From "the pale Boy-Senator" to the regal "Doctor" to the "Tyrant supreme" who can "Teach Kings to fiddle, and make Senates dance," *Dunciad* 4 is organized by the metaphor of political miseducation. Ultimately, it is that "'Tyrant supreme!'" who "'shall three Estates command, / and MAKE ONE MIGHTY DUNCIAD OF THE LAND!'" He is the valedictorian of the "*Academy* for the Instruction of young Gentlemen in the Art and Mystery of *Government*" ironically promoted by *The Craftsman* (no. 170, 30 August 1729).[32]

The inversion of the proper ends of education in *Dunciad* 4 is reflected in the uses to which Pope puts traditional iconography. Conventional icons are usurped or parodied in this "new moral World" (15n.) of Dulness restored. The poem is framed by allusions to such familiar emblems as those of winged Time (6) and "Self-conceit" (533), now associated with the victorious forces of a universe overturned. In line 71—"And now had Fame's posterior Trumpet blown"—Pope parodies the common notion of Fame's having two trumpets—one for good Fame, the other for bad. Such casual references to common emblems, like Pope's mention of "Folly's Cap" (240), suggest the audience's easy familiarity with several visual traditions. Consequently, Pope can economically parody the heraldic or armorial tradition in his line and note on "the Arms of Venice": "And Cupids ride the Lyon of the Deeps" (308).

A bit more complicated perhaps is Pope's allusion to the emblem of "the Samian letter" Y in lines 150–51: "When Reason doubtful, like the Samian letter, / Points him two ways, the narrower is the better." As S. K. Heninger, Jr., reminds us, "One curious bit of Pythagorean lore employed the letter Y . . . to symbolize the moral choice between a life of virtue or of vice, a choice which a young man faces upon reaching adulthood."[33] In emblematic representations of the Pythagorean letter, Hercules at the Crossroads is frequently associated with the choice between virtue and vice. Pope clearly expects his readers to keep in mind "the Samian letter" as a choice of roads to be taken, since he returns to the image in lines 470–72: "Mother of Arrogance, and Source of Pride! / We nobly take the high Priori Road, / And reason downward, till we doubt of God."

In his notes as well as in the poem itself, Pope repeatedly calls our attention to the emblematic side of *Dunciad* 4. For example, the note to lines 11 and 12 tells us that "the Sun is the *Emblem* of that intellectual light which dies before the face of Dulness," or the note to line 18, when Dulness "mounts the Throne," turns the image of the godhead upside-down, since, according to the "vet. Adag., The higher you climb, the more you shew your A——; Verified in no instance more than in Dulness aspiring. Emblematized also by an Ape climbing and exposing his posteriors." The reference to the ape recalls how commonly artists used this animal as an emblem of foolish imitation and hypocrisy.[34] "We are next presented with the pictures of those whom the Goddess leads in Captivity" (21, 22n.). Here, the icons are usurped. To recognize fully the "pictures" Pope gives us, we must *see* the allusion made in lines 24 and 26. "There, stript, fair *Rhet'ric* languish'd on the ground . . . / And shameless *Billingsgate* her Robes adorn." The briefest reference to the clothing of "fair *Rhet'ric*" shows that Pope expects his readers to remember the proper icon of this figure, as described in Ripa's *Iconologia* (fig. 319, p. 80):

Rettorica: RHETORICK

A fair Lady, richly cloth'd, with a noble Head-dress; very complaisant; holds up her right Hand open; a Scepter in her left, with a Book, on the Skirt of her Petticoat are these Words, ORNATUS PERSUASIO; of a ruddy Complexion, with a Chimera at her Feet.

Fair and complaisant, because there is none so ill bred that is not sensible of the *Charms* of Eloquence. Her open Hand shews Rhetoric discourses in a more open Way than Logic. The Scepter, her Sway over Mens Minds. The Book, *Study* requisite. The Motto denotes its *Business*: The Chimera, the three *Precepts* of it; judicial, demonstrative, and deliberative.

The usurpers, in turn, are icons of Pope's own creation, such as *"Chicane* in Furs, and *Casuistry* in Lawn" (28). Pope returns to the misuse of the iconography of clothing in lines 585–86 ("The Cap and Switch be sacred to his Grace; / With Staff and Pumps the Marquis lead the Race") when the nobility foolishly assume the dress of their inferiors and underlings, thus overturning the proper social hierarchy. The greatest usurper of all, of course, is Dulness herself, the parody of the godhead. Pope's note to line 27 makes clear that Dulness is in part a parody of *Astraea*, or Justice, in this new age of Gold and Lead. Thus, the enthroning of Dulness reverses the order depicted in Geffrey Whitney's emblem "Sine iustitia, confusio," whose explanatory verses instruct us that men degenerated from "the goulden worlde" into such a state of moral confusion and disordered values

That nowe, into the worlde, an other CHAOS came:
But GOD, that of the former heape: the heaven and earthe did
    frame.
And all thinges plac'd therein, his glorye to declare:
Sente IUSTICE downe into the earthe.
                                    (*A Choice of Emblems*, Leyden, 1568)

Similarly, Dulness's usurpation is reflected in Pope's parodic treatments of the icon of the bee, common emblem of ideal kingship, as well as of Copernican cosmography in the note to lines 76–101, which again underscore the universal disorder the enthroning of Dulness represents.[35] Opera's likening of Handel to Briareus, defender of Jove against his fellow Titans, and her warning that if he is not exiled "Jove's own Thunders follow Mar's Drums" (65–68) invite us to see Dulness as a mockery of the enthroned Jove or Justice so frequently depicted by artists.[36] Dulness becomes a kind of Titan triumphant in this "new moral world" of perverted values.

In this role of mock-Jove, Dulness presides over the rest of the poem, meting out mock-justice to her petitioners and mock-degrees to her scholars. In the scene in which Dulness judges between Annius and Mummius, we find one inversion of traditional iconography—the enthroned Jove or Justice—facing another inversion—the iconography of medals or coins. This passage in *Dunciad* 4 (347–96) is appropriate to the theme of education because in the eighteenth century the iconography of medals, as an art, was recognized as a sister of poetry. In *Dialogues Upon the Usefulness of Ancient Medals; Especially in Relation to the Latin and Greek Poets*, Addison describes the making of coins as "a kind of printing, before the art was invented." Both arts should instruct as well as please, and since "there is a great affinity between coins and poetry," "poetry being in some respects an art of designing, as well as painting or sculpture, they may serve as comments on each other." Pope's *To Mr Addison, Occasioned by his Dialogues on Medals* (1720) is the touchstone by which we can measure the reversal of iconographic values found in *Dunciad* 4. Pope's earlier poem makes it clear that coins should convey visually the lessons of history. For Mummius and Annius, the only value of ancient coins is financial; their didactic value is ignored.

In addition to the rather direct transmogrifications found in *Dunciad* 4 of the visual traditions already discussed, we can detect several more general parallels in Pope's poem to contemporary engraved satires. For example, Pope's depiction of Opera as an allegorical female and the theme of opera as a means of miseducation are both to be found in the 1731 print *The Stage's Glory* (B.M. 1869), one of whose medallions (labelled "O") shows a tiny woman, perhaps Madame Cuzzoni, placed in a scene representing Italian opera. Verses explain the medallion:

Little Syren of the stage,
Charmer of an idle age,
Empty warbler, breathing lyre,
Wanton gale of fond desire,
Bane of every manly art,
Sweet enfeebler of the heart,
Oh, too pleasing is thy strain,
Hence, to southern climes again:
Tuneful mischief, vocal spell,
To this island bid farewell;
Leave us, as we ought to be,
Leave the Britons, rough and free.[37]

Another such contemporary engraving which shares a theme with *Dunciad* 4 is the animal print of circa 1730, *A Satire on School-Masters and School-Mistresses* (B.M. 1862), whose lines express its point:

35. *A Satire on School-Masters and School-Mistresses* (B.M. 1862)

Thus many Sensless [*sic*] -flogging Fools,
Are Teachers of our Modern Schooles:
Tho' Void of Learning, Wit, or Parts,
Presume to teach the Lib'ral Arts:
Strange! that such Asses shou'd bestow
On others more than yet they know:
And such the Madness of Mankind,
We're fond of Fools, to Merit blind.

36. The C{a}rd{i}n{a}l Dancing-Master; or, Pl{a}ce-m{e}n in Leading-Strings (B.M. 2530)

Much more closely linked to the imagery of *Dunciad* 4, with its "WIZARD OLD" (517), is the 1739 engraving *The State Pack-Horse* (B.M. 2420), a print that supplements its visual meaning with lines from Pope. Nearly at the center of this engraving presides the wizard-Walpole figure of political corruption. Of all the contemporary prints, perhaps the 1742 *The C{a}rd{i}n{a}l* [i.e., Fleury] *Dancing-Master; or, Pl{a}ce-m{e}n in Leading-Strings* (B.M. 2530) is, as its title indicates, most like the representation in *Dunciad* 4 of the political abuse of education to serve the ends of Dulness and tyranny: "Others import yet nobler arts from France, / Teach Kings to fiddle, and make Senates dance" (579–98).

37. Geffrey Whitney, *A Choice of Emblems*, "Tempus omnia terminat"

38. John Gay, "Fable XLVII: The Court of Death"

39. Geffrey Whitney, *A Choice of Emblems*, "Veritas temporis filia"

Pope's reversals of traditional iconography find their grandest illustrations in the last thirty lines of *Dunciad* 4, which celebrate the enthroning of yet another usurper, "C H A O S." Critics have long noted the parody of *Genesis* in these lines, but no one has remarked their relationship to the tradition of emblem books. Ronald Paulson plausibly suggests that Hogarth's 1764 *Tailpiece; or, The Bathos* (B.M. 4106) may have been influenced by these final lines of *Dunciad* 4.[38] But Pope's own ending is a variation of the tailpieces often seen before in emblem books. Emblem books frequently conclude with an image of Time or Death, as does Geffrey Whitney's *A Choice of Emblems*:

> Tempus omnia terminat.
> The longest daye, in time resignes to nighte,
> The greatest oke, in time to dust doth turne,
> The Raven dies, the Egle failes of flighte.
> The Phoenix rare, in time her selfe doth burne.
> The princelie stagge at lengthe his race doth ronne.

40. *The Doctrine of Morality*, frontispiece

41. *The Doctrine of Morality*, plate 46

And all must ende, that ever was begonne.
Even so, I, here doe ende this simple book. . . .   (P. 230)

Whitney's is a rather mild image of the Ovidian figure of *Tempus edax Rerum* ("Time, gluttonous of things") Pope uses to end his poem. Indeed, Pope's tone is harsher than that found in most emblem books, and he seems willing to undercut the icon of Time, an ambivalent figure in the emblematic tradition. The sinister side of Time appears in a print Pope certainly knew and one that may have influenced Pope's depiction of the satiric enthroning, the wand, and the distribution of awards in *Dunciad* 4. The engraving, designed by Pope's friend William Kent, is the emblem for Gay's "Fable XLVII: The Court of Death" (1727):

DEATH, on a solemn night of state,
In all his pomp of terrors sate:
Th' attendants of his gloomy reign,
Diseases dire, a ghastly train,
Croud the vast court. With hollow tone
A voice thus thunder'd from the throne.
    This night our minister we name,
Let ev'ry servant speak his claim;
Merit shall bear this eban wand.
All, at the word, stretch'd forth their hand.   (1–10)

In *Dunciad* 4 we "See skulking *Truth* to her old Cavern fled" (641), just as Pope himself retreats to his grotto, defeated by Time, on whose "rapid wing" (6) the poet is borne throughout the poem.[39] Is Pope here intentionally perverting the commonly depicted relationship of Time and Truth as father and daughter he could have found, for example, in the fourth of Whitney's *Choice of Emblems?*:

Three furies fell, which turne the worlde to ruthe,
Both Enuie, Strife, and Slaunder, heare appeare,
In dungeon darke they longe inclosed truthe,
But Time at lengthe, did loose his daughter deare,
And setts alofte, that sacred ladie brighte,
Whoe things longe hidd, reveales, and bringes to lighte.

The conventional notion that Time is the revealer of Truth can be seen again in "LE MIROIR QUI NE FLATE POINT," the *memento mori* frontispiece to *The Doctrine of Morality; or, A View of Human Life, According to the Stoick Philosophy* (London, 1721). Here Time pulls back the curtain to enable the viewer to see his own skeletal reflection in the mirror; in *Dunciad* 4, Time and the curtain hide Truth. Indeed, in many ways, *Dunciad* 4

42. *The Doctrine of Morality*, plate 50

inverts the iconographic teachings of *The Doctrine of Morality*. Like *Dunciad* 4, *The Doctrine* is a book about education: the first four plates show that education must assist nature to guide us to follow virtue and avoid vice (pp. 2–9). Plate 17, "God alone has no Superior," offers us the positive image of the good king enthroned: "Draw near and take notice of this good King here represented for your Imitation, He is surrounded with his Subjects, ren'dring Justice. . . . Behold who are the Ministers and Counsellors that he consults. He lifts up his Eyes to Heaven, and contemplates the supreme Justice, who is the Rule and Perfection of all Things" (p. 34). Even closer to what Pope does in *Dunciad* 4 is plate 46, "All yield to the Daemon of Riches," in which the enthroned Daemon is surrounded by perverted images of Virtue, Piety, and Wisdom, as well as by Fame with her two trumpets:

Monster! whose Head a Diadem does grace,
Thou vile Corrupter of the Mind;
Fierce, cruel, Tyrant o'er Mankind,
Who boldly do'st usurp bright Virtue's Place:
Who can resist thy Charms since here we see,
Virtue forget her self, and worship Thee?   (P. 93)

Another usurpation image appears in plate 50, "Fortune cannot give Desert," whose reference to a monkey reminds us of Pope's use of the ape image in *Dunciad* 4: "It is true, Fortune, that fickle Goddess, to try the Patience of great Souls, often takes delight to leave the Wise neglected in Obscurity and Want, and seats the Idiot on the Throne. But 'tis not in her Power to disguise the Monkey she has crown'd so well, but that through all the gaudy Robes and Ornaments with which she has endeavour'd to conceal his Deformities, he still appears to be such as Nature has made him" (p. 100).

Book 2 of *The Doctrine of Morality* displays several emblems that can be the touchstones for the inverted or subverted icons of what I have called Pope's tailpiece, the final thirty lines of *Dunciad* 4. Thus, where "*Art* after *Art* goes out, and all is Night" (640), in plate 15, "Eternal Honours are the Fruits of elaborate Studies," "[Virtue] constrains Time, maugre his Ill-Nature and Aversion to preserve things from Decay, to lend her his hand to place her Favourites above perishing things, and to record from Age to Age the Acts of these illustrious Men; proclaiming aloud, that thus shall all those be honoured, whom Vertue judges worthy of Eternity" (p. 154). In the emblem book, "Vertue triumphs over all her Enemies" (plate 23, pp. 170–71) just as Dulness does in the poem. Pope's images of decay, collapse, and death are found in the emblem of "We ought to make use of Time" (plate 26, pp. 176–77), but one of the lessons of "Everything perishes with Time" (plate 29, pp. 182–83)—that "Wit lives to all Eternity, / And all things else do die"—is denied in *Dunciad* 4 by the line: "*Wit* shoots in vain its momentary fires" (633). And, ultimately, Pope transcends the didactic temporal perspective of the last emblem of *The Doctrine of Morality*, "Death is the End of all things" (plate 43, pp. 210–11), to "let the curtain fall" on his own satiric doctrine of immorality with all its eschatological implications of "Universal Darkness."

CHAPTER VI

After the Fall: Political Satire, 1742–60

Pope and poetry are dead! Patriotism has kissed hands on accepting a place.
—Horace Walpole to Horace Mann, 21 March 1746

The preceding chapter describes *Dunciad* 4 as standing in an emblematic relation to the previous three books of the *Dunciad*. We may go further and see *Dunciad* 4 as a fitting emblematic conclusion to Pope's whole career as an Opposition political satirist. Pope's last poem sums up many of the political and historiographic assumptions he shared with Bolingbroke, *The Crafts-man*, and others who had opposed in prints and verse the ministry of the last twenty years. And, as the present chapter will show, *Dunciad* 4 marks an abrupt turning point in the development of eighteenth-century English political satire.

In the final version of the *Dunciad*, the poet reassumes the pose of historian we saw in *Windsor Forest*. More precisely, in the *Dunciad* Pope fuses the role of historian he adopted in his first political poem with the role of satirist he adopted in the *Imitations of Horace*. History and satire are the only means left to oppose Dulness because they are the only Muses that remain unconquered:

> There to her heart sad Tragedy addrest
> The dagger wont to pierce the Tyrant's breast;
> But sober History restrain'd her rage,
> And promis'd Vengeance on a barb'rous age.
> There sunk Thalia, nerveless, cold, and dead,
> Had not her Sister Satyr held her head. (4:37–42)[1]

As historian-satirist, Pope creates in the *New Dunciad* a poem of which the conception and organization are strikingly like those of *Windsor Forest*. Both are progress poems celebrating restorations. In his earliest political poem, Pope celebrates the progress of "Fair *Liberty*, Britannia's Goddess" (91), achieved by the Stuart succession; in his last poem Pope ironically celebrates the triumph of Dulness, who restores her reign over the world. Astrea-like, Anne and Dulness inaugurate, respectively, "Albion's Golden Days" (424) and "Saturnian days of Lead and Gold" (16). The *New Dunciad* represents the reverse image of *Windsor Forest*. The poems share the same historical assumptions, but on the cycle of history the *New Dunciad* is the nadir opposite the zenith of the earlier poem.

These similarities in conception and organization are reflected in the imagery of both poems. The integration of spatial and temporal dimensions we discussed in relation to *Windsor Forest* is again apparent in Pope's last poem; book 4 is another mixture of progress piece and history painting.[2] Just as the sovereigns in *Windsor Forest* were shown in their official attire, Dulness is presented in her regal glory. Thus the state portrait seen in *Windsor Forest* (413–22) or in Thornhill's *Allegory of the Protestant Succession* reappears, satirically inverted, in book 4, when Dulness is described on her throne:

> Beneath her foot-stool, *Science* groans in Chains,
> And *Wit* dreads Exile, Penalties and Pains.
> There foam'd rebellious *Logic*, gagg'd and bound,
> There, strip't, fair *Rhet'ric* languish'd on the ground;
> His blunted Arms by *Sophistry* are born,
> And shameless *Billingsgate* her Robes adorn,
> *Morality*, by her false Guardians drawn,
> *Chicane* in Furs, and *Casuistry* in Lawn,
> Gasps, as they straiten at each end the cord,
> And dies, when Dulness gives her Page the word.   (21–30)

This allegorical tableau is indicative of the generalized descriptions in book 4.

As we have seen, the political implications of Pope's emphasis on music, education, and learning in *Dunciad* 4 become more apparent when we compare his last poem with his earlier works. Let us look at just two more examples. The political significance of Opera's dissonant introduction of Dulness's reign gains importance when we recall a stanza of Pope's *Ode for Musick. On St. Cecilia's Day*, a stanza that appears only in the 1730 edition:

> *Amphion* thus bade wild Dissention cease,
> And soften'd Mortals learn'd the Arts of Peace.
> > *Amphion* taught contending Kings,
> > From various Discords to create
> > The Musick of a well-tun'd State,
> Nor slack nor strain the tender Strings;

Those useful Touches to impart
That strike the Subjects answ'ring Heart;
And the soft, silent Harmony, that springs
From Sacred Union and consent of Things.

Similarly, the close relation of learning to politics in *Dunciad* 4 already exists in "Two Chorus's to the Tragedy of Brutus" (1717):

> *Antistrophe* 2.
> Ye Gods! what justice rules the ball?
> Freedom and Arts together fall;
> Fools grant whate'er ambition craves,
> And men, once ignorant, are slaves.
> Oh curs'd effects of civil hate,
> In every age, in every state!
> Still, when the lust of tyrant pow'r succeeds,
> Some *Athens* perishes, some *Tully* bleeds.

The references to history and satire, as well as the cyclical concept of restoration in *Dunciad* 4, seem to suggest the possibility of the eventual return of Freedom. The suggestion, however, may be more illusory than real. The ending of Pope's last poem is very similar to that of *Windsor Forest*, but the major difference in the structural organization of the two poems lies in the point at which Pope arrests the historical cycle. In *Windsor Forest* Pope stops the cyclical movement at its highest point and then replaces it with a linear progression in time and space. In *Dunciad* 4 Pope appears to arrest the cyclical movement at its lowest point. Walpole ("Sir Blue") finds both his poet and his historian in Pope and thus loses even the "Fame" he had been ironically advised to seek:

> POETS, Sir *Blue* have maul'd Thee fore,
> Just like great *Burleigh* heretofore;
> Spencer to Him a Foe We see,
> And *P—pe* was never Friend to Thee;
> But Prose extolls a *Cecil's* Name,
> And *Cambden* gives a Right to Fame;
> Who then, *most* admirable *Knight*,
> Thy matchless Actions shall recite?
> Say, what Historian will Thou fix on,
> *Pitt, Norton, Arnal*, or *Oldmixon*?
> (Anonymous, "to HIM, whom it may concern" [1735?])

But, as we have seen, by 1742 Pope is more concerned with Walpole's legacy than with the minister himself. Pope, in *Dunciad* 4, accepts as accomplished fact the dire warnings uttered by the Opposition for the past twenty years. The redemptive qualities of the patriot king extolled in his own unpublished "1740" and in Bolingbroke's not-yet-published *The Idea of a Patriot King* do not appear in Pope's last poem. Pope agrees in the end only with the negative stress Bolingbroke places on the kind of education the teacher Walpole has allegedly given England. Bolingbroke soon makes clear his faith in the future, which Pope no longer shared in 1742:

> Let us not flatter ourselves: I did so too long. It is more to be wished than to be hoped, that the contagion should spread no further than that leprous race, who carry on their skins, exposed to public sight, the scabs and blotches of their distemper. The minister preaches corruption aloud and constantly, like an impudent missionary of vice: and some there are who not only insinuate, but teach the same occasionally. . . . I say, some; because I am as far from thinking, that all those who join with him, as that any of those who oppose him, wait only to be more authorized, that they may propagate it with greater success, and apply it to their own use, in their turn."[3]

The philosopher Bolingbroke stands no more prominently behind Pope's *Essay on Man* than the historian Bolingbroke stands behind what I have called Pope's ironic *Essay on Man*. For example, Dulness's call for "'Some gentle JAMES'" to preach "'The RIGHT DIVINE of Kings to govern wrong'" ironically echoes a passage in *The Idea of a Patriot King*: "But the principles we have laid down do not stop here. A divine right in kings is to be deduced evidently from them: a divine right to govern well, and conformably to the constitution at the head of which they are placed. A divine right to govern ill, is an absurdity: to assert it, is blasphemy."[4] More generally, *Dunciad* 4 is the poetic expression of the current state of England Bolingbroke outlined at the very end of his *Letters on the Study and Use of History*:

> . . . the state is become, under ancient and known forms, a new and undefinable monster; composed of a king without monarchical splendor, a senate of nobles without aristocratical independency, and a senate of commons without democratical freedom. . . . the very idea of wit, and all that can be called taste, has been lost among the great; arts and sciences are scarce alive; luxury has been increased but not refined; corruption has been established, and is avowed. When governments are worn out, thus it is: the decay appears in every instance. Public and private virtue, public and private spirit, science and wit, decline altogether.[5]

The student Pope has learned his lessons on the study and use of history from his mentor Bolingbroke and put them to use in the greatest publication of the Opposition wits.

Publication of the 1743 *Dunciad* marks an abrupt end to an era of political satire. In the aftermath of Walpole's fall from power and the consequent collapse of the strategy developed by the Opposition, English political satire rapidly became more personal and restrictedly topical. Thus, although we can easily name great satirists (e.g., Pope, Gay, Swift, and Johnson) writing from 1720 to 1743, it is difficult to find satirists of any significance working between 1743 and the emergence of Charles Churchill. Pope believed, in the last years of his life, that no real differences in principle divided Walpole from his opponents. This belief resulted in a poem that portrayed individuals as far less important than the forms of corruption they commonly pursued. Most of Pope's contemporaries and successors in satire apparently felt that if indeed there were no differences of principle among political rivals, then only personalities were left to attack. Namier's thesis that personalities were more important than principles in mid-eighteenth-century English politics is lent considerable support by literary and artistic evidence.

To a greater extent than we have done heretofore, we shall observe political developments in the decades between Walpole's fall in 1742 and the accession of George III in 1760 principally through the words and pictures of the satirists.[6] As I shall demonstrate, however, the relative political stability of the period led to the virtual stagnation of political satire, and so we shall look only briefly at each particular poem or print. The existing satiric material simply does not deserve the detailed attention we have given each work in earlier chapters. Yet, to understand the differences between the poetry and prints of Pope's time and those of Churchill's we must consider some of the satiric productions of the interregnum.

Pope's disappointment, if not despair, at the events surrounding Walpole's fall from power was shared by many of his contemporaries. For years, ministerial apologists had contended that the Opposition attacks on Walpole were motivated by his being "in" while they were "out." Walpole's defenders had long described his attackers' claims of virtue and sincerity in attacking measures not men as so much political cant. William Arnall's attitude in *Opposition no Proof of Patriotism: with Some Observations and Advice Concerning Party-Writings* (London, 1735) is typical: "It requires but a small Degree of Sagacity to distinguish between publick Zeal and private Passion, however the latter may assume the Name of the former; and in an Opposition which *continually* rages, it will easily be seen that it is *Men* and not *Measures* that give the real Offence, especially when the Opposers have themselves formerly approved and promoted the very same Measures which they afterwards oppose" (p. 12).

The shaky nature of the Opposition coalition of Tories and disaffected Whigs and the unreliability of some of its leaders were obvious to Bolingbroke years before Walpole actually fell from power. Bolingbroke expressed his own growing disillusionment to Polwarth on 1 January 1740 when he asked, "[Is it] not manifest, that two or three men have been labouring some years to turn a virtuous defence of the constitution, and a virtuous opposition to maladministration into a dirty intrigue of low ambition? that they are preparing to continue Walpole's scheme of government in other hands, and that the sole object of their pretended patriotism is to deliver over the government of their country from faction to faction?"[7] We have already seen that Pope's unfinished "1740" expressed similar distrust of Carteret and Pulteney. By late 1741 Pulteney was indicating in the House of Commons that he sought to oust only Walpole himself and not his whole administration.

Events seemed to justify the doubts about the fidelity of Carteret and Pulteney. Even before Walpole left office, George II, through Newcastle, began negotiations with Pulteney to form a new government composed of the remnant of Walpole's administration—the Old Whigs—and a few New Whigs like Carteret and Pulteney separated from the bulk of the Opposition. The new ministry simply continued Walpolean war policy, protected the former minister from prosecution, and opposed popular Country legislation. By March 1742 Carteret and Pulteney were voting to support the Septennial Act, so long attacked by the Opposition as a principal support of Walpole's corrupt system of rule. Opposition wits themselves had set the standards by which Walpole's attackers would be judged were they to achieve office. *The Bystander. A Poem* (London, 1741), after devoting a verse paragraph of praise to each leading member of the Opposition, had confidently predicted:

> Good Patriot Statesmen, (sure there are such things!)
> Promote their Country's Welfare and the KING's:
> *These*, Time hath prov'd and further Time will tell,
> If *Actions* with their *Words* run Parallel;
> If so, Be these your *faithful Guides*, if not,
> Let 'em ignobly with their Baseness rot;
>
> . . . .
>
> Not *One* here mention'd's tainted with a Crime;
> Knowing no Guilt, till charg'd they must be free,
> And stil'd *Preservers of our LIBERTY.*   (Pp. 14–15)

Pulteney, rendered politically impotent by his own public vow not to seek office and by his elevation to the House of Lords as the earl of Bath in July 1742, was the primary target of the politically dissatisfied. Erstwhile allies like Lyttelton, Chesterfield, and Pitt, who had not been brought into the new coalition, and Old Whigs like Hervey, who had been sacrificed to make way for the New, joined to assail Pulteney as the arch-opportunist of

English politics. He retained the stigma for the rest of his life.[8] His former prominence in the Opposition to Walpole made him an easy target for charges of desertion and hypocrisy. Quotations (presumed to be his own) from *The Craftsman* were ironically used to reveal Bath's lack of principles in *A New Year's Gift for the R——t H——e, the E—— of Bath; In a Letter from R{ichar}d F{ranckli}n* [printer of *The Craftsman*] (London, 1744), published after he had lost all effective power.

Pulteney was not completely without apologists. His "Self-denial rare" of refusing office is praised in *An Epistle to the Right Honourable William Pulteney, Esq.; Upon His Late Conduct in Publick Affairs* (London, 1742), a poem clearly inspired by the *Dunciad*. In lines said to "represent the State of *Great Britain* in the Year 1741" (p. 6) the poet agrees with Pope's dark vision of England:

> *Britannia's* Sun now shot a *parting* Ray,
> Just on the Point of putting out her Day;
> Now, half *enslav'd*, half bankrupt, *Albion's* Realm,
> Had neither *Weight* nor *Wisdom* at the *Helm*,
> But *W——e*, like a boding *Screech-Owl* sate
> Close to the Window of the dying State.   (Pp. 6–7)

Pope's despair, however, is replaced in the next few lines with hope:

> Now all things tow'rds their pristine *Chaos* lean'd,
> No Seed of Art or Science to be glean'd;
> St. Stephen's *Curfew* toll'd—*put out the Light*,
> And the P——s Chimes play'd round—*let there be Night*.
> Now the last Times of *Peril* seem'd begun,
> For fatal *Discord* reign'd 'twixt *Sire* and *Son*;
> Each *Nation* against *Nation* fierce rose up,
> And *Britons* drank the dregs of *Circe's* Cup;
> Whilst ev'ry *Patriot* Eye distill'd a Tear,
> And Bourbon rung his *Shackles* in our Ear.
> Then, in that very *Crisis* of our *Fate*,
> Just at the *Point* when 'twas not *quite* too *late*,
> Pultney step'd forth the Saviour of the State.   (P. 8)

But such defense of Pulteney was very rare. Far more common was the satirists' elaboration of Pope's theatrical metaphor in the *Dunciad* to attack what they saw as the continuation of Walpole's system of government. Ironically enough, Pulteney was one of the first to accuse Walpole of stage-managing from behind the scenes. Pulteney, assuming Walpole himself had been the author of a prose defense of his ministry, says in *A Proper Answer to the By-Stander* (London, 1742), "People are very much mistaken, if you are not more properly to be called a Behind-Stander; because, though you do not appear upon the Stage, you direct all behind the Scene" (p. 1). Very soon, however, Pulteney was being portrayed as one of the stars on the stage of Walpole (now Lord Orford), performing with Carteret, despite Carteret's statement to Lord Egmont that he had no intention "of coming in as a screen to Sir Robert Walpole, or that Sir Robert should . . . play still the game behind the curtain."

Carteret had also told Egmont that, "considering his Majesty's temper, it would have been impossible to make the intended changes if all at once a number of gentlemen whom Sir Robert Walpole had possessed his Majesty with an ill opinion of, had offered to force themselves upon him before the aspersions cast on them were removed."[9] The exclusion of this "number of gentlemen" guaranteed the new ministry an opposition. Carteret and Pulteney are the targets of the ironic *A Congratulatory Letter to a Certain Right Honourable Person, Upon His Late Disappointment* (London, 1742). Carteret is seen as a friend who saved Pulteney from charges of hypocrisy by retiring him to domestic bliss (Pulteney's wife was a notorious termagant). The anonymous author suggests that the Roman tradition of appending to a hero's name that of his conquest should be revived and applied to Pulteney: "Your famous Conquest over Sir *R——t W——e*, and your kind Treatment of him afterwards (so much to the Satisfaction of these injured Kingdoms) deserv'd to have you made known to the present Age, and render'd immortal to Posterity by the Name of *P——y* the *Walpolian*" (pp. 30–31).

The weakness of the verse satire written immediately after the fall of Walpole may conveniently be seen in *The New Ministry: Containing a Collection of All the Satyrical Poems, Songs, Etc., Since the Beginning of 1742* (London, 1742). Many of these verses are by Sir Charles Hanbury Williams, whom Horace Walpole considered (unfortunately, with justification) the most important political satirist after Pope's death. Active from 1739 until 1747, when he entered diplomatic service on the Continent, Williams concentrated his attacks on Pulteney. In a footnote to Williams's "The Country Girl; An Ode: Humbly Inscribed to the Earl of Bath," Horace Walpole remarks: "The pen of Sir Charles Hanbury Williams inflicted deeper wounds in three months on this Lord than a series of Craftsmen, aided by Lord Bolingbroke, for several years, could imprint on Sir Robert Walpole: the latter lost his power, but lived to see justice done to his character—his rival acquired no power, but died very rich; he is supposed to have had the principal hand in Mist and Fog's Journals, and the Craftsman."[10] Williams had been a fervent supporter of Sir Robert and remained a close friend of Horace. A professed admirer of Pope, whom he encouraged to attack the new ministry with him (*An Ode: Inscribed to the Right Honourable the Viscount Lonsdale*, May 1743), Williams did not try to imitate England's master of political satire. Williams was content to write strictly topical, ephemeral, and personal satire in a variety of verse forms. One senses a joy in the discomfort of his enemies rather than the anger Pope felt in his later satire. We find little in the way of historical allusions or generalized satire in the verse of Williams or others in the years after Pope.

Williams's methods may be illustrated from just a few examples. In "The Country Girl" he compares Bath to a country wench who guards her virtue until the price is right:

> So virtuous Pult'ney, who had long
> By speech, by pamphlet, and by song,
> Held patriotism's steerage,
> Yields to ambition mixt with gain,
> A treasury gets for Harry Vane,
> And for himself a peerage.

"A Dialogue Between the Earl of Bath and his Countess" becomes more personal, attributing Bath's political impotence to his wife's greed and envy. Williams's opinions about the fall of Walpole and the new ministry are summarized in lines from "A New Ode":

> O Walpole, Walpole, blush for shame,
> With all your tools around you!
> Does not each glorious patriot name,
> Quite dazzle and confound you?
>
> Had you sought out this patriot race,
> Triumphant still you'd been;
> By only putting them in place,
> You had yourself kept in.

Walpole's mistake was not repeated by those Old Whigs, like Pelham and Newcastle, who had themselves kept in despite his removal from office. Once Pelham and Newcastle had forced Carteret out of office as secretary of state in November 1744, and especially after they had consolidated their power in the wake of Pulteney and Carteret's abortive "forty-eight hour ministry" (10–12 February 1746), Walpole's former colleagues followed a policy of comprehension. Walpole had helped create the formidable opposition to himself by expelling from office those who seemed a threat to his own preeminence in the administration. Throughout the 1740s and 1750s his successors placated their opponents by bringing them into office. The ministry sought to "broaden its bottom" by adopting the advice of "Jeffrey Broad-Bottom, Esq.," pseudonymous editor of Chesterfield's weekly paper *Old England; or, The Constitutional Journal* (published from 5 February 1743 until December 1744), to accept both Tories and Whigs in office. Since 1742, the "Broad-Bottoms" had been encouraging the Old Whigs to cast out Carteret and Pulteney and to bring them in. As soon as they were brought in they supported the very "Hanoverian measures" and the war policy they had been assailing when they were out of power. Such apparent hypocrisy led Horace Walpole to decry "the impudent prostitution of patriots, going to market with their honesty."[11]

Dismaying as it was to some, the Pelhamite policy of comprehension resulted in the most tranquil period of domestic English politics in the eighteenth century. Horace Walpole's observation in 1746 that politically "now we are said to be all of a mind" and his description of Parliament as "all harmony" would remain accurate until the accession of George III. This political stability justified Walpole's analysis of the state of political satire: "Pope and poetry are dead! Patriotism has kissed hands on accepting a place."[12] Pelham, who was *primus inter pares* from 1747 until his death in 1754, extended his policy of comprehension to include his literary opponents. Sir Robert Walpole had either ignored the Opposition wits or hired hacks to combat them; Pelham, however, according to Horace Walpole, "employed any means to get able men out of the Opposition; he always bought off enemies to avoid their satire."[13] Such strategy certainly weakened the formerly strong tradition of English verse satire.

Voices were still raised against the ministry, and the accusation that only men and not measures were changed became a constant refrain. *In and Out and Turn About, a New C——t Dance* (London, 1745) notes that when the Opposition came in "They alter'd a Note, / Yet the same Tune was play'd" (p. 3). The anonymous author of *One Thousand, Seven Hundred, and Forty-five. A Satiric-Epistle; After the Manner of Mr. Pope* (London, 1746) asks, "Why, in rotation, still the splendid rout / Are *Prostitutes* while in, and *Patriots* out?" His own answer reflects the apparent lack of principles on the part of those in opposition: "I know no cause—but that they're *out* or *in*: / For just alike who or applaud or blame, / I hold at bottom—*all are much the same*" (pp. 1–2). In 1747, *An Expostulatory Letter to a Certain Right Honourable Person upon His Late Promotion* warned Chesterfield not to be corrupted by the Walpolean political miseducation satirized in the *Dunciad*: "What think you of the *School* of W[alpol]e, whom you formerly for many Years opposed with so much Eloquence and Applause? Does it not still exist in his *Disciples*, Men greatly inferior to him in Abilities, and yet without any Principles but what they derived from him?" (p. 6).

So efficient was the Pelhamite system of political comprehension in bringing virtually all potential rivals into the ministry that by the end of George II's reign, Horace Walpole predicted, "The Opposition will be chiefly composed of men in place: you know we always refine; it used to be an imputation on our senators, that they opposed to get places; they now oppose to get better places!"[14] Events proved him correct when Pitt and Fox sought more power from within the ministry. Lord Waldegrave observed that since they were already a part of the ministry they could hardly attack policy: "They might attack persons, though not things."[15] Many would have agreed with Sir Charles Hanbury Williams's sentiments in his *Place-Book for the Year Seventeen-Hundred, Forty-Five. A New Ballad* (London, 1745):

> Gods! how we're perplex'd by Promotions and Claims!
> I'd sing of new Measures, I'm sick of new Names,
> To write of fresh Placemen each Year was a Folly,
> I'm tir'd of the Text,—leave the Subject to *Colly*.

The transition from Bolingbroke's rhetorical strategy of attacking measures not men to one of attacking men not measures was complete by the end of George II's reign and the effect on political satire was revolutionary. *The Craftsman* had encouraged what might be called the high road of satire, satire which, at its best, combined the particular with the general, using historical parallels to render political allegory allusively complex. Satirists of the interregnum did write allegorical verse satire, but these productions strike one as disappointingly simple-minded after the richly complex satires of the 1730s. In the satire of the 1740s and 1750s allegory tends not to have any historical or allusive depth, as titles often indicate: *A Dialogue on the Late Downfall of Metophis* (London, 1742); *The Farce is Over; or, The Plot Discover'd without an Enquiry: A Poem* (London, 1742); *Politicks in Miniature; or, The Humours of Punch's Resignation. A Tragi-Comi-Farcical-Operatical Puppet-Show* (London, 1742); *Court and Country; or, The Changelings. A New Ballad Opera* (London, 1743); *The Usurpers; or, The Coffee-House Politicians. A Farce* (London, 1749).

Political satirists during Walpole's ministry had many advantages available to them that disappeared after his fall. For the twenty years of his ministry, many of the most eloquent politicians were turned out of office only to enter the Opposition. Walpole's long rule gave his opponents the time to develop the most important satiric rhetorical strategy in English history; conversely his long rule meant that the sincerity of the Opposition's assertions of virtue and high principles could not be tested if they were not in power. Walpole's preeminence gave the Opposition one principal target at which to aim, and his development of the not yet legally recognized office of the prime minister encouraged his enemies to stress the historical implications of his power. Constitutional issues were foremost in the debate between the ministry and its opponents at least in part because Walpole's was a reign of unprecedented peace, with foreign affairs playing a relatively minor role.

The events that followed Walpole's ouster certainly seemed to prove his apologists correct in their accusation that political satire is motivated by self-interest. The apostacy of Pulteney and Carteret was too glaring to be successfully defended. One would not exaggerate very much to say that political events in mid-century caused the rapid decline of political verse satire, and by extension of verse satire in general. For twenty years verse satire had become increasingly political in its applicability. *The Craftsman* saw to it that a political dimension could be found in virtually any human activity during the Walpole years. Economics, history, art, music, literature, and education all became liable to political interpretation. At the same time, satire in general gradually became virtually identified with political satire. By 1742, Pope was able to see the whole of contemporary English culture in political terms, and the corruption of politics became in his eyes a greater force than the mere mortals who ruled. But satire lost its credibility because of the actions of Walpole's opponents in the years after his fall. The former grand claims of the Opposition sounded hollow once its members attained office and revealed that they were unwilling or unable to change the quality of either measures or men. Consequently, the satirists were seen as having prostituted their art to support hypocrites—the very charge Walpole's defenders had made against them.

Circumstances were such that it was impossible for political satirists of the 1740s and 1750s to regain the stature they had enjoyed in the previous decades. Some of their difficulties lay in the differences in character between Sir Robert Walpole and Henry Pelham, until his death in 1754 the most important of Walpole's successors. Horace Walpole compares the two ministers:

> Sir Robert loved power so much, that he would not endure a rival; Mr. Pelham loved it so well, that he would endure anything. The one would risk his Administration, by driving every considerable man from Court, rather than venture their being well there; the other would employ any means to take able men out of the Opposition, though he ventured their engrossing his authority and outshining his capacity; but he dreaded abuse more than competition, and always bought off his enemies to avoid their satire, rather than to acquire their support; whereas, Sir Robert Walpole never trading but for numbers, and despising invectives, and dreading rivals, gained but weak, uncertain assistance, and always kept up a formidable Opposition.[16]

Although we must discount the son's biases in favor of his father and against Pelham, much truth remains.

Pelham's broad-bottomed politics of comprehension meant that no potential rival remained out of office for long. Even Pitt, despite George II's animosity toward him, was brought in. Pitt's career exemplifies the tactics of opposition in mid-century. Since no significant politician was kept in the wilderness, no new rhetorical strategy was developed to replace the essentially Country program espoused by Bolingbroke and *The Craftsman*. Out of office, Pitt gathered arguments from dissident Whigs and Tories alike in his attempt to force his way into the ministry. His indiscriminate use of the arguments of all sides incidentally caused them to be perceived as mere cant and catch-phrases. Unconcerned about contradicting himself, he realized that all a politician out of office need do was be annoying enough to be bought off. George II's dislike of Pitt was prompted mainly by Pitt's vocal opposition to England's Hanoverian ties, but as soon as Pitt came into the government he supported the Hanoverian policy. Satirists quicky perceived him as no more principled than any other politician. "Short Verses, in Imitation of Long Verses: in an Epistle to W——m P——tt, Esq.," attack Pitt for shifting his beliefs; "A D——ss's Ghost to Orator H——r Pitt" accuses the new minister of treachery and hypocrisy in changing sides after having received money from the Dutchess of Marlborough as a reward for his opposition to Walpolean measures.[17] To be fair to Pitt, we should note that he may simply have discovered once he was in office that many of the supposedly ministerial measures were in fact regal. Particularly in foreign affairs, George II exerted far more direct influence than was or is often realized.[18]

The twenty years of peace that had marked Walpole's ministry were followed by more than two decades of almost continuous wars. Because of George II's strong foreign interests, ministries found themselves relatively less free to influence foreign affairs than Walpole had been in molding domestic policies. For the satirist, the continuing emphasis on events external to England meant that he must deal with occasional issues alien to the experience of his readers. The primarily domestic and constitutional arguments of the Walpole years enabled satirists to allude concisely and economically to a common fund of knowledge. All were familiar, or became so in the years of the Opposition rhetorical strategy, with such notions as that of balanced government, the ancient constitution, or prime ministers. Foreign issues meant that readers must continually be taught the context of the satirist's remarks. As allies and enemies shifted at mid-century, the concision and economy of verse satire gradually was replaced by the elaboration and explanation of prose. Even in the 1720s and 1730s, prose had been the dominant medium for attacking the ministry in foreign affairs because of the necessity of explaining unfamiliar references and events.

The continuous emphasis on foreign rather than domestic matters increased the appeal of a government of national consensus like that of Pelham's system. After having only one target for so many years in the previous decades, satirists had to deal with a succession of coalition governments at mid-century. There was no one-man rule comparable to that of Walpole: the ministry of Carteret and Pulteney was followed by that of Pelham and Newcastle, which was in turn succeeded by that of Newcastle and Pitt. Satirists of Walpole had developed a kind of satire of aggrandizement, emphasizing the allegedly overbearing and unconstitutional power of the prime ministerial colossus. Such a model of the "Great Man" could not be applied to the later period; satirists were forced to develop a strategy of satiric diminution, in effect emphasizing their targets as men rather than ministers. Targets kept moving as figures went in and out of office, adjusting their principles accordingly. As Charles Hanbury Williams lamented in his *Place-Book for the Year Seventeen-Hundred, Forty-Five*, office-holders increasingly came to resemble a jumble of interchangeable names, but with policies never changing.

First reduced from powerful ministers to mere names, office-holders were soon denied any distinguishing characteristics whatsoever. Macnamara Morgan, writing under the pseudonym Porcupinus Pelagius, ridiculed the Pelhamite system of political comprehension in *The Triumvirade; or, Broad-Bottomry. A Panegyri-Satiri-Serio-Comi-Dramatical Poem* (London, 1745). When replacements are sought for the ousted Carteret and Pulteney, the choices are to be made on the basis of whoever has the longest head. Unfortunately, "they were all short and round, / Of equal Dimensions, than deep rather shallow" (p. 6). As the 1750s drew to a close, satires of diminution became satires of dehumanization. Some titles indicate the technique: *The Rival Politician; or, The Fox Triumphant. A Fable* (London, 1757); *The Insects Chuse a Minister. A Fable* (London, 1757); and *The Beavers: a Fable* (London, 1760).

The development of political verse satire during the middle decades of the eighteenth century is paralleled by the changes that take place in graphic political satire, changes that result in the dominance of caricature, a recent form. The conception and execution of *The Dunciad* is similar to such a representative print of the 1730s as *The Present State of a Certain Great Kingdom* (B.M. 2336), published in 1739. At the center of the print is an emblematic painting of England, displayed by its creator, "Danvers," who wears a mask to represent his concealed identity. Behind the painting, Time breaks a chain; in front of the painting, a reclining Britannia holds a newly broken olive branch. The print is "Humbly Inscribed" to "all True

Lovers of Liberty, Merchants, Land-holders, Freeholders, and other Electors to parliament, to Returning Officers, & to all Clear-Sighted Honest Men" "by their Most Obedient Servant Dry Bob." Danvers's painting illustrates the "*Robinocracy*" attacked in *The Dunciad*. The results of Walpolean measures are seen in depictions of "*Arts Starving*," "*Trade Sinking*," and "*Magna Carta*" outweighed by "*Bribery*." The emblematic quality of *The Present State* is reflected in the general satire of *The Dunciad* because both are more concerned with satirizing a method of government and its effects than with mocking an individual.

If I am correct in earlier suggesting that the depiction of Sir Robert Walpole in the prints of the 1720s and 1730s reflects the influence of the Opposition's rhetorical strategy of attacking measures not men, we should expect to find a shift from more general representations of the minister and his policies to more specific attacks on the man and his personal life after he fell from power. And indeed we do. The transition toward caricatured illustrations of the former minister is quite sudden and marked.

The words that accompany *The Anti-Crafts Man unmask'd* (1742, subtitled "A Man May Be Known By His Looks") (B.M. 2558) clearly express the meaning of the print:

Britons behold! your petty Tyrant here,
Observe his honest Face, Observe his sneer,
Observe that *Hand*, which do's the *Patriot* hold
That Hand by which we've oft' been bought & sold:
Sold Once too oft, as sure the Traitor'll find,
Whene'er *Vienna* Treaties come in Mind.

Another kind of facial distortion appears in *The late P———m———r M———n———r* (1743, subtitled "Lo! What are all your Schemes come to?") (B.M. 2607), which Atherton accurately labels "a form of proto-caricature."[19] Its inscription is taken from the "Yawn of Gods" passage near the end of Pope's *Dunciad*.

The prints become more personal in their accusations. In *The Treasury; or, His Honour Bit* (B.M. 2560), a 1742 engraving reminiscent of the second of the *Robin's Reign* frontispieces to *The Craftsman*, Walpole is portrayed as both corruptor and corrupted:

Satan a while his Votaries deceives
And Places, Honours and high Titles gives:
But why you'll say is all this Favour shown?
Only more surely to confirm his Own,
The plund'rer thus by his own Bags o'erweigh'd
Is by the steps he rais'd himself betray'd

43. *The Anti-Crafts Man Unmask'd* (B.M. 2558)

44. *The late P——m——r M——n——r* (B.M. 2607)

45. *The Treasury; or, His Honour Bit* (B.M. 2560)

Hence learn, the wicked Man for all his hast
Will be deserted by his Dev'l at last.

The corruptor-corrupted theme reappears in another 1742 print, *Bro'
Robert under his Last Purgation* (B.M. 2533), in which Cardinal Fleury
unsuccessfully— "My Labour's in Vain, its all over ye Glyster Returns"—
tries to apply a clyster to a complaining "friar" Walpole—"O I am Grip'd
with ye heavy weight of ye nation." Walpole is surrounded by bags of
money and papers which represent his alleged attempts to bribe members of
Parliament. The figure of Avarice reveals an empty chest inscribed "The
Treasure is Gone" and implies that Walpole has used public funds to enrich
his family: "nothing left for poor miss" (i.e., Walpole's daughter, Lady
Mary Churchill, shown in the print). The vision in the clouds of the devil
driving Walpole "for France" anticipates the minister's expected destiny.
The "Last Purgation" of the title refers to Walpole's being purged from
office. A later 1742 print, *Bob The Political Ballance Master. Gone throw* [sic]
his first Purgation and ready for the Second (B.M. 2576), apparently a sequel to
Bro' Robert, calls for Walpole's punishment now that he has lost office.

46. *Bro' Robert under his Last Purgation* (B.M. 2533)

47. *BOB THE POLITICAL BALLANCE MASTER* (B.M. 2576)

Walpole's loss of eminence is reflected in the caricature of his physique. The more traditional iconography of earlier engraved attacks of Walpole includes the sorrowing Britannia with "Trade" at her feet; the figure of Justice weighed down by "Treasury," "Exchequer," and "Sinking" [fund] bags; and the devil, whom Walpole implores, "Oh Help thy Faithfull Servant, Bob." The devil holds an axe, which he tells Walpole is "This thy due," and thus expresses the message of the print:

> Tho' Crafty Knaves may for a While defer
> The Punishment their Horrid crimes incur

THE POLITICAL VOMIT FOR THE EASE OF BRITAIN

He hath Swallowed down Riches and he shall Vomit them up again; GOD.shall cast them out of his Belly. Job XX. 15.

48. *The Political Vomit For the Ease of Britain* (B.M. 2531)

> A Secret Horrer [*sic*] still their conscience knaws
> Justice has Leaden Feet but Iron Claws.

Caricature and corruption join in *The Political Vomit For the Ease of Britain* (B.M. 2531). Its engraved motto reads, "He hath Swallowed down Riches and he shall Vomit them up again; God Shall cast them out of his Belly. —*Job*. XX. 15th." The grotesque Sir Robert Walpole vomits forth the election reverses forced on him by the Opposition, represented here by the physician with his drenching horn. Walpole is discharging into "The Gulph of Secret Iniquity" at the same time. Opposition members collect the purged honors, offices, and pensions in the foreground, while the sinister earl of Winchelsea, lord of the Admiralty, lurks in the background, under the emblematic anchor that identifies his demonic nature as well as his office.

Walpole's family soon became the target for graphic satire. *The Norfolk Dumplin* (B.M. 2616) of 1744 shows a grotesque little man, apparently drunken and simple-minded. The square object on the left identifies him as

Edw. Taylor,
alias
W–lp–le.
Born at
LYNN,
in
Norfolk.
1703

THE DOG

HONOURS VOID OF...

THE PENSION...

...DUCKS MY TASTE

Exod. Chap XX.
And Visit the Sins of the Fathers
Upon the Children unto the third
& Fourth Generation of them
that hate me.

49. *The Norfolk Dumplin* (B.M. 2616)

50. *A Courier just Setting out* (B.M. 2629)

51. *Touch me not; or, B——bs Defiance* (B.M. 2551)

52. *The Screen* (B.M. 2539)

an illegitimate off-shoot of the Walpole family. The print displays the arms of the earls of Orford with a *baton* of illegitimacy added. Within a cartouche is the following quotation: "*Exod.* Chap. XX. And Visit the Sins of the Fathers, Upon the Children, Unto the third & Fourth Generation of them that hate me." The 1745 engraving *A Courier just Setting out* (B.M. 2629) reviles Walpole for corruption even after his death.

The satiric pursuit of Walpole into the afterlife seems surprising until we recall the charges by verse satirists that Walpole retained power although he had lost office. Pope's comprehensive assault on the longevity of the "*Robinarchy*" becomes clearer when we realize that many saw Walpole as maintaining political power, directly as well as indirectly, even after February 1742. Walpole's satiric career began and ended behind "screens." The "Skreen-Master General" had allegedly risen to power by protecting the malefactors of the South Sea Scheme from condign punishment; he lost power only to be saved from prosecution by George II. Two months after his fall, we find Walpole portrayed in double face with George II in the engraving *Touch me not; or, B———bs Defiance* (B.M. 2551). The accompanying verses link the king to his minister's crimes and use *The Craftsman's* tactic of comparing Walpole to Wolsey:

Behold two Patriots of our British Land,
Join'd Head to Head, instead of Hand to Hand!
When two such Noddles are laid close together,

The SCREEN. A SIMILE.

DEAR *William*, did'st thou never go
To mimic Farce, call'd *Puppet-Shew?*
There, *William*, did'st thou never see
Of Figures great Variety?
With a big Belly comes a Fellow,
In blustering Mood, call'd *Punchinello*;
He roars and swaggers, bounces, swears,
Giving himself a thousand Airs;
Knocks Puppets down, and makes a Boast,
That he alone will rule the Roast.
  But when *Punch* is turn'd off the Stage,
Some other Puppets come t'engage:
With other Motions, other Faces,
Act some new Part, to shew their Graces.

Alas! dear *William*, all this while,
A Trickster does your Sense beguile:
Behind that SCREEN there stands a Wight,
Safely conceal'd from publick Sight:
He was the *Punch* at first you saw;
He gives the other Puppets Law;
And by his secret Strings he still
Governs the others as he will;
And all the Difference that is known,
You only hear *another Tone*:
The *Puppet Man*,——behind the *Screen*,
Is the same Man,——although not seen.

53. *The Screen. A Simile. A New Screen for an Old One; or, The Screen of Screens*
(B.M. 2540)

54. William Hogarth, *Four Prints of an Election*, plate 2, *Canvassing for Votes* (B.M. 3298)

What tempests in ye State can Shatter Either?
I and the K——g the haughty W——lsey cry'd,
And All ye Malice of his Foes defy'd;
But R——n, haughtier still, (t'evade Disaster)
Cries, Touch me if you can,—and not my Ma——r.

The metaphor of George II's screening Walpole becomes more concrete in *The Screen* (B.M. 2539), published in 1742. Here Walpole appears as Punch, exclaiming "O! the Glorious 244." He refers to the 244 members of the House of Commons who voted on 9 March against a proposed Secret Committee of Inquiry into Walpole's alleged ministerial crimes. A large crown hanging tenuously from a spider's web in the center of the room represents the royal protection of the fallen minister. Names of offices and preferments on the crown and the eager politicians scrambling beneath it for them indicate how George II defended Walpole.

55. *The Motion* (B.M. 2479)

The screen metaphor becomes more complex in *The Screen. A Simile. A New Screen for an Old One; or, The Screen of Screens* (B.M. 2540), published in 1742. Here the screen both protects Walpole from prosecution and enables him to manage affairs from behind the scenes. The engraving is divided into three vertical main sections. The first depicts the reconciliation of Prince Frederick and George II, which helped to assure Walpole's dismissal. The second shows a large folding screen of nine distinct designs, each exhibiting past events in Walpole's political career. For example, the first of these is entitled "The Scum of the South Sea." A mirror reveals that behind the screen Sir Robert Walpole works the strings of the parliamentary puppets displayed in the third section of the engraving. The accompanying verses, probably addressed to William Pulteney, are from the *London Evening Post* (9–11 March 1742):

> Alas! dear *William*, all this while,
> A Trickster does your Sense beguile:
> Behind that SCREEN there stands a Wight,
> Safely conceal'd from public Sight:

56. *A Cheap and Easy Method of Improving English Swine's Flesh by a German Method of Feeding* (B.M. 2604)

> He was the *Punch* at first you saw;
> He gives the other Puppets Law;
> And by his secret Strings he still
> Governs the others as he will;
> And all the Difference that is known,
> You only hear *another Tone*:
> The *Puppet* Man,—behind the *Screen*,
> Is the same Man,—although not seen.

Punch, Pulteney, and Walpole apparently become linked in Hogarth's great political progress, *Four Prints of an Election* (B.M. 3285, 3298, 3309, 3318). The four prints comprise a general attack on the corruption of both sides in the Oxfordshire election of 1754. Except for the appearance of Britannia in her coach in the last print, *The Polling*, naturalism has almost completely replaced the kind of emblematic representation dominant in the *South Sea Scheme*. The earlier style of representation, however, still plays a major role in *Canvassing for Votes*, the second of the *Election* prints. In the center of the engraving are a sign and a show-cloth. The sign with Charles

II's head surrounded by three crowns identifies the Royal Oak, headquarters of the Tory part. Overshadowing this visual reference to the seventeenth-century distinction between politican parties is a satire on modern Whig-gery. The show-cloth, entitled "Punch Candidate for Guzzledown," recalls earlier prints depicting Walpole as a corrupting Punch training politicians in the school of Walpole. The system flourishes. But if, as I suspect, Hogarth's Punch with his wheelbarrow is a visual allusion to Pulteney and his wheelbarrow in the 1741 print *The Motion* (B.M. 2479), then Hogarth is mocking all the students of Walpole, including his erstwhile "patriotic" opponents. The formerly clear distinction between Whigs and Tories be-comes confused if we consider all their adherents as would-be recipients of Punch's largess.

Other prints, with their suggestion that the "Robinocracy" outlasted its creator, are perhaps closer in spirit to *The Dunciad*. Inspired by Pope's "Westphaly Hogs" passage in Dialogue 2 of the *Epilogue to the Satires*, the print *A Cheap and Easy Method of Improving English Swine's Flesh by a German Method of Feeding* (B.M. 2604), portrays the continuation of political cor-ruption after Walpole's retirement. Published in 1743, *A Cheap and Easy Method* is produced "By a Norfolk man [i.e., Walpole] for the Use of the Royal Society." While George II, whip in hand, oversees the farm, Carteret feeds offices and places to the first in a line of pigs. Each succeeding pig devours the office discharged by its predecessor. At the end of the line, a caricatured duke of Newcastle sweeps together more ordure, bearing the names of officers of "Salt Customs," "Excise," and "Stamps." As he does so, he remarks, "Not eat it—damn 'em there's nothing two [*sic*] nasty for 'em." On the left, other hogs eat out of a place-filled trough. In a shed on the right, the scrolls "Mag[na] Char[t]er," "Habeas Corpus," and "Bill of Rights" are to be burned to cure in smoke newly created peers like those represented by the "Orford Flitch" and the "Bath Flitch." Equally cynical is the 1746 print *The Noble Game of Bob Cherry* (B.M. 2850), which shows office-seekers jumping for ministerial cherries hanging from the signboard of the Crown tavern in front of St. James's Palace. Seated on a bench in front of the tavern, Carteret vomits forth the cherry labeled "Sec. of State." Pulteney lies on the ground, unsuccessful in his attempt at the "High Treasurer" cherry. Others await their turns while Pelham and Newcastle at the front of the group observe the game.

In the prints after the fall of Walpole we have considered so far, the most marked difference from those of the 1730s is the increased number of individuals represented. Political events dictated that Walpole be removed from center stage if not from the playhouse altogether. The colossus of previous engravings has been replaced by a swarm of aspiring politicians. As a rhetorical strategy based on attacking measures not men was perforce

57. *The Noble Game of Bob Cherry* (B.M. 2850)

replaced by one attacking men not measures, artists, like the satirists in verse, had to develop new methods of attack. The results were a loss for verse satire, which too often dwindled into ephemeral invective, but a gain for engraved satire, which encouraged the new form of caricature. Caricature—the exaggeration of a person's external appearance to express his internal condition—appeared fitfully but continually during the 1740s and 1750s. By 1760 caricature had become the dominant form, surpassing but not eradicating the earlier, more emblematic mode of engraved satire. The nature of politics at mid-century promoted this development and from the results in verses and prints we may confidently say that visual satire benefited more from events than did verbal satire. As Atherton notes, "Satire and caricature grasp the individual more easily than the group. This, in part, explains why the prints of the era concentrated their attention on individuals—not parties, not factions, not coalitions. The phenomenon

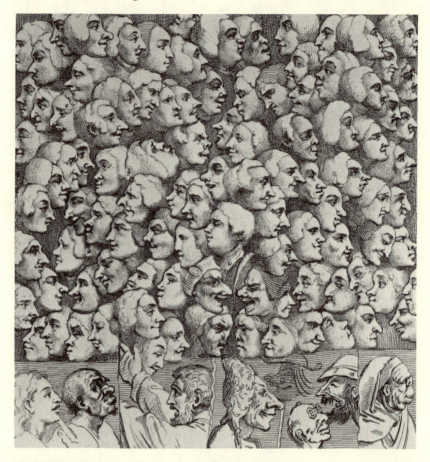

58. William Hogarth, *Characters Caricaturas* (B.M. 2591)

also reflects an historical truth: the politics of the mid-eighteenth century had reached a marked degree of atomization."[20]

We have noticed the sudden interest in Walpole's personal life and in him as a man rather than minister after his dismissal from office. Many saw this change as a sign of the times. On 28 August 1742, Horace Walpole observed to Horace Mann, "Indeed, everybody's name now is published at length: last week the *Champion* mentioned the Earl of Orford and his *natural daughter* Lady Mary at length (for which he had a great mind to prosecute the printer)."[21] Precisely this naming of names and emphasis on individuals led to the remarkable rise in "caricatures" Thomas Gray mentioned to Chute on 24 May 1742.[22] Hogarth's own unsuccessful attempt in 1743 to

John Wilkes Esqr.

Drawn from the Life and Etch'd in Aquafortis by Willm Hogarth.

Price 1 Shilling.   *Publish'd according to Act of Parliament May 16. 1763.*

59. William Hogarth, *John Wilkes Esqr.* (B.M. 4050)

60. *The Treacherous Patriot—Unmask'd* (B.M. 2538)

61. *A Very Extraordinary Motion* (B.M. 2613)

avoid the label of caricaturist with his *Characters Caricaturas* (B.M. 2591) must be seen against the contemporary political background. Much of the confusion about Hogarth's role in the development of caricature comes from his own misleading distinction between "characters" and "caricaturas." Seeking to defend himself as a comic history painter of "characters," Hogarth describes "caricaturas" as if they were restricted purely to physiological distortion with no intention of expressing the psychological truths revealed by the creators of "characters." In practice, however, caricature combines physiological with psychological revelation, as Hogarth's satiric *John Wilkes Esqr.* (B.M. 4050), published in 1763, demonstrates.

Ernst Kris and E. H. Gombrich describe the relationship between portrait painting and caricature: "The portrait painter's task was to reveal the character, the essence of the man in an heroic sense; that of the caricaturist provided the natural counterpart—to reveal the true man behind the mask of pretense and to show up his 'essential' littleness and ugliness."[23] We saw the caricaturist's method in the rather stylized *The Anti-Crafts Man Unmask'd* (B.M. 2558). The technique is perhaps best seen by comparing this print with its original, *The Treacherous Patriot—Unmask'd* (B.M. 2538), an anti-Pulteney engraving of 1742. I call B.M. 2558 stylized because the design used to attack the inner nature of Walpole unmasked is

62. *Broad-bottoms* (B.M. 2621)

63. *The Political Clyster* (B.M. 3557)

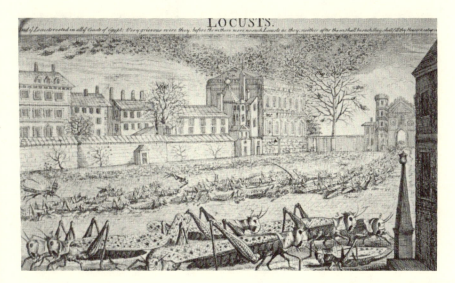

64. *Locusts* (B.M. 3018)

taken directly from the illustration of Pulteney (who physically resembled Walpole) in B.M. 2538. In 1742 caricature had not yet reached much beyond a generalized sense of ugliness beneath the mask of pretense. The same picture could be used to attack either Walpole or Pulteney. Perhaps the satirist of B.M. 2558 copied the earlier print to show that the continuity of measures rendered the two former political enemies essentially identical.

Although the figure of the duke of Newcastle in *A Cheap and Easy Method of Improving English Swine's Flesh* anticipates the later caricatures of George Townshend, such individualized caricatures were still rare before Townshend's work appeared in the 1750s.[24] Like their counterparts in verse, print satirists in the 1740s and 1750s played with several methods to achieve the goal of diminution the new political realities seemed to call for. One such method was scatological, as in *The Political Vomit for the Ease of Britain*. A print of 1744, *A Very Extraordinary Motion* (B.M. 2613), shows George II defecating Lord Hobart, as Newcastle and Pelham are about to cram Sir John Hynde Cotton down the king's throat. Others await their turns to be forced on the king in this attack on the "storming of the closet" by the Broad-Bottoms. Print satirists can hardly be expected to have ignored the possibilities such a political label offered, especially when one of its leaders, Cotton, was renowned for his girth. In *The Last Will and Testament of R. Walpole* (London, 1745) Cotton is bequeathed the minister's legs "to bear up the enormous weight of his *broad bottom* and his most unwieldly corporation" (p. 15).

Cotton's ample buttocks are prominently displayed in *Broad-bottoms* (B.M. 2621), the frontispiece to the satiric pamphlet *An Address of Thanks to the Broad-Bottoms, for the Good Things They Have Done, and the Evil Things They Have Not Done, Since Their Elevation: Wherein is Stated, A Fair Account of Their Promises and Performances; Preceded by an Introductory Discourse on Ingratitude, a Sketch of the History of the Broad-Bottoms, and a Resembling Portrait of Their Chiefs. To Which is Prefix'd, A Curious Emblematic Frontispiece, Taken from an Original Painting of the Ingenious Mr. H——th* (1745). Cotton's is one of many human posteriors seated on an arch and defecating on tax-laden asses below. Subscribed are the lines "Believing, we lifted ye up among the Mighty; / Yet our Drivers have ye join'd, increasing our Loads." Once again, in office the new ministers practice the same measures they had formerly opposed. Mid-century interest in scatological satire was so great that Hogarth's *The Punishment Inflicted on Lemuel Gulliver* (B.M. 1797), a general satire of 1726, reappeared as a more specifically political print, *The Political Clyster* (B.M. 3557), aimed at the ministry in 1757.

The animal figures of verse satire are also found in the prints, particularly during the dark, early years of the Seven Years' War. We saw animal

THE RECRUITING SERJEANT   OR BRITTANNIAIS HAPPY PROSPECT

65. *The Recruiting Serjeant; or, Brittanniais* [sic] *Happy Prospect* (B.M. 3581)

figures in *A Cheap and Easy Method*, where ministerial supporters are likened to swine. Henry Fox's name had invited animal prints at least since 1734, when he appeared in the frontispiece to *A Tryal of Skill*. Fortuitously, the visual pun on his name aptly expressed his basically vulpine nature. The fable of the fox and geese inevitably led to representations of Newcastle as a goose in his relations with Fox. Because of his avarice, Lord Hardwicke often becomes a vulture in the prints.[25] The tactic of engraved dehumanization reaches its most extreme form in the 1748 print *Locusts* (B.M. 3018). Prompted no doubt by the swarms of locusts that appeared in various parts of England during the summer of 1748, *Locusts* gives us a view of Whitehall, Westminster, and their environs. Locusts fill the air and have already eaten the leaves of the trees of Habeas Corpus and Magna Charta. Among the locusts on the ground are lawyers, attorneys, priests, commissioners, and excisemen; others bear symbols of place or power. A key to the print identifies the eight great locusts in the foreground. They include: Cumberland, Gower, Bedford, Newcastle, Pelham, the countess of Yarmouth (the king's mistress), Sandwich, and possibly Sandys. Visual satirists were able to go further than verbal satirists in diminishing their victims: engravers could reduce their subjects to the briefest outline sketches necessary to express their real natures. Probably the best example of the new technique of caricatured diminution is George Townshend's *The Recruiting Serjeant; or, Brittanniais* [sic] *Happy Prospect* (B.M. 3581), a 1757 satire on Fox's unsuccessful attempt to form a new government. The animal caricature of "Serjeant" Fox leads outline caricatures of Winchelsea, Dodington, Sandwich, and Ellis to a mock Temple of Fame containing a statue of the duke of Cumberland, who has been distilled—in Horace Walpole's words—to a "lump of fat."[26]

The distance between Pope's grandly general satire on Walpolean England and George Townshend's narrowly personal caricatures of political figures at mid-century could not be greater. The age of satiric exaggeration had been succeeded by that of satiric reduction. Pope emphasizes the school of Walpole; later satirists in verse and prints aim at the students. The Pelhamite rule by political comprehension, the dominance of foreign policy, and the absence of a "prime minister" of Walpole's stature, all contributed to the collapse of *The Craftsman*'s rhetorical strategy. A new rhetorical strategy, seen in Williams's poetry or in prints like *The Noble Game of Bob Cherry* (B.M. 2850) (1746), emphasized that if anything at all mattered in government it was men rather than measures because the latter never seemed to change. All candidates were said to be motivated solely by the chance to bite the cherry of place. As a result, political verse satire quickly became timebound, personal, and ephemeral during the interregnum between Pope and Churchill, rarely rising above invective. The effect on graphic satire was happier because caricature proved to be a more efficient means than verse of impaling a personality: one need not know the offender to appreciate his execution. In 1743, the most important form of political satire was verse. At mid-century, this leading position was lost, never to be regained.

CHAPTER VII

The Writing of History
at Mid-Century

Don Quixote believed; but even Sancho doubted.
—Bolingbroke, *Letters on the Study and Use of History*

The philosophy of government, accompanying a narration of
its revolutions, may render history more intelligible as well
as instructive. And nothing will tend more to abate the
acrimony of party-disputes than to show men, that those
events, which they impute to their adversaries as the deepest
crimes, were the natural, if not the necessary result of the
situation, in which the nation was placed, during any period.
—Hume, *History of Great Britain*

During the interregnum between Pope and Churchill the greatest shift in
the development of English historiography, the transition from uniformitarianism to relativism, undermined one of the principal supports—
exemplar history—of Bolingbroke's campaign against Walpole. In the new
strategy interregnum satirists developed of emphasizing personalities more
than principles, poets and artists tended far less to rely on historical parallels in attacking contemporary politicians than had their predecessors.
Interregnum satirists more often sought to diminish their victims and
display them as foolish operatives of an all-pervasive system of corruption
than to stress their individual significance by comparing them to past
historical figures. The great villains of the past were succeeded by the
insects of the present.

Coincident with the changes in satire was the change in historiography
which would increasingly make history less available as a weapon in the
satirist's arsenal. Bolingbroke himself was an important figure in the transition from a humanist, uniformitarian historiography to one based on a more
skeptical attitude toward the past and its relation to the present. Given
Bolingbroke's writings in *The Craftsman* and other anti-Walpole tracts, it is

ironic that he should have had a major voice in this change. As we saw earlier, he had skillfully adopted the Whig assumptions about uniformitarianism and the immemorial constitution we looked at in *Windsor Forest* and turned them against Walpole's ministry. So effective had been his rhetorical strategy that Walpolean apologists like Walsingham, Osborne, and Hervey had been forced to counterattack with the previously Tory historical arguments of Brady.

In the historical writings Bolingbroke published during the 1730s, it is difficult to judge his disinterested beliefs about how the past should be handled. If for no other reason than to make a point about the current political situation, he embraced humanist history with its emphasis on the individual's direction of events. In his *Remarks on the History of England*, Bolingbroke seems to have little doubt that history consists of the actions of heroes and villains. Furthermore, uniformitarianism enabled Bolingbroke and his readers to see these heroes and villains virtually as types of contemporary political figures. Bolingbroke as humanist historian probably appears at his most extreme in *The Idea of a Patriot King*. Written for Prince Frederick in 1739, the essay was not published until 1749, just two years before the death of the prince ended whatever meager hopes remained of his becoming the nation's political saviour. Bolingbroke depicted his patriot king as one who singlehandedly could alter the course of English history as Elizabeth and James I had done—she for the better, he for the worse.

Bolingbroke's published historical writings before 1750 may reveal more about his appreciation of rhetoric than about his own historiographic premises. His *Letters on the Study and Use of History* did not appear until 1752, although it had been written between 1735 and 1738, during a retirement to France. The transition in his *Letters* from the humanism of the Renaissance to the historicism of the next century is not complete. Indeed, in this work we find the statement "history is philosophy teaching by examples," even though much of his argument undermines the notion of exemplar history. Repeatedly in his *Remarks*, his *Dissertation upon Parties*, and in other political writings of the 1730s, Bolingbroke assumes that his audience shares the belief that all of previous history was available as a source from which parallels could be drawn with the present. In the 1730s, classical Rome and Anglo-Saxon England, as much as seventeenth-century France and contemporary Spain, offered illustrative exempla that could be profitably applied to eighteenth-century Britain. Such simplistic and extreme uniformitarian exemplar history was well-suited to the rhetorical strategy the Opposition aimed at Walpole.

The *Letters on the Study and Use of History* reveals that Bolingbroke was aware of the dangers in such a partisan view of the past. In one passage

Bolingbroke sounds remarkably like David Hume in his advocacy of historical relativism and in his qualification of uniformitarianism:

> These are certain general principles, and rules of life and conduct, which always must be true, because they are conformable to the invariable nature of things. He who studies history as he would study philosophy, will soon distinguish and collect them, and by doing so will soon form to himself a general system of ethics and politics on the surest foundations, on the trial of them by universal experience. I said he will distinguish them; for once more I must say, that as to particular modes of actions, and measures of conduct, which the customs of different countries, the manners of different ages, and the circumstances of different conjunctures, have appropriated, as it were; it is always ridiculous, or imprudent and dangerous to employ them. But this is not all. By contemplating the vast variety of particular characters and events; by examining the strange combination of causes, different, remote, and seemingly opposite, that often concur in producing one effect; and the surprising fertility of one single and uniform cause in the producing of a multitude of effects, as different, as remote, and seemingly as opposite; by tracing carefully, as carefully as if the subject he considers were of personal and immediate concern to him, all the minute and sometimes scarce perceivable circumstances, either in the characters of actors, or in the course of actions, that history enables him to trace, and according to which the success of affairs, even the greatest, is mostly determined; by these, and such methods as these, for I might descend into a much greater detail, a man of parts may improve the study of history to its proper and principal use; he may sharpen the penetration, fix the attention of his mind, and strengthen his judgment; he may acquire the faculty and the habit of discerning quicker, and looking farther; and of exerting that flexibility, and steadiness, which are necessary to be joined in the conduct of all affairs that depend on the concurrence or opposition of other men.[1]

History is now far more difficult to deal with than it had been in the 1730s. Even though we may be able to recognize "certain general principles, and rules of life and conduct," we are not guaranteed that "the customs of different countries, the manners of different ages, and the circumstances of different conjunctures" can be reconstructed. Men are no longer seen as universal in their actions and thoughts. The earlier humanist faith in the individual's ability to control events is now tempered by the skeptic's acknowledgement that there may well be a "strange combination of causes, different, remote, and seemingly opposite, that often concur in producing one effect" and that causes and effects must be looked at in their unique historical contexts. The "faculty and the habit of discerning quicker, and looking farther" is essential because of the demands the study of the past makes upon us. No longer is history merely a fund of examples on which we can draw at will. The would-be historian must first learn "that history has been purposely and systematically falsified in all ages, and that partiality and prejudice have occasioned both voluntary and involuntary errors, even in the best" (p. 51).

History is still a teacher, but no longer is every former time equally applicable to the present. One need not trace precedents back to an immemorial past. Bolingbroke, in the *Letters*, instructs Lord Cornbury in "how little need there is of going up higher than the beginning of the sixteenth century in the study of history, to acquire all the knowledge necessary at this time in ecclesiastical policy, or in civil policy as far as it is relative to this" (p. 86). Elsewhere, he advises his reader that one should not know too much about times before 1500: "To be learned about them is a ridiculous affectation in any man who means to be useful to the present age" (p. 83). Change has become at least as important as continuity, and in the *Letters* he says, "We are not much concerned to know with critical accuracy what were the ancient forms of our parliaments" (p. 90). Similarly, England's political system should not be so readily compared to that of other European states as it had been by *The Craftsman*, "for the nature of our government, the political principles in which we are bred, our distinct interests as islanders, and the complicated various interests and humors of our parties, all these are so peculiar to ourselves, and so different from the notions, manners, and habits of other nations" (p. 91). We must still learn from history but her lessons have become much more difficult than they were in previous decades. The historical certainties of *The Craftsman* have given way to the probabilities of the *Letters on the Study and Use of History*.

Bolingbroke's *Letters* might have played a far more significant role in mid-century historiographic developments than they did if he had not argued that religion was the primary culprit in distorting the past: "Let me say without offence, my lord, since I may say it with truth and am able to prove it, that ecclesiastical authority has led the way to this corruption in all ages, and all religions" (p. 51). Bolingbroke's contributions to the study of history have been obscured by the wrath of clergymen who emphasized only one aspect of his work. But even William Warburton, one of Bolingbroke's most outspoken opponents, was arguing in 1746 for a kind of historical relativism and against uniformitarianism. Although for him "the greatest Part of the Old Testament is historical, and chiefly written for our Information," he seeks in *The Nature of National Offences Truly Stated* to prove that Biblical events do not have direct, specific applications to contemporary

England.[2] Warburton is concerned lest the historical precedent of the special Jewish dispensation for the title of "Lord's anointed" be used to justify the divine right theory of English kingship (p. 8). Such a historiographic assumption makes unlikely the creation in the eighteenth century of such a typological political satire as *Absalom and Achitophel* (1681).[3]

Roman history, no less than the Biblical and English past, was studied in mid-century with increasing skepticism. Historical realities had already undercut the usefulness of Horace for political myth by the 1730s.[4] Similarly, the Whig or Republican view of Roman history, perhaps best exemplified in Swift's *A Discourse of the Contests and Dissentions Between the Nobles and the Commons in Athens and Rome* (1701), came under greater scrutiny as the century advanced.[5] According to the traditional view Cato was the hero of the virtuous Senate in opposition to the tyrannical Caesar. Caesar became less and less available as a stock political villain, however (e.g., he appears so in Fielding's *The Life of Mr. Jonathan Wild The Great* [1743] and in Johnson's *Adventurer*, no. 99 [1753]), in the light of new facts, which also cast into doubt Cicero's former role as a Roman hero. The revision of Roman history reached a peak with Nathaniel Hooke's *Roman History* (4 vols, 1738–71), which argued that the Senate had been the oppressor of Roman liberty, not her protector, as Swift and others had maintained. Although Hooke's views did not replace completely the traditional Whig interpretation, they made it increasingly difficult for a satirist to assume his audience would automatically accept particular classical figures as heroes or villains. Many of the political satires Bolingbroke and the Opposition encouraged and inspired during the 1730s had depended on such ready acceptance of the Whig interpretation of Roman history. The potential loss to would-be satirists caused by more sophisticated handling of classical history is apparent when we appreciate "that there is no correlation between literary merit and historical impartiality: indeed the unhistorical Republican 'myth' with its heroes and villains is a far more imaginative vehicle than the detailed causal structure a modern historian must erect."[6]

The relative stability and calm—or perhaps, recalling the "Yawn of Gods" passage in the *Dunciad* and the anti-Walpole print it inspired, one might say boredom—of mid-eighteenth-century politics probably encouraged to some extent the historiographic freethinking of the 1740s and 1750s. The study of history was now somewhat less politically charged than it had been in earlier decades, and the mid-century shift in historiography, once it gained speed with the publication of Hume's major work, *The History of England* (6 vols., 1754–62) made Clio less vulnerable to political manhandling. Bolingbroke expressed a common complaint when he lamented in his *Letters on the Study and Use of History* that the English "have no general history to be compared with some of other countries" (p. 91). Most

Englishmen would have agreed with Montesquieu's explanation in *The Spirit of the Laws* for this lack: "In monarchies extremely absolute, historians betray the truth, because they are not at liberty to speak it; in states remarkably free, they betray the truth, because of their liberty itself; which always produces divisions, everyone becoming as great a slave to the prejudices of his faction as he could be in a despotic state."[7]

Any attempt to supply the need for a general history of England was a political act. Until the triumph in the nineteenth century of historicism—the view that each event in history is unique and must be reconstructed within its own context—the past was still seen as serving the present as model or paradigm. Thus Thomas Carte's *A General History of England* (4 vols., 1747–55) was received as Jacobitical and William Guthrie's *A General History of England, from the Invasion of Julius Caesar, to the Revolution in 1688* (4 vols., 1744–51) as Whiggish. Neither Carte nor Guthrie was a worthy successor to Rapin, whom Hume in 1748 called "the most judicious of historians."[8] Although establishment Whigs like Lord Hervey in *Ancient and Modern Liberty Stated and Compared* (1734) had in the 1730s tried to refute Rapin's interpretation of English history, once the Opposition campaign against Walpole collapsed, establishment historians generally re-embraced the traditional Whig notion of the ancient, immemorial constitution with its accompanying set of heroes and villains. Hume, in effect (though perhaps unknowingly), took up the argument where Hervey and others had left it two decades earlier.[9]

Hume chose to confront the Whig interpretation of English history in its most extreme—almost caricatured—form, as promoted by Bolingbroke in Rapin's name at the height of the Opposition rhetorical campaign against Walpole. The notions of the immemorial constitution, the antiquity of Parliament, the uniqueness of English liberty, and the political conflict of the seventeenth century as one between a virtuous Parliament seeking to uphold its ancient rights against an evil king set on usurping them and unconstitutionally extending his prerogative all came under the skeptical gaze of Hume's "philosophical" history. Even as he was praising Rapin in 1748 as "the most judicious of historians," Hume added that his predecessor "seems sometimes to treat them ["the two first Princes of the House of Stuarts"] with too much severity" (*Essays*, p. 491). By 1757, Hume had altered his opinion: "To tell the truth, I was carry'd away with the usual Esteem pay'd to that Historian [Rapin], till I came to examine him more particularly when I found him altogether despicable; & I was not asham'd to acknowledge my Mistake."[10] Even when Hume's own *History* began to appear in 1754, he felt that England was still awaiting her historian: "'Tis well known, that the English have not much excelled in that kind of literature."[11]

Richard Hurd described the order of composition and publication of the *History* in striking but disapproving language: "For having undertaken to conjure up the spirit of absolute power, [Hume] judged it necessary to the charm, to reverse the order of things, and to evoke this frightful spectre by writing (as witches use to say their prayers) *backwards*."[12] Hume's *History of Great Britain, Volume One, Containing the Reigns of James I and Charles I* was followed by a second volume in December 1756 (dated 1757), which brought the *History* up to 1688. The two volumes of the *History of England under the House of Tudor* came out in 1759. The final pair of volumes, covering the period from the invasion of Julius Caesar through the reign of Henry VII, were published in November 1761 (dated 1762). The *History* was rearranged chronologically and published in eight volumes in 1763.

Hume admitted to William Strahan, "In my private Judgement, the first volume of my History is by far the best; the subject was more noble, and admitted both of greater Ornaments of Eloquence, and nicer Distinctions of Reasoning" (*Letters* 1:240). Hume chose to begin his *History* "backwards" because to do so allowed him to confront the Rapin-Bolingbroke-Pope view of the English past as dramatically as possible. In his essay "Of the Coalition of Parties" (1758), published while he was writing the Tudor volumes, Hume indicates his aim as a historian: "The greater moderation we now employ in representing past events, the nearer shall we be to produce a full coalition of the parties and an entire acquiescence in our present establishment" (*Essays*, p. 485). Hume's purpose was to write an establishment history based on an impartial investigation of the available evidence. To do so he had to overturn the received interpretation of seventeenth-century events.

Such an undertaking was daring because, as James Hampton notes in his *Reflections on Ancient and Modern History* (1746), recent history was confused by faction. The sixteenth and seventeenth centuries, according to Edward Gibbon in 1762, were particularly prone to misinterpretation. Since "every character is a problem, and every reader a friend or an enemy, . . . every writer is expected to hang out a badge of party, and is devoted to destruction by the opposite faction."[13] Hume intended to deal less severely with the Stuarts—those villains of the Whig historians—than Rapin had done, and the result created an uproar. Warburton went so far as to call the Stuart volume "Jacobite," but the faithful Whig Horace Walpole was more accurate about the "book, which, though more decried than ever book was, and certainly with faults, I cannot help liking much. It is called Jacobite—but in my opinion is only not *George-abite:* where others abuse the Stuarts, he laughs at them; I am sure he does not spare their ministers."[14] Hume himself said of his work: "With regard to politics and the character of princes and great men, I think I am very moderate. My views of *things* are more conformable to Whig principles; my representations of *persons* to Tory prejudices. Nothing can so much prove that men commonly regard more persons than things, as to find that I am commonly numbered among the Tories" (*Letters* 1 : 237). So entrenched was the Whig interpretation of the previous century that even the slightest deviations from it prompted charges of Tory, if not Jacobite, bias.

Hume accepted the logical extension of Hervey's 1734 argument that the Glorious Revolution of 1688 was not a restoration of an immemorial constitution; rather, it marked an abrupt break with the past and put the English system of government on a new foundation. The establishment Whigs, Hervey argued, were the heirs and protectors of this new constitution. Hervey did not, however, go on to argue that if the events of 1688 led to a new constitution, how could the Stuarts fairly be accused of trying to usurp the constitution by extending the royal prerogative? Hume seeks in his *History* to show that the actions of the Stuart kings may not have been unprecedented. He calls into question the convenient Whig assumptions about the past that underlie the uses of history in *Windsor Forest*, *The Craftsman*, and *The Dunciad*. There should be no question that Hume is a firm supporter of such establishment Whig beliefs and ideals as a limited, constitutional monarchy, the Protestant succession of the Hanoverians, a "Mixt Government," and a balance between liberty and authority. His break with the current establishment lay in his interpretation of how these desirable concepts came to be put into practice:

> The revolution forms a new epoch in the constitution; and was attended with consequences much more advantageous to the people, than the barely freeing them from a bad administration. By deciding many important questions in favour of liberty, and still more, by the great precedent of deposing one King, and establishing a new family, it gave such an ascendent to the popular principles, as has put the nature of the English constitution beyond all controversy, And it may safely be affirmed, without any danger of exaggeration, that we in this island have ever since enjoyed, if not the best system of government, at least the most entire system of liberty, that ever was known amongst mankind. (2 [1759] 441)

The very success of the Whig establishment has led to the need for an impartial history. In an important passage written at the end of the same later-Stuart volume, which consequently appears at the end of the whole *History* as rearranged in 1763, Hume explains his intentions:

> The whig party, for a course of near seventy years, have, almost without interruption, enjoyed the whole authority of the government;

and no honours nor offices could be obtained but by their countenance and protection. But this event, which has been advantageous to the state, has been destructive to the truth of history, and has established many gross falsehoods, which it is unaccountable how any civilized nation could have embraced with regard to its domestic occurrences. Compositions the most despicable, both for style and matter, have been extolled, and propagated, and read; as if they had equalled the most celebrated remains of antiquity. And because the ruling party had obtained an advantage over their antagonists in the philosophical disputes concerning some of their general principles, they thence assumed a right to impose on the public their account of all particular transactions, and to represent the other party as governed entirely by the lowest and most vulgar prejudices. But extremes of all kinds are to be avoided; and tho' no-one will ever please either faction by moderate opinions, it is there we are most likely to meet with truth and certainty. (P. 443)

Hume's recognition of his own strong inclination to Whig beliefs and ideals may explain his statement in his concise autobiography, *My Own Life*, "that in above a hundred Alterations, which farther Study, Reading, or Reflection engaged me to make in the Reigns of the two first Stuarts, I have made all of them invariably to the Tory Side" (*Essays*, pp. 612–13), as well as his complaint to Gilbert Elliot in 1763 that "several Mistakes & Oversights" in the Stuart volumes "proceeded from the plaguy Prejudices of Whiggism, with which I was too much infected when I began this Work."[15]

Two quotations from Hume's account of the reign of James I must suffice to illustrate his contention that, in the seventeenth century, Parliament gained new rights and privileges rather than reasserted traditional ones, especially when the basis of government was unsettled. Discussing the legal force of James I's proclamations, Hume says that "in this instance, as in many others, it is easy to see, how unintelligible the English constitution was, before the parliament was able, by continued acquisitions or encroachments, to establish it on fixt principles of liberty" (1 [1754]:711). Hume repeatedly argues throughout the *History* that we must evaluate past actions not from a modern perspective but by trying to recreate the contexts in which they occurred. We must not assume that James I acted in a period equivalent to that under the current Whig establishment:

But so low, at that time, ran the inclination towards liberty, that Elizabeth, the last of that arbitrary line [the Tudors], herself no less arbitrary, was yet the most renowned and most popular of all the princes, who had ever filled the throne of England. It was natural for James to take the government as he found it, and to pursue her measures, which he had so much applauded; nor did his penetration extend so far as to discover, that neither his circumstances nor his character could support so extensive an authority. (1 [1754]:171)

We would be more correct to say, according to Hume, that James I acted by precedent than to assert that he was an unconstitutional monarch.

As the last quotation indicates, Hume is not reluctant to question the standard Whig views of the supposedly heroic Elizabeth of *Windsor Forest* and the villainous James I of *Dunciad* 4. For Hume, Elizabeth was "that arbitrary Princess" (1 [1754]:79), a despotic ruler who was hardly the great defender of liberty *The Craftsman* celebrated. The Tudor volumes of the *History* show that absolute monarchy was firmly established in English politics by the beginning of the seventeenth century. Hume is "Toryish" about persons insofar as he is willing to judge actions in light of precedents rather than by reference to posterity and insofar as he is willing to distinguish between the king's two bodies of man and ruler. Hume's "characters" of the Stuarts are unlikely to strike twentieth-century readers as adulatory, but any attempt at a balanced representation of almost sterotyped exemplars in the mid-eighteenth century was bound to arouse partisan rage. Of James I, Hume says: "His intentions were just; but more adapted to the conduct of private life, than to the government of kingdoms. . . . Of a feeble temper more than of a frail judgment: Exposed to our ridicule from his vanity; but exempt from our hatred by his freedom from pride and arrogance" (1 [1754]:216). Even James II, at least in his private capacity, deserves some praise: "In domestic life, his conduct was irreproachable, and is intitled to our approbation." But as a ruler, his virtues of steadiness, diligence, bravery, and sincerity were "swallowed up in bigotry and arbitrary principles" (2 [1759]:432).

Hume's more balanced approach to the Stuarts, like his challenge to the Whig interpretation of English history in general, was founded on a skeptical attitude toward the past. Like Bolingbroke's Sancho, Hume doubted. He agreed with Bolingbroke that the past would never fully be recaptured, in part because of intentional distortions by its recorders. Repeatedly throughout his *History* Hume comments on the unreliability and inadequacy of chroniclers and their evidence. When data have not simply been lost or overlooked, they have been misrepresented or suppressed for ecclesiastical or political reasons. Such incomplete evidence called into question the received notions of uniformitarianism and humanistic exemplar history.

In a passage from the *Enquiry Concerning Human Understanding* (first published in 1748 under the title *Philosophical Essays Concerning Human Understanding*) Hume presents a view of history that is as uniformitarian and didactic as the one Bolingbroke maintained in the 1730s:

Its chief use is only to discover the constant and universal principles of human nature, by shewing men in all varieties of circumstances
and situations, and furnishing us with materials, from which we may
form our observations, and become acquainted with the regular springs
of human action and behaviour. These records of wars, intrigues, factions, and revolutions, are so many collections of experiments, by
which the politician or moral philosopher fixes the principles of his
science; in the same manner as the physician or natural philosopher
becomes acquainted with the nature of plants, minerals, and other
external objects, by the experiments, which he forms concerning
them.[16]

Hume, however, like Bolingbroke in the passage quoted earlier from *Letters
on the Study and Use of History*, found that uniformitarian history was not
easy either to put into practice or to reconcile with a skeptical view of the
past. Certain general statements about human nature, both men (and most
modern historians) would agree, could be drawn from the study of history.
All men, past and present, are motivated by such universal passions as lust,
greed, and ambition, but the complexity of ever-changing events and
influences either suppresses or encourages these passions. Moreover, as
Bolingbroke points out, a multitude of possible causes, external as well as
psychological, may contribute to a seemingly simple effect.

Hume emphasizes more than once that "the movements of great states
are often directed by as slender springs as those of individuals" (2 [1759]:
38). Even a complete knowledge of a man's character, were such knowledge
possible, would not be enough to predict his activities. Thus, Cromwell's
election to Parliament depended upon a combination of "accident and
intrigue." Hume agreed with Bolingbroke that in the face of incomplete or
conflicting evidence the historian must identify the probable causes for
known effects, but he also warns us that "what is most probable in human
affairs is not always true; and a very minute circumstance, overlooked in our
speculations, serves often to explain events, which may seem the most
surprizing and unaccountable" (2 [1759]: 47, 238). Hume seems to take
particular interest in the effects of accidents or apparently insignificant
details on the course of history, as he does when he stresses that "the poniard
of the fanatical Ravaillac" probably altered European history (1 [1754]:
114). Hume's syntax suggests that the instrument was as important as the
assassin.

Because Hume, who was naturally skeptical, sought to challenge conventional wisdom about the past, it was appropriate that he question the
available data and received interpretation. His thesis that the present Whig
establishment and constitution were the result of revolution rather than of

continuity from an immemorial past had to rely on historical relativism, not uniformitarianism, for its justification. To demonstrate that the present Whig establishment did not exist by some teleological law or as the only possible heirs to an unchanging theory of government, Hume argued that "each century had its peculiar mode of conducting business" (2 [1803]: 471) and that the political basis of English goverment has undergone many changes. History shows us that "all human institutions . . . require continual amendments" (2 [1759]: 243) and are subject to abrupt and unexpected alterations. Thus Hume insists that William I was indeed a conqueror and that only those (like Pope in *Windsor Forest*) who are politically motivated dispute this fact (1 [1803]: 375–80). The myth of the Norman Yoke must fall, along with the legend of the immemorial constitution.

Hume's historical relativism challenged accepted ideas about exemplar history, uniformitarianism, and the belief in the ancient constitution. His emphasis on accidents and external causes as influences of events tends to reduce greatly the individual's responsibility for history. Hume's Tory attitude toward the early Stuarts, and his contention that their actions were not unprecedented usurpations of long-standing parliamentary rights, are based on historical relativism. We must realize, he says, that "it was the fate of the house of Stuart to govern England at a period, when the former source of authority [the Crown] was already much diminished, and before the latter [Parliament] began to flow in any tolerable abundance." The Stuarts, no longer the villains they had been seen as in 1730s, are now seen as victims of "fate." Elsewhere, Hume tells us, "'Tis the situation which decides intirely of the fortunes and characters of men. The King [Charles I], it must be owned, tho' laudable in many respects, was not endowed with that masterly genius, which might enable him to perceive, in their infancy, the changes that arose in natural manners, and know how to accommodate his conduct to them." Hume's ironic reference to those who judge by hindsight their predecessors is repeated in his analysis of Oliver Cromwell. Hume reminds those of his readers who attribute Cromwell's success to his cunning and foresight that "this opinion, so much warranted by the exorbitant ambition and profound dissimulation of his character, meets with ready belief; tho 'tis more agreeable to the narrowness of human views, and the natural darkness of futurity, to suppose, that this daring usurper was guided by events, and did not, as yet, foresee, with any assurance, that unparalleled greatness, which he afterwards attained" (1 [1754]: 390, 381, 645). True to his belief that each period of history is unique, Hume sees Cromwell as "suited to the age in which he lived, and to that alone" (2 [1759]: 3).

Historical figures so controlled by their situations and so affected by accidents were not very useful to the eighteenth century as exemplars of

behavior. Consequently, one of the didactic purposes of the study of history
was undercut. As Edmund Burke notices in his positive review of Hume's
History for the *Annual Register* (4 [1761]: 301 4), by the time Hume wrote
the medieval volumes, he was attributing to men less power than he had in
the earlier volumes: "The third part seems to evince, that this pitch, which
the prerogative had attained, was not the effect of the abilities, or the
violence, of this or that family, so much as the natural course of things."
Nearly the last thing Hume wrote in his *History*, a passage at the end of the
reign of Richard III, summarizes Hume's conclusions about the usefulness
of history. The passage merits full quotation because it indicates how much
less applicable to the present historical relativism is than uniformitarianism
had been. The past, especially the distant past, contrasts with, rather than
parallels, the present:

> In each of these successive alterations, the only rule of government
> which is intelligible or carries any authority with it, is the established
> practice of the age, and the maxims of administration which are at that
> time prevalent and universally assented to. Those who, from a pre-
> tended respect to antiquity, appeal at every turn to an original plan of
> the constitution, only cover their turbulent spirit and their private
> ambition under the appearance of venerable forms; and whatever period
> they pitch on for their model, they may still be carried back to a more
> ancient period, where they will find the measures of power entirely
> different, and where every circumstance, by reason of the greater bar-
> barity of the times, will appear still less worthy of imitation. Above all,
> a civilized nation, like the English, who have happily established the
> most perfect and most accurate system of liberty that was ever found
> compatible with government, ought to be cautious in appealing to the
> practice of their ancestors, or regarding the maxims of uncultivated
> ages as certain rules for their present conduct. An acquaintance with
> the ancient periods of their government is chiefly *useful*, by instructing
> them to cherish their present constitution, from a comparison or con-
> trast with the condition of those distant times. And it is also *curious*, by
> shewing them the remote and commonly faint and disfigured originals
> of the most finished and most noble institutions, and by instructing
> them in the great mixture of accident which commonly concurs with a
> small ingredient of wisdom and foresight in erecting the complicated
> fabric of the most perfect government. (4 [1803]:54–55)

Hume's research leads him to conclude, as Bolingbroke had done in *Letters
on the Study and Use of History*, that only the recent past (since about 1500)
can help us understand the present: "Whoever carries his anxious researches
into preceding periods is moved by a curiosity, liberal indeed and com-

mendable; not by any necessity for acquiring knowledge of public affairs, or the arts of civil government" (4 [1803]: 191).

The mid-century shift in English historiography Bolingbroke and Hume represented did not suddenly convert establishment Whigs to a skeptical view of their past. William Blackstone supports the notion of the Norman Yoke and denies in his *Commentaries* (1765–69) that William was a conqueror. Blackstone's views were widely available after 1758—circulated as manuscript notes of his Vinerian lectures. Hume's *History* was greeted, particularly at first, by many dissenting voices. Hurd, for example, took exception to Hume's contention that 1688 marked a change in the English political structure. Speaking for many, Hurd objects that the Glorious Revolution "has not created a *new plan of policy*, but perfected the old one," though he traces the present constitution only back to "the *Norman* establishment." Even Hurd, however, recognizes the appeal of the *History*. Although "on the whole, it is to be lamented that Mr. HUME's too zealous concern for the honour of the house of STUART, operating uniformly through all the volumes of his history, has brought disgrace . . . , in the main, [the *History*] is agreeably written, and is indeed the most readable *general* account of the *English* affairs, that has yet been given to the public." [17] So quickly did Hume's *History* gain an "unrivaled popularity in the walk of English history" that Catherine Graham Macaulay, the radical historian, felt the need in 1763 to refute the Stuart volumes. [18]

There is reason to believe that Hume's *History* appeared just at the time when his audience was most receptive to such a revisionist approach to their past. As we have seen, Carte and Guthrie had recently reopened the past for investigation. The minor historian Samuel Squire switched his allegiance from the immemorial constitution to Brady's findings in the course of works published between 1745 and 1753. [19] Continuous appeals in *The Monitor* (1755–65) to the authority of the ancient constitution attest to the vitality of the myth at mid-century. [20] Historians of the time, including Tobias Smollett, Hume's principal competitor for the popular market, had to deal with the Whig myth. [21] In his *A Complete History of England, from the Descent of Julius Caesar to the Treaty of Aix la Chapelle, 1748* (11 vols., 1757–60) Smollett expresses little doubt that the myth is invalid: "We are not to look for a settled constitution among the Saxons, who first landed in Britain" (1:155). The events of 1688–89 marked a distinct break with the past: "The constitution of England had now assumed a new aspect." Smollett feels that the Glorious Revolution probably did not go far enough in changing the English political structure: "In a word, the settlement was finished with some precipitation, before the plan had been properly digested and matured" (8:291). Generally speaking, however, Smollett's *History* is far less innovative than Hume's. Smollett admits that his work does not contain any new information which "must alter the received opinions of mankind" (vol. 1, "Plan of the Complete History of England," unpaginated). Nevertheless, Smollett's contemporaries inaccurately labelled his *History* "Tory," as they had Hume's.

Had Hume's *History* not appeared, Edmund Burke probably would have published one perhaps very similar to it. Burke had contracted with Robert Dodsley to produce a single-volume history of England by 1759. We know from Burke's *Annual Register* review that he believed Hume had proven himself the equal of Italian and French historians: Burke calls Hume a "very ingenious and elegant writer . . . certainly a very profound thinker." Burke obviously agreed with Hume's controversial treatment of "the Stuarts, who, we imagine with this ingenious author, erred not so much in extending the prerogative, as in not having had sagacity enough to see that they had fallen in the times, when . . . it behoved them to slacken and remit of the authority exercised by their predecessors." Hume could not have hoped for higher praise than Burke's judgment that "no man perhaps has come nearer to that so requisite and so rare a quality in an historian of unprejudiced partiality."

Although Burke's own *An Essay towards an Abridgment of the English History in Three Books* (1757, published 1811) is incomplete, enough exists to indicate that he would have been no more charitable to the Whig myth of the immemorial constitution than Hume is. In the section of Burke's *Essay* entitled "An Essay towards an History of the Laws of England," he makes clear his attitude toward those who argue for the antiquity of precedent:

> The spirit of party, which has misled us in so many other particulars, has tended greatly to perplex us in this matter. For as the advocates for prerogative would, by a very absurd consequence drawn from the Norman Conquest, have made all our national rights and liberties to have arisen from the grants, and therefore to be revocable at the will of the sovereign, so, on the other hand, those who maintained the cause of liberty did not support it upon more solid principles. They would hear of no beginning to any of our privileges, orders, or laws, and, in order to gain them a reverence, would prove that they were as old as the nation; and to support that opinion, they put to the torture all the ancient monuments. . . . In reality, that ancient Constitution and those Saxon laws make little or nothing for any of our modern parties, and, when fairly laid open, will be found to compose such a system as none, I believe, would think it neither practicable or desirable to establish.[22]

The implications of the mid-century shift in historiography for the production of satire were enormous. Hume's assumptions about history undercut the very bases of the rhetorical strategy Bolingbroke and his circle developed against Walpole. Poets and printmakers could no longer so easily call the past into the service of the present. Uniformitarianism and exemplar history had given them a fund of historical precedents and parallels on which to draw to create metaphors in their satire. When Pope wanted to praise Anne or damn George II he needed only suggest a likeness with Elizabeth or James I. Hume challenged the validity of classifying historical figures as heroes or villains. Not even Cardinal Wolsey was completely evil in Hume's *History* (4 [1803]: 265, 384), and historical analogies, like the one Gilbert Burnet made between Charles II and Tiberius, were challenged (2 [1759]: 371–72). Consequently, the concision of historical allusion became less and less available to the satirists. In a way, they were losing the past. The importance of the loss of the constitutional myth to political satirists was probably even greater in its significance than the loss of the Roman myth: "The concept of the immemorial constitution encouraged the fabrication of myths about immensely remote times, and the fact that the appeal to early national history took the form of partisan controversy between sovereign and constitution enhanced this tendency."[23] To be sure, a satirist could choose to ignore the implications of the new history writing, but he could never again assume as easily as Pope had been able to that his audience shared his view of the past. The impact of the new history writing on political satire was not immediate, in part because it did not conflict with the dominant policy of attacking personalities rather than issues. As we have seen, in the 1740s and 1750s satirists tended to diminish and dehumanize their subjects in ways that did not depend very heavily on humanistic assumptions about history or on appeals to the past. The loss of history does not become truly noticeable until we try to account for the nature of Charles Churchill's poetry and the engraved political satire of the early 1760s.

CHAPTER VIII

Charles Churchill and Political Satire of the Early 1760s

If thou a fortune woulds't atchieve [*sic*],
Write, write *politic rhymes*, and thrive:
Abuse the Ministers, and whirl
Keen venom at a certain Earl;
Invent new slanders, forge fresh hints
For Blasphemy—to aid my *prints*;
Write Histories, and Libels too,
And copious Novels not a few.
    —*Folly, a Satire on the Times*, 1763

Although the narrowly partisan nature of political satires during the 1740s and 1750s makes them unfamiliar today to any but the most specialized of eighteenth-century scholars, their contribution to the development of caricature and satire cannot be overlooked if we are to understand and appreciate the eclectic nature of political satire in the first years of George III's reign. The mid-century changes in satire and historiography discussed earlier help to explain the differences between the poetry and prints of Pope's times and those of Churchill's. Political realities during the interregnum between Pope and Churchill led to a very different rhetorical strategy than the one Bolingbroke and his allies had developed against Sir Robert Walpole, one not as consciously promoted as Bolingbroke's had been. Also during the interregnum the trend toward historicism meant that the past was becoming less accessible to satirists as a means for attacking the present. Herbert Atherton is one of a growing number of scholars who argue that the reign of George III led to a renewal of the importance of political principles:

In the 1760s new blood began to flow in the body politic. The *cause célèbre* of Wilkes, the birth of radicalism, the organization on a mass scale of 'opinion without doors,' and the contests of George III with his ministers and would-be ministers produced real constitutional issues. The American Revolution and the events leading up to it introduced an entirely new issue. Imperial affairs are generally absent from the prints before 1760. The return of a degree of factionalism to graphic satire in the sharp exchange of prints was another sign of the revival of issues.[1]

If these scholars are correct about the renewed importance of principles, why do we not then find as glorious a flowering of satire as we saw in Pope's day? The present chapter attempts to answer this question.

The relative political tranquillity of the 1740s and 1750s was succeeded by the increased domestic turmoil of the early 1760s. So peaceful at times was the mid-century domestic political scene that at one point—when Parliament reassembled on 14 November 1751—Henry Fox predicted, "There never was such a session as this is likely to be. The halcyon days the poets write of cannot exceed its calmness. A bird might build her nest in the Speaker's chair, or in his peruke. There won't be a debate that can disturb her."[2] There were certainly some times that would have disturbed her nest—times such as the shameful events surrounding the Jewish Naturalization Bill of 1753 and Admiral Byng's loss of Minorca in 1756—when popular discontent had ignoble results. The last gasp of Jacobitism in 1745–46 caused a flurry of excitement. But on the whole, the Pelhamite refinement of the school of Walpole helped create a consensus about the basic principles of the British government. The brief three-year period of ministerial instability following Henry Pelham's death in 1754 was resolved by the formation of the grand alliance of Pitt and Newcastle, which George III inherited in 1760 from his grandfather.

The new reign began auspiciously. Englishmen were reveling in the aftermath of Pitt's *annus mirabilis* of 1759, when British success in the Seven Years' War with France seemed unlimited. Although George III was expected to exert more power than George II, especially in his later years, was thought to have wielded, Horace Walpole predicted that "services will be pretensions in *this* reign."[3] George III's professed pride in being the first British-born Hanoverian delighted his subjects, but all were aware that his closest advisor and friend was John Stuart, Earl of Bute, a Scotsman and distant relative of the Jacobite Pretender. Bute, with no parliamentary base of political support, was clearly an ousider to the Pelhamite political establishment, and its members perceived him as a threat. Walpole thought it worth mentioning to Horace Mann at the very beginning of the new reign that "Lord Bute avoids preferring his countrymen."[4] Walpole's opinion of

Bute's impartiality was not shared by most of his fellow Englishmen, who saw him as favoring Scotsmen and others from outside the political coterie that had administered England since 1720. Equally damaging to Bute's popularity was his advocacy of George III's policy of seeking peace with the defeated French. Bute officially took control of the government as first lord of the Treasury on 29 May 1762, after the resignations of William Pitt on 9 October 1761 and the duke of Newcastle on 29 May 1762. The Pelhamite policy of comprehension was quickly replaced by the Butean system of exclusion. The response to Bute's acquisition of power at the expense of the Old Whig establishment was the formation of the most organized and effective verbal and visual opposition since the fall of Walpole.

At first glance, there is a sense of déjà vu about the satiric attacks on Bute and his ministry. One might be tempted to see the campaign against him as a repetition of the Opposition propaganda against Walpole. Horace Walpole compared the two ministries when he observed in 1762, "The new administration begins tempestuously. My father was not more abused after twenty years than Lord Bute is in twenty days. Weekly papers swarm, and like other swarms of insects, sting."[5] As Horace Walpole remarks, the attacks on Bute were more numerous and strident than those on Sir Robert Walpole. As in the 1730s, historical parallels were employed in the 1760s, but now clearly for more personal abuse: "Parallels, you know, are the food of all party writings: we have Queen Isabel and Mortimer, Queen Margaret and the Duke of Suffolk, every week. You will allow that abuse does not set out tamely, when it even begins with the King's mother."[6]

There were a striking number of similarities between Walpole and Bute, which the latter's opponents exploited. Both ministers were accused of rising undeservedly from humble origins; both were awarded the Garter; both were seen as favorites; both proposed excise taxes; both were called corrupters of the constitution. Given the apparent similarities, we might expect to find an opposition rhetorical strategy aimed at Bute very like the one used against Walpole. Indeed, there is some evidence that satirists tried to apply the previous strategy to the new political situation. For example, probably in 1762, the print *The Stature of a Great Man; or, The Scotch Colossus* (B.M. 4000) appeared; it is simply a republication of the 1740 print *The Stature of a Great Man; or, The English Colossus* (B.M. 2458) with Bute's face substituted for that of Walpole.

A closer study of political satire during the early 1760s, however, impresses one with the differences in strategy from that of the 1730s. We notice first the increased level of personal abuse, a development we traced in the work of those I have labeled interregnum satirists. By 1760, invective had become generally more acceptable in poetry and prints than ever before. When Henry Fielding dropped his persona in *The Jacobite's Journal* of

66. *The Scotch Broomstick and the Female Beesom, a German Tale, by Sawney Gesner* (B.M. 3852)

26 March 1748, one of the reasons he gave for doing so was the public's distaste for irony:

> there is no species of Wit or Humour so little adapted to the Palat [*sic*] of the present Age. I am firmly persuaded, that if many of those who have formerly gained such Reputation this Way, were to revive and publish their Words *de novo*, they would have few Readers, and acquire but little Credit. This is indeed too plain and simple a Food, and wants all that high Seasoning which recommends the Works of modern Authors. Ridicule is not sufficiently poignant; nothing but downright Abuse will whet up and stimulate the pall'd Appetite of the Public; nor will the World at present swallow any Characters that are not well ragoo'd and carbonaded. The general Taste in Reading, at this Time, very much resembles that of some particular Men in Eating, who would never willingly devour what doth not stink. When a new Book, Pamphlet, or Poem is published, the Enquiry is not, as formerly, What is the Subject? Who writ it? Is there Wit or Humour in it? But, who is abused? Whom is the Author at now? Doth he lay about him well? and such-like; and according to the Answer received to these Questions, the Performance is cherish'd or rejected.[7]

67. William Hogarth, *The Bruiser* (B.M. 4084)

We can add engravings to the list of publications in which Fielding's contemporaries hoped to find personal abuse. A glance at a few of the prints of the early 1760s quickly impresses one with the continued expectation of invective and caricature in Georgian political satire. *The Scotch Broomstick and the Female Beesom, a German Tale, by Sawney Gesner* (B.M. 3852), a 1762 print attributed to Townshend, is typical of the numerous engravings attacking the alleged illicit sexual and political relationship between Lord Bute and George III's mother, the Princess of Wales. This print and the many others like it, with their thinly veiled sexual suggestions, their often obscene language, and their reiteration of the princess's attraction to Bute's exaggerated staff or bagpipe, can only be called political pornography. The rhetorical appeal is obvious and representative of the same audience taste for personal abuse Hogarth acknowledged with his satires of John Wilkes (B.M. 4050) and Charles Churchill (B.M. 4084). The great importance of the mid-century development of political caricature and its probable relationship to the recent trends in historiography are more fully appreciated when we recognize that the caricaturists' stress on the nonheroic individual anticipated a similar emphasis in history painting after 1770. Edgar Wind observes that developments in historiography by Voltaire, Gibbon, and Hume indirectly affected the subject matter and style of history painting, because "while the Academicians refused to depict ordinary men as heroes, the new historians refused to believe in heroes who could not be depicted as ordinary men."[8] I suggest that popular engravings, because of the mid-century political climate, responded more directly and immediately to the new historiography and in turn probably had an as yet unrecognized influence on later history painting.

The legacy of interregnum personal satire helps explain the weakness of the poetry of Churchill, the most important political satirist after Pope. We saw Pope transform his attack on Hervey in the *Epistle to Dr. Arbuthnot* from one on an individual to one on the principles Hervey was allegedly fostering: the measures replace the man. How different is Churchill's tactic in *An Epistle to William Hogarth* (1763), which could easily be instructions to a caricaturist:

> WITH all the symptoms of assur'd decay,
> With age and sickness pinch'd, and worn away,
> Pale quiv'ring lips, lank cheeks, and falt'ring tongue,
> The Spirits out of tune, the Nerves unstrung,
> Thy Body shrivell'd up, thy dim eyes sunk
> Within their sockets deep, thy weak hams shrunk
> The body's weight unable to sustain,
> The stream of life scarce trembling thro' the vein,

68. William Hogarth, *The Times*, plate 1 (B.M. 3970)

More than half-kill'd by honest truths, which fell,
Thro' thy own fault, from men who wish'd thee well,
Can'st thou, e'en thus, thy thoughts to vengeance give,
And, dead to all things else, to Malice live?
Hence, Dotard, to thy closet, shut thee in,
By deep repentance wash away thy sin,
From haunts of men to shame and sorrow fly,
And, on the verge of death, learn how to die.   (419–34)

One must have a great love for invective and personal abuse if one is not to be repelled by Churchill's treatment here of his aged victim Hogarth.[9] Churchill names names and exploits his victims' physical weaknesses in his satires in ways Pope avoided.

The growth of caricature and invective in political satire at mid-century was at the expense of the emblematic tradition. In earlier chapters we saw how often Pope used what he called in *The Rape of the Lock* "Th' expressive Emblem" (3:40) as a structuring device in his political satires from *Windsor Forest* to the *New Dunciad*. For Pope, the emblematic tradition we first looked at in Hogarth's *South Sea Scheme* was an economical way to appear to draw logically deductive conclusions from the evidence offered earlier in a political poem. Thus, the emblematic tale of Balaam sums up and expresses in a general way the meaning of the particular data Pope gives us earlier in the *Epistle to Bathurst*. Hogarth's own work—if we compare the *South Sea Scheme* with *Four Prints of an Election*—illustrates the shift Ronald Paulson has described as one from "emblem to expression," a gradual transition from the Hercules figure in *A Tryal of Skill* to the fox figure. Although emblematic prints can still be found after the fall of Walpole, so rapidly are they supplanted by caricatures that at least one scholar contends that after 1760 the earlier method of representation is rarely found.[10] We can see the shift in two states of Hogarth's *The Times*, plate 1 (B.M. 3970), a proministerial engraving of 1762. In the first state, Hogarth attacks Pitt in the person of Henry VIII amidst a cityscape peopled by naturalistic figures. The image of Henry VIII as an emblem of despotic tyranny reminds us of Hogarth's work in the 1720s and 1730s. Very soon, however, Hogarth produced another state of the print in which a naturalistic Pitt replaces the Henrician figure. The desuetude in the 1740s and 1750s of the emblematic tradition that had served Pope so well as a means of structural economy in political satire may well explain a Churchillian fault his critics often remark: Churchill seems not to know how to end a poem.[11] Pope's method of emblematic summation, or what I have called rising to a general conclusion, seems to have been unavailable to Churchill and his contemporaries. Churchill's tendency to write verse caricatures gives his poetry the appearance of a series of separate portraits strung together.

The digressive and long-winded nature of Churchill's satire probably results as much from the loss of the concise allusions of historical references as it does from the loss of emblematic economy. Pope, Bolingbroke, and their circle had the great advantage in the campaign against Walpole of being able to enlist Rapin, generally recognized as the greatest and most objective contemporary historian. Walpole's apologists were forced into the embarrassing position of having to refute the Whiggish Rapin by embracing the Tory historian Brady of the seventeenth century. But whichever historian one side or the other espoused, both agreed on the value of humanistic and uniformitarian history. Bolingbroke and Hume at mid-century questioned these long-standing verities. Hume in particular challenged the assumptions underlying anti-Walpole satire. He disputed the accepted facts as well. During the 1720s and 1730s history and satire complemented one another insofar as the political satirists based their attacks on what was certainly arguably the best available interpretation of the past. Bolingbroke's *Remarks on the History of England,* which first appeared in *The Craftsman*, partisan and simplistic though it seems to us now, was a not too greatly distorted popularization of Rapin's work.

Churchill and his fellow satirists found themselves in a very different situation. They tended to see the recent histories by Hume and Smollett, influential and popular though they undeniably were, as threats to their own satires, as interpretations that might best serve the ministry, and as Scottish productions. In *The Apology* (1761), Churchill clothes an attack on Smollett in irony:

> From LIVY'S temples tear th' historic crown
> Which with more justice blooms upon thine own.
> Compar'd with thee, be all life-writers dumb,
> But he who wrote the Life of TOMMY THUMB,
> Who ever read the REGICIDE but swore
> The author wrote as man ne'er wrote before?   (152–57)

Churchill discloses his feelings about Hume in the unfinished *The Journey. A Fragment*, which appeared posthumously in 1765:

> If fashionable grown, and fond of pow'r
> With hum'rous SCOTS let Them disport their hour;
> Let Them dance, fairy like, round OSSIAN's tomb;
> Let Them forge *lies*, and *histories* for HUME.   (119–22)

Hume, with his alleged Tory prejudices, is almost certainly the historian referred to in Churchill's long political poem *Gotham* (1764), when the poet recounts in book 2 the history of the Stuarts, ending with James II:

> No matter *how*—he slept amongst the dead,
> And JAMES his Brother reigned in his stead.
> But such a reign—so glaring an offence
> In ev'ry step 'gainst Freedom, Law, and Sense,
> 'Gainst all the rights of Nature's gen'ral plan,
> 'Gainst all which constitutes an Englishman,
> That the Relation would mere fiction seem,
> The mock creation of a Poet's dream,
> And the poor Bard's would, in this sceptic age,
> Appear as false as *their* Historian's page.   (2:639–58)

Churchill's lengthy summary of English history, which comprises more than half of the 678 lines of book 2, is significant because it illustrates one of the problems satirists faced. To refute Hume's *History*, Churchill must offer his own. Increasingly, a satirist's audience must be told which particular interpretation of the past is the basis for the work being read or looked at. Just as Hogarth in 1762 no longer safely could assume that his audience would agree with his view of Henry VIII and apply it properly to William Pitt, Churchill felt the need to confront Hume if he were to offer his readers the traditional view of the Stuarts as villains. The poet of *The Scourge, A Satire. Part I* (1765) felt the same compulsion to summarize Stuart history, as did Edward Burnaby Greene in his *Privilege. A Poem* (1764). Greene intends to treat the Stuarts as they deserve, not as Tory historians have dealt with them:

> Hence be *such* rulers, let the bigot praise
> The gloomy records of those guilty days,
> Let frantic TORIES, whose rebellious ire
> Would spread their native land with flames of fire,
> On regal vileness venal flatt'ry roll,
> No spark of FREEDOM glimm'ring in their soul.   (P. 19)

Greene later in the poem (p. 25) indicates that Hogarth and Johnson are included among the incendiary Tories.

By 1764, readers of political satire must be warned away from particular historians and advised to follow others. In *Privilege* the "vagrant HUME" is treated contemptuously as a philosopher who "Deals wanton paradox in headlong rage; / *Who*, what he thinks, with confidence can bawl / Freely, as that, he never thought at all" (p. 3). Greene, in response to those who "rake the *Grecian* for th' historic lye" (p. 5), turns to the more recent English past for "true" historical parallels to the present. But to do so he must turn his readers from Smollett's *History*, which had been dedicated to William Pitt, to that of Catherine Graham Macaulay, written, we should recall, expressly to refute the interpretation found in Hume's Stuart volumes:

> But chiefly ye, whose learning's sob'rer rage
> Points the full beauties of th' historic page,
> Not rous'd by SMOLLET's pride, with partial views,
> Dealing each faithless anecdote from *news*,
> Changing, like vanes, before the changing wind,
> Where faction bids, who fly with giddy mind,
> 'Gainst honest Pitt's unsully'd virtues roar,
> That Pitt your int'rest deem'd a God before,
> Who madly vaunting in the Tory's name,
> Throw vilain slanders on a William's fame,
> William, whose worth shall triumph, when the Scot,
> Of All disdain'd, shall in oblivion rot,
> Howe'er the wretches labor to survive,
> Prop'd on the rebel-deeds of *forty-five*;
> But Ye, inspir'd by truth's severer laws,
> Who rush undaunted in your country's cause,

Macaulays firm, who soar on Freedom's wings,
No dupes to statesmen, and no slaves to Kings,
Who frown on Stuarts with a gen'rous zeal,
Each thought directed to the public weal;
Distinguish'd patriots! in whose strains we find
The purest language of a manly mind;
—Attend the muse, which fearless of control,
Speaks the strong dictates of an ENGLISH soul,
On vile corruption swells th' indignant stream,
FREEDOM her boast, and PRIVILEGE her theme.   (Pp. 7—8)

Horace Walpole's description of Macaulay's abilities as a historian indicates why she appealed so strongly to Bute's enemies and how different her treatment of the past was from Hume's emphases on accidents and the "situation" of events:

> The female historian, as partial in the cause of liberty as bigots to the Church and royalists to tyranny, exerted manly strength with the gravity of a philosopher. Too prejudiced to dive into causes, she imputes everything to tyrannic views, nothing to passions, weakness, error, prejudice, and still less to what operates oftenest, and her ignorance of which qualified her yet less for a historian,—to accident and little motives. She seems to think men have acted from no views but those of establishing a despotism or a republic.[12]

The antiministerial writers expressed their continued faith in the didactic uses of exemplar history, even in the face of recent historiography. Churchill calls history to his aid in book 3 of *Gotham*:

> Let me the page of History turn o'er,
> Th' instructive page, and heedfully explore
> What faithful pens of former times have wrote
> Of former kings; what they did worthy note,
> What worthy blame, and from the sacred tomb
> Where righteous Monarchs sleep, where laurels bloom
> Unhurt by Time, let me a garland twine,
> Which, robbing not their Fame, may add to mine.   (3:461—68)

Similarly, in the *North Briton*, no. 39 (26 February 1763), which John Wilkes wrote and Churchill edited, the usefulness of parallel history is asserted as if Hume's *History* had never appeared:

> There is a great resemblance between the histories of most nations, whose forms of government are nearly similar. . . . The resemblance between particular periods of history, in different states as well as in the

same body politic, is sometimes remarkably striking. There are few passages in the *Roman* history but find their exact parallels in our own. *Oliver Cromwell* plays the same poor farce (and acts it as ill) in his refusal of the crown from a committee of parliament, as *Julius Caesar* had before done on a like offer from Mark Anthony. The comparison of particular periods of the history of the same nation is still more just, and an argument may be drawn from it with more truth and precision, because it is founded in the genius of the people and the form of the government.[13]

But compared to *The Craftsman*, the *North Briton* rarely employs ancient history, be it classical or English, in its satire on the Bute ministry. Far more common is the use of English history since 1600. Apparently Wilkes and Churchill agreed with Bolingbroke and Hume, who had argued that one no longer need go back further than the sixteenth century if one seeks to understand contemporary events. Even *North Briton*, no. 39, beginning as it does with an assertion of the relevance of Roman history to modern times, expends most of its energy on a comparison of the present Peace of Paris to the Peace of Utrecht and the last years of Queen Anne's reign. The old Whig myths of the ancient constitution and Magna Carta still are called into service: Churchill refers to both in book 2 of *The Duellist* (1764). Increasingly, however, in the prints and poems, the earlier myths are treated as legends rather than facts generally accepted. They frequently become little more than political slogans, as in Joseph Massie's attack on the malt tax in *Magna Charta—or—Magna Farta* (1762). The notion of an immemorial constitution can still be found in the nineteenth century, but after 1760 the idea received less and less credence as a historical rather than mythical reality.

The one historical parallel political satirists most often used in prose, prints, and poetry—that between Bute and the seventeenth-century Stuarts—demonstrates how unsuitable *The Craftsman*'s rhetorical strategy was to the early 1760s. Churchill and his contemporaries enjoyed identifying Lord Bute with the Stuart despots of the past and the Jacobites of the present. Bute, however, clearly served only at the king's pleasure. His enemies were correct in labeling him a "favourite": indeed, he was the last "favourite" England would have and the first since the seventeenth century. Without a seat in the Commons, Bute had little political base other than the king's favor. Unlike Walpole, Bute could not create a school or system of government. Unlike Walpole, Bute was only in a very restricted sense of the phrase a prime minister, and then for less than a year, since he quit after the Peace of Paris formally took effect in April 1763. Bute's opposition spent a great deal of energy on a target that did not enjoy the power attributed to it. Moreover, the *North Briton*'s constant expression and observation of the traditional notion that the Hanoverian George III could do no wrong made it impossible for Wilkes and Churchill to transfer all their anti-Stuart propaganda from the fallen Bute to the reigning king. Political satirists of the early 1760s restricted themselves to a historical parallel that was too limited in its applicability, especially when coupled as it was with personal attacks on Bute's alleged relationship with the Princess of Wales. When Bute left office he lost power, despite his enemies' charges that, as Walpole had supposedly done, Bute still ran the government.[14]

The principal response of political satirists in the early 1760s to what I have called the loss of history was an attempt to replace historical fact with literary myth as a means to generalize particular satire. The print "Andrews-Cross" (B.M. 3964) of 1762 and the unacted play *The Three Conjurors, a Political Interlude. Stolen from Shakespeare* (1763) are just two of a number of engravings and verses that draw a parallel between Bute and Macbeth, a comparison that enabled satirists to emphasize Bute's ancestry as well as his alleged ambitions. *The Three Conjurors* demonstrates, moreover, the strong appeal personal abuse had for satirists. Amidst stock references to Magna Carta and praise for Wilkes and Churchill we find many references to the sexual relationship between the characters Macboote and Hecate. The play ends with praise for George III. Miltonic allusions and imitations begin to appear in political satires like Theophilus Hogarth's *Liberty in the Suds; or, Modern Characters* (1764) and the anonymous *An Epistle to the Irreverend Mr. C{harle}s C{hurchil}l, in His Own Style and Manner* (1764), two verse satires aimed at Bute's opposition. Such appeals to literary history were encouraged by the publication of James Macpherson's Ossianic forgeries, themselves nonpolitical. The Ossianic poems (mainly because a Scotsman created them) seemed to invite imitation and political application as literary history took the place allusions to the past had in the anti-Walpole satires.

Probably the most influential political imitation of Ossianic verse was the virulently anti-Bute *Gisbal, An Hyperborean Tale* (1762), a long prose satire in mock Biblical style on the alleged relationship between Bute and the Princess of Wales. Gisbal (Bute) and his staff inspired several scandalous 1762 prints, including "*Gisbal, Lord of Hebron*" (B.M. 3848), *Gisbal's Preferment; or, The Importation of the Hebronites* (B.M. 3849), and *Gisbal and Bathsheba, in the Hyperborean Tale* (B.M. 3850). *Gisbal* is just one of the many satirical attempts to replace history with literature. Political satirists—both pro- and antiministerial—produced allegorical pieces in which a combination of original allegory and realistic figures was used to duplicate the earlier tactic of generalizing and distancing through the use of historical allusions. Quasi-allegories like *Gisbal* and Churchill's *The Prophecy of Famine*

THE

STAFF of GISBAL:

An Hyperborean SONG,

Tranflated from the Fragments of OSSIAN, the Son of FINGAL.

By a YOUNG LADY.

" *Arma virumque cano.*" VIRGIL.

N. B. This SONG is a fuitable Companion to the Book of GISBAL.

I.

YE frolickfome Laffes in Country and City,
Attend for a while to a frolickfome Ditty!
Thou Spirit of OSSIAN, great Son of FINGAL,
Affift me to fing of the STAFF of GISBAL!
Derry down, &c.

II.

When this notable Chief of the HEBRONITES Land
Before BATHSHEBA ftood, with his STAFF in his Hand,
The Damfels around her cry'd out, one and all,
" What a *wonderful* STAFF is the STAFF of GISBAL" !
Derry down, &c.

III.

From the Days of old ADAM there has not been found,
Thro' the World's ample Circuit, a STAFF fo renown'd:
Not the CHEROKEE KING, or NABOB of BENGAL,
Can boaft fuch a STAFF as the STAFF of GISBAL.
Derry down, &c.

IV.

If Madame Pompadour had this Prodigy feen,
She'd have own'd it was fit for the Ufe of a Queen;
And that LOUIS LE GRAND, with his BATON ROYAL,
Was lefs *magnifique* than the STAFF of GISBAL.
Derry down, &c.

V.

Of fuch exquifite Virtue this STAFF is poffeft,
It will kindle Emotions of Love in your Breaft:
For a proof of this Truth, I appeal to them all,
Who have ever beheld the fam'd STAFF of GISBAL.
Derry down, &c.

VI.

No STAFF ever made of *Gold, Silver,* or *Wood,*
Could compare with this Compound of pure *Flefh* and *Blood:*
A STAFF fo upright, I may venture to call,
A STAFF for a PRINCESS — this STAFF of GISBAL.
Derry down, &c.

VII.

Entomb'd with his Fathers when GISBAL lies rotten,
Though worn to a *Stump,* it fhall ne'er be forgotten:
As a *Trophy* we'll bear it to WESTMINSTER HALL,
And hang up the *Remains* of the STAFF of GISBAL.
Derry down, &c.

VIII.

If Critics fhould cenfure, or Witlings fhould laugh,
And fay " furely MISS ftands in Need of a STAFF,"
I defy the moft fwaggering Blade of them all,
To produce fuch a STAFF as the STAFF of GISBAL.
Derry down, &c.

LONDON: Printed for the AUTHOR, and Sold by the Bookfellers and Print-fellers.
[Price Six Pence.]

69. *"Gisbal, Lord of Hebron"* (B.M. 3848)

70. *Gisbal's Preferment; or, The Importation of the Hebronites* (B.M. 3849)

71. *Gisbal and Bathsheba, in the Hyperborean Tale* (B.M. 3850)

(1763), which satirized the ministry, were counterattacked in similarly conceived poems like *The Wilkiad, a Tale* (1763) and Hugh Baillie's *Patriotism! A Farce* (1763). All the members of this class of political satires shared the faults Horace Walpole recognized in Hugh Dalrymple's *Rodondo; or, The State Jugglers* and Richard Bentley's *Patriotism, A Mock-Heroic*, two 1763 anti-opposition poems Walpole judged to be "of uncommon merit." One of the "greatest faults" of *Patriotism*, Walpole wrote,

> seems to be, that though all the personages appear under allegoric names, all were meant for living characters, till the last canto, when Fate is introduced in its own essence, and though maintained with as sublime dignity as the nature of burlesque would allow, still produces a confusion by not being a piece with the rest of the work. It has the same misfortune with Rodondo of being written on transient ridicules. (*Memoirs*, 3:119)

The confusion Walpole speaks of is very evident in Churchill's *The Prophecy of Famine*, one of his better poems: Churchill seems uncertain whether he is writing "A Scots Pastoral," an epistle to Wilkes, or a narration of Famine's Prophecy. It is difficult to determine at times whether he is addressing an allegorical figure or a human listener. Churchill is confused as well about his relationship to the tradition of political verse satire. *The Prophecy of Famine* is just one example of how uncertain Churchill seems to be about what position he speaks from. Modern critics have noted his apparent lack of positive beliefs and his preoccupation with self. Both, I think, may be traced at least in part to his ambivalent attitude toward the past, an attitude he shared with his contemporaries in satire.

Bolingbroke and his circle espoused a "politics of nostalgia," which enabled them to judge the actions and principles of contemporary politicians against standards of behavior and belief inherited from the past. The rhetorical poses of latter-day Horace, clergyman, and country gentleman, each with a number of received associations, were available to Pope as positions from which to speak. As we have seen, Horace quickly became less desirable to eighteenth-century satirists as a rhetorical mask; Churchill's personal life and own preferences made the mask of clergyman inappropriate; and the role of country gentleman could not be reconciled with the kind of urban political opposition Wilkes and Churchill represented in the early 1760s. As historians have increasingly come to see, 1760 marks a major turning point in British political history. Churchill and his fellow anti-ministerial satirists had more in common with the future development of British politics than with the past Bolingbroke and his circle so often invoked.

The rapid growth after 1760 of extraparliamentary pressures for more popular influence on the British government made satirists' attempts to portray themselves as conservers of former political traditions increasingly difficult to maintain. The accusation in the prominsterial journal *The Briton* (11 September 1762) that the opposition sought to create "an ochlocracy, or mob-commonwealth" now seems not too farfetched in light of recent historical research on the period. Political satire was addressed more consistently than it had ever been before to a mass audience composed mainly of the unenfranchised. Satirists, like the designer of the 1762 print *The Boot & the Bruisers; or, Scotch Politicks 1762* (B.M. 3818), clearly enjoyed the power of the mob. Many political observers came to see a new threat to the constitution arising from increased aristocratic power that had few precedents in recent English history because it was a result of mid-century political and economic developments. Early in the reign of George III, Horace Walpole expressed to Horace Mann his hope that "the Crown can reduce the exorbitance of the peers."[15] Churchill, too, in *The Farewell* (1764) warned against the growth of what Disraeli would later call the "Venetian oligarchy":

> Let not a Mob of Tyrants seize the helm
> Nor titled upstarts league to rob the realm,
> Let not, whatever other ills assail,
> A damned ARISTOCRACY prevail.   (361–64)

And yet, as everyone knew, Wilkes and Churchill depended heavily on the aristocratic earl of Temple for political and financial support and sought to associate themselves with the duke of Newcastle, whom the *North Briton*, no. 37 (12 February 1763), called "the ancient bulwark of the house of *Hanover.*" Similarly, Churchill was both attracted and repelled by England's rapid economic and imperial growth, which the triumphs of the Seven Years' War accelerated. *Gotham* opens with a long passage attacking imperialism while admitting that imperialism rather than tradition or historical precedent is the basis for the poet's own right to rule his imaginary kingdom.

The period 1760–65 was one of rapid political transition, involving changes contemporaries saw only dimly and consequently expressed confusedly. The increased importance of extraparliamentary forces was recognized by many, but politicians were not yet ready to accept the revolutionary implications of a wider franchise. Not even the "Great Commoner" Pitt sought anything resembling democratic government.[16] Satirists like Churchill seemed uncomfortable with the past and unclear about the future: the result was what some have called a preoccupation with the self, or what I think of as a present-mindedness. No new satiric formula had yet been devised to replace the tradition of Pope, which had undergone so many

72. *The Boot & the Bruisers; or, Scotch Politicks* 1762 (B.M. 3818)

transformations in the 1740s and 1750s. But until the unprecedented political issues that arose in George III's reign were fully appreciated, satirists could not develop a new strategy; they had to try to adapt their eclectic inheritance to the new situation. And yet, as if recognizing that the "Old England" so dear to earlier political satirists was no longer desirable after 1760, men like Churchill and Wilkes saw as their enemies most of those earlier satirists who were still living: Hogarth, Johnson, and Paul Whitehead. As the print *"The Irish Stubble alias Bubble Goose"* (B.M. 4068) of 1763 illustrates, the essentially conservative Samuel Johnson and the incipient radical Charles Churchill were no longer members of one family of political satire. Churchill's ambivalent attitude toward Pope expresses the same uncertain sense of a satiric tradition. At times seeing Pope as little more than a maker of sweet music, Churchill also acknowledged him as the standard of satire against which Churchill himself must be measured. On at least one occasion—in "Verses Written in Windsor Park" (1763)—Churchill acknowledged the importance of political satire in Pope's *Windsor Forest* and sought to enlist his great predecessor in the current political struggle.

73. *"The Irish Stubble alias Bubble Goose"* (B.M. 4068)

Janus-like, Churchill's satire looked forward as well. In it we may detect the signs of the future which would succeed the older tradition of political verse satire. Uncomfortable with appeals to the past, Churchill turns in *Gotham* to himself as the ultimate judge of political systems. Increasingly, satirists would appeal not so much to tradition to validate their political positions as to what they thought rationally just. This appeal to reason, in combination with the shift in historiography and the decline of the emblematic tradition, only accelerated the supremacy of prose as the political medium. Here, too, Churchill's work anticipated the future: his contemporary fame as a journalist was almost as great as his fame as a poet.

Appropriately, after Churchill's death the anonymous poet of "A Character" predicted that the satirist's mantle would pass to a writer of prose:

What, tho' inimitable Churchill's hearse
Sav'd thee from all the vengeance of his verse,

Macaulay shall in nervous prose relate
Whence flows the venom that distracts the state.
Thy name will stink in hist'ry's awful page,
Curs'd by thy native land from age to age.

Indicative of the influence of mid-century historiography on political satire
is the poet's specification of Macaulay rather than simply the abstraction
history to carry on from Churchill. Significant, too, is the anonymous poet's
association of England's last important eighteenth-century political satirist
with a historian whose republican principles and faith in rationally based
political systems would have repelled Pope as much as they did Horace
Walpole, whose philosophy is outlined in his *Memoirs*.

> To such absurdities are they reduced whose prejudices hurry them to
> extremes! If the Parliament were not the legal authority for controlling
> the King, where shall we say legality resides? She would answer, In the
> natural right of mankind to be free. That right, then, must be vindi-
> cated by force. Thence we revert to a state of nature. What did that
> state of nature produce? System-builders will tell me, it produced
> deliberation on the right method of governing nations. The answer is
> not true. Time, accident, and events produced government. . . . Mrs.
> Macaulay will allow that there is no check upon an absolute monarch.
> In an aristocracy, the pride, ambition, and jealousy of the nobles are
> some check upon each individual grandee. But what is a check upon the
> people in a republic? In what republic have not the best citizens fallen
> a sacrifice to the ambition and envy of the worst? God grant that, with
> all its deficiencies, we may preserve our own mixed government!
> (3:122–23)

At the same time as prose was becoming a preferred vehicle for political
writing, graphic satire, especially in the form of caricature, continued to
become more important than verse satire. The anonymous author of the
poem *Folly, a Satire on the Times. Written by a Fool, and Younger Brother to
Tristram Shandy* (1763) has John Pridden, publisher of *Folly* itself as well as
many satiric engravings, advise an imaginary author:

> "If thou a fortune woulds't atchieve [*sic*],
> Write, write *politic rhymes*, and thrive:
> Abuse the Ministers, and whirl
> Keen venom at a certain Earl;
> Invent new slanders, forge fresh hints
> For Blasphemy—to aid my *prints*;
> Write Histories, and Libels too,
> And copious Novels not a few."   (Pp. 8–9)

At least for so important a publisher as Pridden, prints have become an essential medium of political satire. Churchill implicitly acknowledges the superiority of graphics when he attempts to duplicate caricature in his verse portraits of Hogarth in *An Epistle to William Hogarth* (1763) and of Lyttelton in *Independence. A Poem, Addressed to the Minority* (1764). Wilkes and Churchill themselves appear as characters in many prints as the media of political satire overlap in the early years of George III's reign. The battle of Churchill and Wilkes on the one hand and Hogarth on the other is a kind of vulgar version of the Renaissance *paragone* between poets and painters over whose art was most important.[17]

The earlier tradition of advice-to-painter poems now includes advice-to-printmaker poems, a demonstration of the poets' recognition, even if unwilling, of the new stature of graphic satire. The unfriendly anonymous author of "A Genuine Receipt to Cure a Mad Dog: In Answer to Mr. Hogarth's Print of the *Bruiser* [i.e., of Churchill]. An Address to Pug the Painter, Who Was Sometime Since Bit by a Scotch Cur" (in *The Scot's Scourge*, 1765) suggests that the artist "Take a print call'd the Times, as a vomit or purge" and be beaten with "a good oaken stick." Then, ". . . I shall send you a hint, / Which will, if pursu'd, make an excellent print." The suggested engraving includes a combination of allegorical and naturalistic figures:

> This Recipe taken, this method pursu'd,
> You'll find, my dear Puggy, will be for your good;
> 'Twill serve to attone for your errors and crimes,
> And rub out your *Bruisers*, your *Wilkes*, and your *Times*.

By the time James Gillray's political engravings began to appear after 1770, the victory for graphic satire was indisputable.

The rhetorical strategy so influential during Pope's life was virtually untenable by the early 1760s. Churchill and his contemporaries could no longer use the older traditions of verbal and visual political satire. Increasingly, the new times demanded new forms. Prose, like that of Junius and Thomas Paine, soon became the dominant method of verbal political statements, as appeals to reason supplanted appeals to tradition as ways to justify ideologies. Gillray and Thomas Rowlandson applied the powers of caricature in depicting new events. The revolutionary upheavals in America and France encouraged artists like William Blake to look to the future rather than the past for political guidance. Even though issues and principles once again became important after 1760, recent historiography made the "politics of nostalgia," which was so rhetorically effective in the 1730s, more and more unattractive to satirists.

Epilogue

Writing an interdisciplinary study like *The Snarling Muse* requires the setting of arbitrary boundaries. To keep the book within manageable limits, I chose to concentrate on but a few of the visual traditions accessible to writers. I have argued that we can better understand one medium of satire, political verse, by comparing and contrasting it with another, political engravings. At the beginning of the period this book covers, satirists enjoyed their inheritance of common iconographic and historiographic traditions that were almost universally recognized by their audiences. Poets and engravers were able to convey particular attacks with a great deal of rhetorical economy. Since virtually all participants agreed on the kind of game and on the rules of the game—in this instance, a belief in constitutional monarchy as the best form of government and a common typology and emblematic iconography—often the briefest allusion to a historical figure or to a conventional image could have political significance. Deviations from recognized iconographic patterns would be recognized by even the illiterate.

After the death of Pope and the fall of Walpole, the rules of the game seemed increasingly inappropriate or untenable. As complicated foreign issues invaded the domestic field, satirists had greater difficulty treating rapidly shifting new problems with traditional rhetorical means. To be understood, foreign relationships needed the expansiveness of prose, not the concision of poetry. In domestic politics, the ministries that succeeded Walpole's did not lend themselves to attacks on the convenient target of a "Great Man" or on a set of measures associated only with ministerial supporters. The Pelhamite system of inclusion of opponents, which replaced the Walpolean system of expulsion of rivals, meant that any politician with a chance of joining the government was soon espousing ministerial programs. If the measures were always the same, then the men were all that were left to attack.

The growing emphasis on individual men was disastrous for the sort of elevated political verse satire Pope and Johnson had written. Typology, which seems to inflate or extend the significance of a particular target—as in the Sporus portrait—became less appropriate as satirists sought to de-flate or restrict the target, usually by either verbal caricature or reductive animal imagery. Typology continued to be used, as in Johnson's Wolsey exemplum, but usually only for general targets, not specific individuals. Lampoons, squibs, and other verbal ephemera were the representative forms of political verse satire in the 1740s and 1750s.

The results for political engravings were vastly different. Before 1742, verbal and visual satirists used quite similar tactics and strategy. After Walpole's fall, as verse satire declined, engraved satire experienced a rebirth in the form of caricature. In the prints, expression replaced content as the method became the message. The target's appearance was rendered so idiosyncratic that he was isolated from his fellow men. He became a locust, a "lump of fat," and finally, a line silhouette which reduced him to a likeness solely his own. So singular does the target become that the artist does not want him to have a context. In traditional iconography there is necessarily a context external to the self.

Just as the rules of the game were becoming less appropriate, they were becoming less defensible as well. The challenges Hume and Smollett were raising to conventional typological historiography were paralleled by challenges to traditional iconography. Works like Joseph Spence's *Polymetis* (1747) and Thomas Blackwell's *Letters Concerning Mythology* (1748) sought to demystify and rationalize the sources of classical icons. We can judge the effect of the challenges in Ronald Paulson's description of a 1775 deck of cards:

> A single-sequence deck of 1775 (Cary Collection, Yale) is intended to teach iconography, but while Justice still appears as a blindfolded woman in Roman dress, Fidelity is now a dog being tempted by a housebreaker with a bone, Wit is Sir John Falstaff, and a Parson is simply a country parson. The old Ripan system of correspondences is being interrupted, not only by biblical equations (Flattery or Deceit is Eve and the serpent) but by rational equations from contemporary experience, decidedly English in reference.[1]

By the early 1760s, when the circumstances seemed ideal for a renaissance of political satire, the rhetorical methods available to Pope and his friends were now, through disuse and attacks on their validity, no longer so readily available to Churchill and his contemporaries. A satirist no longer could safely assume that his audience shared his historiographic premises or his iconographic vocabulary. The rules had to change.

Moreover, the game itself was changing. I chose to end *The Snarling Muse* at 1764 because after the deaths of Churchill and Hogarth the English political scene was dramatically transformed, especially by distant events. Challenges to the very game of constitutional monarchy arose in America and France. Churchill and Wilkes anticipated the kind of radical questionings of the English political system that would soon be taken up overseas. From 1764 to 1783, particularly, when one speaks of the development of English political satire, one must include the colonists who tried, in their rhetorical strategy, to present themselves as what might be called conservative radicals. They attempted to apply some of the rules of the old game to the new one by imitating tactics of *The Craftsman* in order to undermine their government. Prints published in London were reissued in Philadelphia with appropriate modifications. At the same time, however, many, like Paine, showed that new tactics were needed. A study of post-1764 verbal and visual political satire would have to consider the growing political influence of the less educated and unenfranchised, the rise of Methodism, the divided domestic political response to the French Revolution and its aftermath, and the efficiency of political censorship during the war with France. All influenced the kinds of iconography satirists could use and the availability of the past to those who wanted to alter the present. The confluence of causes that led to the flowering of verbal and visual political satire during Walpole's ministry would never recur. Never again would the game and its rules be so universally agreed upon.

Notes

Preface

1. Paul J. Korshin, "The Development of Abstracted Typology in England, 1650–1820," in Earl Miner, ed., *Literary Uses of Typology from the Late Middle Ages to the Present* (Princeton: Princeton Univ. Press, 1977), pp. 147–203.

2. Ronald Paulson, *Popular and Polite Art in the Age of Hogarth and Fielding* (Notre Dame: Univ. of Notre Dame Press, 1979), p. 31.

3. E.g., see Betty Willsher and Doreen Hunter, *Stones: A Guide to Some Remarkable Eighteenth Century Gravestones* (New York: Taplinger Publishing Company, 1979).

4. Jean H. Hagstrum, *The Sister Arts: The Tradition of Literary Pictorialism and English Poetry from Dryden to Gray* (Chicago: Univ. of Chicago Press, 1958); Lawrence Lipking, *The Ordering of the Arts in Eighteenth-Century England* (Princeton: Princeton Univ. Press, 1970); James S. Malek, *The Arts Compared: An Aspect of Eighteenth-Century British Aesthetics* (Detroit: Wayne State Univ. Press, 1974); Ronald Paulson, *Emblem and Expression: Meaning in English Art of the Eighteenth Century* (London: Thames and Hudson, 1975); Morris R. Brownell, *Alexander Pope and the Arts of Georgian England* (Oxford: Clarendon Press, 1978).

5. Peter M. Daly, *Literature in the Light of the Emblem: Structural Parallels Between the Emblem and Literature in the Sixteenth and Seventeenth Centuries* (Toronto: Univ. of Toronto Press, 1979); Ernest B. Gilman, *The Curious Perspective: Literary and Pictorial Wit in the Seventeenth Century* (New Haven: Yale Univ. Press, 1978).

6. Maynard Mack, *The Garden and the City: Retirement and Politics in the Later Poetry of Pope 1731–1743* (Toronto: Univ. of Toronto Press, 1969), p. 128.

7. Herbert M. Atherton, *Political Prints in the Age of Hogarth: A Study of the Ideographic Representation of Politics* (Oxford: Clarendon Press, 1974).

8. Bertrand A. Goldgar, *Walpole and the Wits: The Relation of Politics to Literature, 1722–1742* (Lincoln: Univ. of Nebraska Press, 1976); Howard D. Weinbrot, *Augustus Caesar in "Augustan" England: The Decline of a Classical Norm* (Princeton: Princeton Univ. Press, 1978); Thomas Lockwood, *Post-Augustan Satire: Charles Churchill and Satirical Poetry, 1750–1800* (Seattle: Univ. of Washington Press, 1979).

CHAPTER 1 Anne and Elizabeth

1. For general discussions of the tradition of classical historiography consult Zera S. Fink, *The Classical Republicans: An Essay in the Recovery of a Pattern of Thought*

in Seventeenth-Century England, Northwestern Univ. Studies in Humanities, no. 9 (Evanston: Northwestern Univ. Press, 1945); James William Johnson, *The Formation of English Neo-Classical Thought* (Princeton: Princeton Univ. Press, 1967); Isaac Kramnick, ed., *Lord Bolingbroke: Historical Writings* (Chicago: Univ. of Chicago Press, 1972), pp. xi–liii, and the works listed in his bibliography.

2. In addition to the works listed in Kramnick, *Bolingbroke: Historical Writings*, see Samuel Kliger, *The Goths in England: A Study in Seventeenth- and Eighteenth-Century Thought* (Cambridge: Harvard Univ. Press, 1952), pp. 112–209; Christopher Hill, "The Norman Yoke," in *Puritanism and Revolution: Studies in Interpretation of the English Revolution of the Seventeenth-Century* (London: Secker and Warburg, 1958), pp. 50–122; Moses I. Finley, *The Ancestral Constitution: An Inaugural Lecture* (Cambridge: Cambridge University Press, 1971).

3. The relationship between the two Williams is described in the following historical discussions of the poem: J. R. Moore, "*Windsor Forest* and William III," *MLN* 66 (1951): 451–54; Robert M. Schmitz, *Pope's Windsor Forest 1712: A Study of the Washington University Holograph*, Washington, Univ. Studies, no. 21 (St. Louis, 1952); Earl R. Wasserman, *The Subtler Language: Critical Readings of Neoclassic and Romantic Poems* (Baltimore: The Johns Hopkins Press, 1959), pp. 101–68; Alexander Pope, *Pastoral Poetry and an Essay on Criticism*, ed. E. Audra and Aubrey Williams, in The Twickenham Edition (TE) of the Poems of Alexander Pope, general ed. John E. Butt, 11 vols. in 12 (London: Methuen and Co. Ltd.; and New Haven: Yale Univ. Press, 1939–69), vol. 1. Unless otherwise indicated, all quotations from Pope's poetry refer to the TE by line numbers; Rachel A. Miller, "Regal Hunting: Dryden's Influence on *Windsor Forest*," *Eighteenth-Century Studies* 13 (1979–80): 169–88.

4. For a thorough discussion of how traditional classical and English panegyrics combined the themes of restoration and limitation, see James D. Garrison, *Dryden and the Tradition of Panegyric* (Berkeley, Los Angeles, London: Univ. of California Press, 1975).

5. Wasserman, *The Subtler Language*, pp. 109, 111.

6. Polybius, *Histories*, 12, 25b, quoted in George Nadel, "Philosophy of History Before Historicism," *History and Theory* 3 (1964), reprinted in *Studies in the Philosophy of History: Selected Essays from "History and Theory,"* ed. Nadel (New York: Harper and Row, 1965), p. 57.

7. Bolingbroke, *The Works of Lord Bolingbroke*, 4 vols. (1754: reprint, Westmead, Eng.: Gregg International Publishers, 1969), 2:193.

8. Nadel, "Philosophy of History," p. 50. Thomas Akstens, "Pope and Bolingbroke on 'Examples': An Echo of the *Letters of History* in Pope's Correspondence," *PQ* 52 (1973): 232–38; and Achsah Guibbory, "Dryden's Views of History," *PQ* 52 (1973): 187–204, deal with the poetic treatment of "exemplar history."

9. Consult C. R. Kropf, "Libel and Satire in the Eighteenth Century," *ECS* 9 (1974/75): 153–68.

10. TE 1:152.

11. Ibid.

12. Quoted in TE 1:156.

13. See Donald T. Torchiana, "Brutus: Pope's Last Hero," *JEGP* 61 (1962): 853–67.

14. The phrase is taken from Addison's description in 1712 of the British political system as ideally a balance of power maintained among the Crown, the House of Lords, and the House of Commons. See *The Spectator*, ed. Donald F. Bond, 5 vols. (Oxford: Clarendon Press, 1965), 3:19–20.

15. The *OED* describes the phrase *To stand in awe of* as having "a remarkable grammatical development." Pope probably uses the phrase "Aw'd by his Nobles" to mean, according to one seventeenth-century usage, "dreaded by his Nobles." With this usage the phrase balances "by his Commons curst."

16. Schmitz, *Pope's Windsor Forest 1712*, p. 9.

17. Jean Bodin, *Method for the Easy Comprehension of History* (1566), quoted in Johnson, *Formation*, p. 32.

18. See Hill, "The Norman Yoke," pp. 50–122.

19. Addison, *Spectator* 3:21.

20. TE 1:159.

21. Jonathan Swift, *The Prose Works of Jonathan Swift*, ed. Herbert Davis and Irvin Ehrenpreis, 14 vols. (Oxford: Basil Blackwell, 1939–68), 2:63. See Machiavelli's treatment of *ricorso* in *The Discourses of Niccolo Machiavelli*, ed. Leslie J. Walker, 2 vols. (New Haven: Yale Univ. Press, 1950), vol. 1, bk. 3, pt. 1, pp. 459–63. For the later influence of Machiavelli on political thought see J. G. A. Pocock, *The Machiavellian Moment: Florentine Political Thought and the Atlantic Republican Tradition* (Princeton: Princeton Univ. Press, 1975), and his bibliography.

22. Swift, *Prose Works* 1:230. This work was originally published in 1701 but revised and republished in 1711. Thus the concept of *ricorso* could be used as a standard against which to measure both a sovereign seen to deviate from the immemorial constitution and one who was seen to embody the desired *ricorso*.

23. Consult Elkin Calhoun Wilson, *England's Eliza* (Cambridge: Harvard Univ. Press, 1939); Frances A. Yates, "Queen Elizabeth as Astraea," *Journal of the Warburg and Courtauld Institutes* 10 (1947), reprinted in *Astraea: The Imperial Theme in the Sixteenth Century* (London and Boston: Routledge and Kegan Paul, 1975), pp. 29–87; David R. Hauser, "Pope's Lodona and the Uses of Mythology," *SEL* 6 (1966): 465–82.

24. John M. Wallace, "Dryden and History: A Problem in Allegorical Reading," *ELH* 36 (1969): 265–90, deals with the complexity of historical allegory in this period. Irvin Ehrenpreis, "Explicitness in Augustan Literature," in *Literary Meaning and Augustan Values* (Charlottesville: Univ. Press of Virginia, 1974), pp. 28–30, argues against an allegorical reading of the Lodona episode.

25. Wilson, *England's Eliza*, chap. 5, "Diana," pp. 167–229. Pope owned at least two books that would have made him aware of the Diana-Elizabeth and Cynthia-Elizabeth associations: see Maynard Mack, "Pope's Books: A Biographical Survey with a Finding List," in Maximilliam E. Novak, ed., *English Literature in the Age of Disguise* (Berkeley and Los Angeles: Univ. of California Press, 1977), p. 247, item 49; p. 266, item. 99.

26. Wasserman, *The Subtler Language*, p. 135.

27. Swift, *Prose Works* 1:230.

28. TE 1:171.

29. Frances M. Clements, "Lansdowne, Pope, and the Unity of *Windsor Forest*," *MLQ* 33 (1972): 44–53.

30. Pope, *The Correspondence of Alexander Pope*, ed. George Sherburn, 5 vols. (Oxford: Clarendon Press, 1956), 1:319.

31. Abel Boyer, *The History of the Reign of Queen Anne, Digested into Annals, Year the First* (London, 1703), p. 162.

32. See Norman Ault, "Mr. Alexander Pope: Painter," in *New Light on Pope* (London: Methuen, 1949), pp. 68–100; Robert J. Allen, "Pope and the Sister Arts," in *Pope and His Contemporaries*, ed. James L. Clifford and Louis A. Landa (Oxford: Clarendon Press, 1949), pp. 78–89; Hagstrum, *The Sister Arts*, pp. 210–42; Benjamin Boyce, *The Character-Sketches in Pope's Poems* (Durham, N.C.: Duke Univ. Press, 1962); Chester F. Chapin, *Personification in Eighteenth-Century English Poetry* (1954; reprint, New York: Octagon Books, 1968), pp. 116–30; Jean H. Hagstrum, "Verbal and Visual Caricature in the Age of Dryden, Swift, and Pope," in *England in the Restoration and Early Eighteenth Century*, ed. H. T. Swedenberg, Jr. (Berkeley, Los Angeles, London: Univ. of California Press, 1972), pp. 173–95; James Sambrook, "Pope and the Visual Arts," in *Writers and Their Background: Alexander Pope*, ed. Peter Dixon (Athens, Ohio: Ohio Univ. Press, 1972), pp. 143–71.

33. Ault, "Mr. Alexander Pope," p. 85; Allen, "Pope and the Sister Arts," p. 84.

34. Notable exceptions are Maynard Mack, *The Garden and the City*, pp. 94–95; David B. Morris, "Virgilian Attitudes in Pope's *Windsor-Forest*," *TSLL* 15 (1973): 231–50, esp. pp. 241–43; Pat Rogers, "'The Enamelled Ground': The Language of Heraldry and Natural Description in *Windsor-Forest*," *Studia Neophilologica* 45 (1973): 356–71; Elias F. Mengel, Jr., "The *Dunciad* Illustrations," *ECS* 7 (1973/74): 161–78; Cedric D. Reverand II, "*Ut pictura poesis*, and Pope's 'Satire II, i,'" *ECS* 9 (1975/76): 553–68; Alan T. McKenzie, "The Solemn Owl and the Laden Ass: The Iconography of the Frontispieces to *The Dunciad*," *Harvard Library Bulletin* 24 (1976): 25–39; Morris R. Brownell, *Alexander Pope and the Arts of Georgian England*.

35. John M. Aden, "'The Change of Scepters, and impending Woe': Political Allusion in Pope's *Statius*," *PQ* 52 (1973): 728–38, contends that Pope's version of book 1 of the *Thebais* is an earlier political poem. I find Aden's argument unconvincing.

36. For general discussions of the tradition of *ut pictura poesis*, particularly in England, see Ralph Cohen, *The Art of Discrimination: Thomson's "The Seasons" and the Language of Criticism* (Berkeley and Los Angeles: Univ. of California Press, 1964), pp. 188–247; Hagstrum, *The Sister Arts*, passim; Rensselaer W. Lee, *Ut Pictura Poesis: The Humanistic Theory of Painting* (1940; reprint, New York: Norton, 1967); Lawrence Lipking, *The Ordering of the Arts*, pp. 3–65, 109–207.

37. John Dryden, *Of Dramatic Poesy and Other Critical Essays*, ed. George Watson (London: Dent; New York: Dutton, 1962), 2:183. In his "Preface to the *Iliad* of Homer," Pope repeatedly calls Homer a painter.

38. Quoted in Francis H. Dowley, "The Moment in Eighteenth-Century Art

see Robert Withington, *English Pageantry: An Historical Outline*, vol. 1 (1918; reprint, New York: Benjamin Blom, 1963), pp. 58–64.

21. Reproduced, respectively, in Frank H. Ellis, ed., *Poems on Affairs of State: Augustan Satirical Verse, 1660–1714*, vol. 7 (New Haven and London: Yale Univ. Press, 1975), p. 414; J. V. Guerinot, *Pamphlet Attacks on Alexander Pope 1711–1744: A Descriptive Bibliography* (New York: New York Univ. Press, 1969), p. 166.

22. See B.M. 1722. M. Dorothy George, *English Political Caricature to 1792: A Study of Opinion and Propaganda* (Oxford: Clarendon Press, 1959), p. 76, accepts Pope as the dwarf.

23. Paulson, ed., *Hogarth's Graphic Works* 1:95.

24. George A. Aitken, *The Life and Works of John Arbuthnot* (Oxford: Clarendon Press, 1892), p. 166, mentions Arbuthnot's well-known habit of eating excessively; R. L. Hayley, "The Scriblerians and the South Sea Bubble: A Hit by Cibber," *RES*, n.s. 24 (1973), pp. 452–58.

25. Antal, *Hogarth and His Place*, p. 81. For an extended description of Picart's print see B.M. 1629.

26. The best accounts of this debate are found in Holmes, *British Politics in the Age of Anne*, pp. 1–9. Quentin Skinner, "The Principles and Practice of Opposition: The Case of Bolingbroke versus Walpole," in *Historical Perspectives: Studies in English Thought and Society in Honour of J. H. Plumb*, ed. Neil McKendrick (London: Europa Publications, 1974), pp. 93–128. Rather than multiply notes, I encourage readers to consult the citations found in Skinner's article. Good general historical discussions of the early eighteenth century include J. H. Plumb, *Sir Robert Walpole*, 2 vols. (London: The Cresset Press, 1956–60); Dorothy Marshall, *Eighteenth-Century England* (London: Longman, 1962); Basil Williams, *The Whig Supremacy 1714–1760*, 2d ed. (Oxford: Clarendon Press, 1962); Archibald S. Foord, *His Majesty's Opposition 1714–1830* (Oxford: Clarendon Press, 1964); J. H. Plumb, *The Growth of Political Stability in England 1675–1725* (Harmondsworth, Middlesex: Penguin, 1967); John B. Owen, *The Eighteenth Century 1714–1815* (London: Nelson, 1974).

27. G. C. Robertson, *Bolingbroke*, gen'l. ser. pamphlet G6 (London: The Historical Association, 1947), p. 3.

28. Holmes, *British Politics*, p. 114.

29. The phrase is quoted from the subtitle of Isaac Kramnick, *Bolingbroke and His Circle: The Politics of Nostalgia in the Age of Walpole* (Cambridge: Harvard Univ. Press, 1968), a thorough discussion of Opposition ideology, to which my summary is much indebted.

30. See Peter G. M. Dickson, *The Financial Revolution in England: A Study in the Development of Public Credit 1688–1756* (New York: St. Martin's Press, 1967); Howard Erskine-Hill, "Pope and the Financial Revolution," in *Writers and Their Background: Alexander Pope*, ed. Peter Dixon (Athens, Ohio: Ohio Univ. Press, 1972), pp. 200–229.

31. On the increasing importance of the law in eighteenth-century England see E. P. Thompson, *Whigs and Hunters: The Origin of the Black Act* (London: Penguin,

Criticism," in *Studies in Eighteenth-Century Culture*, vol. 5, ed. Ronald C. Rosbottom (Madison: Univ. of Wisconsin Press, 1976), pp. 317–36.

39. Dryden, *Of Dramatic Poesy*, p. 189.

40. The central scene of the painting is reproduced in Ellis Waterhouse, *Painting in Britain 1530–1790*, 3d. ed. (Baltimore: Penguin, 1969), plate 76; Ronald Paulson, *Emblem and Expression*, p. 17.

41. Steele's interpretation appeared in *The Lover*, no. 33 (11 May 1714). Paulson (*Emblem and Expression*, pp. 232, n. 18) believes Thornhill supplied Steele with the interpretation. Thornhill's later explication is found in *An Explanation of the Painting in the Royal Hospital at Greenwich*. Although Thornhill's pamphlet is undated, it was written clearly after the completion of the painting. Edgar de N. Mayhew, *Sketches by Thornhill in the Victoria and Albert Museum* (London: Her Majesty's Stationery Office, 1967), p. 6, suggests the 1730 date. I quote from Steele's description because it explains those portions of the painting that were completed or at least well under way while Pope was writing *Windsor Forest*.

42. Geoffrey Holmes, *British Politics in the Age of Anne* (London: Macmillan; New York: St. Martin's Press, 1967), p. 6.

43. For arguments that *Windsor Forest* reflects a Jacobite bias, see Moore, "*Windsor Forest* and William III"; and Rogers, "'The Enamelled Ground'. . . ."

44. Reproduced in Roy C. Strong, *Portraits of Queen Elizabeth I* (Oxford: Clarendon Press, 1963), plate 17.

45. Mack, *The Garden and the City*, p. 95. W. Gerald Marshall, "Pope's *Windsor Forest* as Providential History," *Tennessee Studies in Literature* 24 (1979): 82–93, argues that Pope uses the static present tense to reflect the providential perspective he finds in the work. An essay that complements my discussion of Pope's visual tactics in *Windsor Forest* is Pat Rogers, "Time and Space in *Windsor Forest*," in *The Art of Alexander Pope*, ed. Howard Erskine-Hill and Anne Smith (New York: Barnes and Noble, 1979), pp. 40–51.

46. Rogers, "Time and Space," pp. 40–51.

47. See Strong, *Portraits*, pp. 33–43.

48. The best discussion of the ways prints were used against James II and the popular audience they were probably designed for is Lois G. Schwoerer, "Propaganda in the Revolution of 1688–89," *American Historical Review* 82 (1979): 843–74. Many of the prints of 1688–89 are described in the *Catalogue of Prints and Drawings in the British Museum: Division I, Political and Personal Satires*, 11 vols. in 12 pts., ed. Frederic George Stephens, Edward Hawkins, and M. Dorothy George (1870–1954; reprint, London, 1978), vol. 1. Hereafter, the number following a print title indicates the *British Museum* [B.M.] *Catalogue* listing.

49. John Hughes's *House of Nassau* (London, 1702), a panegyric ode on the death of William III, also associates Elizabeth with Anne by concluding with a prediction that the reign of Anne would reestablish England's international dominance:

That Glory to a mighty Queen remains,
To triumph o'er th' extinguish'd Foe.
She shall supply the Thunderer's Place;

As Pallas from th' Aetherial Plains
    Warr'd on the Giants impious Race,
And laid their huge demolish'd Works in smoky Ruins low.
    Then ANNE's shall rival Great ELIZA's Reign,
    And *William's* Genius with a grateful Smile
    Look down, and bless this happy Isle,
And Peace restor'd shall wear her Olive Crown again.   (P. 12)

Hughes's footnote to the line in italics identifies it as a translation of "*the Motto on her Majesty's Coronation Medals*," another source of visual imagery available to eighteenth-century authors that could be used with the classical, architectural, historical, and allegorical imagery of this passage.

CHAPTER 2 "Measures Not Men"

1. The best discussions of *The South Sea Scheme* (B.M. 1722) are Frederick Antal, *Hogarth and His Place in European Art* (New York: Basic Books, 1962), pp. 80–82; Ronald Paulson, ed., *Hogarth's Graphic Works*, rev. ed. (New Haven and London: Yale Univ. Press, 1970), 1:94–96; Paulson, *Hogarth: His Life, Art, and Times* (New Haven and London: Yale Univ. Press, 1971), 1:70–77.

2. Robert Withington, *English Pageantry: An Historical Outline*, vol. 2 (1926; reprint, New York: Benjamin Blom, 1963); David M. Bergeron, *English Civic Pageantry 1558–1642* (Columbia, S.C.: Univ. of South Carolina Press, 1971), pp. 273–308; L. J. Morrissey, "English Pageant-Wagons," *ECS* 9 (1975/76): 353–74; the quotation is from p. 374.

3. Thornhill's engraving is reproduced in David Green, *Queen Anne* (New York: Scribner's, 1970), between pp. 328 and 329.

4. The fullest account of English puppet shows is George Speaight, *The History of the English Puppet Theatre* (New York: Hohn De Graff, 1955). For a brief but suggestive discussion of playing cards, see Ronald Paulson, *Popular and Polite Art*, pp. 85–102.

5. Quoted in Speaight, *History of the English Puppet Theatre*, p. 81.

6. John Gay, *Poetry and Prose*, ed. Vinton A. Dearing and Charles E. Beckwith, 2 vols. (Oxford: Clarendon Press, 1974). All quotations of Gay's poetry are from this edition and will be cited in the text by line numbers.

7. Mario Praz, *Studies in Seventeenth-Century Imagery* (Rome: Edizioni Di Storia E Letteratura, 1964), p. 169.

8. In addition to Praz's work, see Robert J. Clements, *Picta Poesis: Literary and Humanistic Theory in Renaissance Emblem Books* (Rome: Edizioni Di Storia E Letteratura, 1960); Rosemary Freeman, *English Emblem Books* (1948; reprint, New York: Octagon Books, 1966); Atherton, *Political Prints*; Paulson, *Emblem and Expression*. For the sake of concision I have oversimplified the range of complexity found in emblem books; many of these works demanded a very sophisticated knowledge of Biblical and classical sources. The satirists, however, usually chose the images their audience would be most likely to recognize and understand.

For an impressive amount of information about emblem books before 1700 see the illustrated Arthur Henckel and Albrecht Schöne, *Emblem Sinnbildkunst des XVI, und XVII, Jahrhunderts* and its *Supplem* gart, 1967–76). Eighteenth-century emblem books include *Emblems by Caesar Ripa . . . Useful for Orators, Poets, and Painte Lovers of Ingenuity* (London, 1709), an English edition of *Iconologia*; two English editions of Otto Van Veen's 1607 *Mo* acknowledged): *The Doctrine of Morality; or, A View of Human Stoick Philosophy* (London, 1721) and *Moral Virtue Delineated, Three Short Lectures, Both in French and English, on the Most Impor* (London, 1726); Nathaniel Crouch, *Choice Emblems, Divine a Modern; or, Delights for the Ingenious* (London, 1732); and *H Emblems, and Ethnick Tales, with Explanatory Notes* (London,

9. On the problem of the frequently alleged arbitrar Daly, *Literature in the Light of the Emblem*, pp. 36–53.

10. For a variety of bubble prints, see prints nos. 161 *Catalogue*.

11. *Epistle to Bathurst*, l. 69.

12. John Carswell, *The South Sea Bubble* (Stanford: Stanf p. 142.

13. Paulson, *Hogarth*, p. 73.

14. Paulson, ed., *Hogarth's Graphic Works*, 1:96.

15. For a representative example, see George Wither, *Ancient and Moderne* (1635; facsimile reprint, Columbia Carolina Press, 1975), p. 209.

16. See Samuel L. Macey, "Hogarth and the Iconogr ald C. Rosbottom, ed., *Studies in Eighteenth-Century C* Univ. of Wisconsin Press, 1976), pp. 41–53.

17. Antal, *Hogarth and His Place in European Art*, p. 8 to Callot. Although the figure in the completed print described as androgynous rather than feminine, in Hoga for *The South Sea Scheme* Honesty is clearly female. Per soften in the print what I see as the more obvious al Fortune of the drawing, because he added to the engr allegorical images of St. Paul's, Trade, the goat, and the earlier sketch. See A. P. Oppé, *The Drawings of William* Press, 1948), plate 2, catalogue no. 3.

18. The tradition of the Ladder of Virtue can be tr For the importance of the image in medieval iconogr bogen, *Allegories of the Virtues and Vices in Medieval Art:* the Thirteenth Century* (1939; rpt. New York: Norton,

19. The medieval figure of the "Rota falsae religio "Rota verae religionis," may have influenced Hogarth round. See ibid., pp. 70–72, on the figure in medi

20. *Revelation* 20:7–10. The analogy between L common one in the seventeenth century: Dryden's best-known example. For the complicated history of

1975); Douglas Hay, "Property, Authority and the Criminal Law," in *Albion's Fatal Tree: Crime and Society in Eighteenth-Century England*, ed. Hay, Peter Linebaugh. E. P. Thompson (London: Penguin, 1975), pp. 17–63.

32. Charles Bachdolt Realey, "The Early Opposition to Sir Robert Walpole 1720–27," *Bulletin of The University of Kansas Humanistic Studies* 4, nos. 2 and 3 (Philadelphia, 1931): 195.

33. Although *The Craftsman* continued to be published into the next decade, it was eventually bought over to the ministerial side, and Bolingbroke's direct association with the journal ended around 1736. All references to *The Craftsman* are taken from the 14-volume collected edition (London, 1737). The rhetorical strategy and tactics of the journal are dealt with in H. T. Dickinson, *Bolingbroke* (London: Constable, 1970), pp. 184–246; and in Walter Kirkpatrick, "Argumentative Strategies of *The Craftsman*: A Case Study of a Rhetorical Campaign," Ph.D. diss., Univ. of Iowa, 1974.

34. See Kramnick, *Bolingbroke and His Circle*, pp. 273–74, and Dickinson, *Bolingbroke*, p. 343.

35. On the popularity of *The Craftsman* see Laurence W. Hanson, *The Government and the Press 1695–1763* (London: Oxford Univ. Press, 1936), p. 85; and Plumb, *Walpole* 2 : 142.

36. Skinner, "The Principles," pp. 126–27.

37. Consult Geoffrey Holmes, "Harley, St. John and the Death of the Tory Party," in *Britain after the Glorious Revolution 1689–1714*, ed. Holmes (New York: St. Martin's Press, 1969), pp. 216–37; Keith Grahame Feiling, *The Second Tory Party 1714–1832* (London: Macmillan, 1938).

38. Skinner's footnotes 80–145 may serve as a bibliography for this tradition of political theory. The most complete treatment of the tradition as found in the eighteenth century is Caroline Robbins, *The Eighteenth-Century Commonwealthman: Studies in the Transmission, Development and Circumstance of English Liberal Thought from the Restoration of Charles II until the War with the Thirteen Colonies* (Cambridge: Harvard Univ. Press, 1961).

39. J. P. Kenyon, "The Revolution of 1688: Resistance and Contract," in McKendrick, ed., *Historical Perspectives*, p. 56.

40. *A Final Answer to the Remarks on the Craftman's Vindication: And to All the Libels, which have come, or may come from the same Quarter against the Person, last mentioned in the Craftsman of the 22d of May* (London, 1731), p. 5.

41. Hanson, *The Government and the Press*, pp. 17, 67, 17.

42. *The Craftsman*, no. 270, discusses the legal dangers.

43. Swift, *Prose Works* 8 : 14–15.

44. For the importance of typology in the eighteenth century see Steven N. Zwicker, "Politics and Panegyric: The Figural Mode from Marvell to Pope"; and Paul J. Korshin, "The Development of Abstracted Typology in England, 1650–1820," in Earl Miner, ed., *Literary Uses of Typology*, pp. 115–203.

45. Atherton, *Political Prints*, pp. 203–4.

46. The Henry referred to in the caption is Henry VIII of England, one of the arch-tyrants in the eyes of the Opposition.

47. (Reprint, Leeds: The Scholar Press Limited, 1966), p. 161.

48. Ernst Kris, and E. H. Gombrich, *Psychoanalytic Explorations in Art* (New York: International Universities Press, 1952), pp. 190–91.

49. Quoted from Harold Williams, ed., *The Poems of Jonathan Swift*, 2d ed., 3 vols. (Oxford: Clarendon Press, 1958). All quotations from Swift's poetry will be cited in the text from this edition by line numbers.

50. John, Lord Hervey, *Some Materials towards Memoirs of the Reign of King George II*, ed. Romney Sedgewick (London, 1931), 1 : 263.

51. The frontispiece to this anonymous poem is not included in the *British Museum's Catalogue of Political and Personal Satires*. William K. Wimsatt, in his *The Portraits of Alexander Pope* (New Havan: Yale University Press, 1965), describes the folio poem as "apparently an attack on Pope's antagonist Lord Hervey [which] has a crudely engraved frontispiece showing a short humpbacked man, wigged and coated (seconded by a wild man with a club) crossing swords with a man in shirt sleeves and open collar, without hair or wig (seconded by a coated figure with fox's head). Pens, ink-pot, and paper litter the ground. Ink spots (?) appear on the face and around the head of the taller duellist, and from his mouth comes a label bearing the words: 'With foul Disgrace—He daubs my face'" (pp. 363–64).

52. For a discussion of the events surrounding the duel and its influence on Hervey's later satiric career see Robert Halsband, *Lord Hervey: Eighteenth-Century Courtier* (New York and Oxford: Oxford Univ. Press, 1974).

53. A shorter version of this poem was originally published 4 December 1733.

54. I am indebted to John Mulryan for first calling my attention to the tradition of Hercules as an emblem of eloquence. For earlier illustrations of this tradition see Henkel and Schöne, *Emblemata*, pp. 1651–52.

55. Sir Lewis Namier, *The Structure of Politics at the Accession of George III*, 2d ed. (1929; reprint, London: Macmillan, 1957), p. 231.

56. I find unconvincing the argument that Walpole alone was intended as the object of attack. See Kathleen Mahaffey, "Timon's Villa: Walpole's Houghton," *TSLL* 9 (1967): 193–222; Mack, *The Garden and the City*, pp. 272–78. Brownell, *Alexander Pope and the Arts of Georgian England*, p. 317, suggests that Timon and his villa represent a conflation of Walpole's character and Marlborough's estate at Blenheim. The Timon portrait is best seen as another example of an allegory which does not "run upon all Four."

CHAPTER 3: The *Epistle to Bathurst*

1. F. W. Bateson, TE 3, pt. 2, p. 81. Readers of Pope criticism will recognize my general debts to Bateson's introduction to the TE as well as to the following scholars: Earl R. Wasserman, *Pope's "Epistle to Bathurst": A Critical Reading with an Edition of the Manuscripts* (Baltimore: The Johns Hopkins Press, 1960); Boyce, *The Character-Sketches in Pope's Poems*; Mack, *The Garden and the City*; and Howard Erskine-Hill, *The Social Milieu of Alexander Pope: Lives, Examples and the Poetic Response* (New Haven and London: Yale Univ. Press, 1975).

2. Although Wasserman did not discuss the fact, he noted that underlying the religious and moral aspects of the poem, the *Epistle to Bathurst* is fundamentally

political in nature. He recognized that it is "Sir Robert Walpole, whose shadowy figure had hovered in the background of the entire poem, just as it hovered over the politico-economic morality of the age. Indeed, it may be said that by indirection the entire poem is really an attack on Walpole, leader of the Whigs, friend of Chartres and other villains in the poem, patron of Phryne, screener of the directors of the South Sea Company, proponent of the Excise Bill" (p. 54). I will show that the poem had a specific occasion which intensifies the political satire.

3. In 1731 William Pulteney anticipated Pope's comparison of Walpole and Chartres as criminals who acquired estates by similar means. He also stressed Walpole's responsibility for Chartres's freedom. Pulteney speaks of Chartres to Walpole: "I know but *one other Estate in England*, which hath been scraped together by such Means; and I make it a question whether all Mankind will not allow the Proprietor of it to be the honester Man; *Him* I mean, whom you lately saved from the Gallows; and it is the only Thing you ever did in your Life for nothing, when you had an opportunity of making a Penny; but perhaps, you might think the Similitude of your Characters and Circumstances made it impolitick to let Him suffer the Punishment, which He deserved" (*An Answer to One Part of a late Infamous Libel*, pp. 43–44).

4. All references to *The Craftsman* are taken from the 14-volume collected edition (London, 1737).

5. Erskine-Hill, *The Social Milieu*, pp. 243–59.

6. Pope's note to line 20, TE 3, pt. 2, p. 83.

7. For some examples of prints associating Walpole with screens, see B.M. 2539, B.M. 2540, and B.M. 2559. For the origin of Walpole's title "the Skreen-Master General," see J. H. Plumb, *Sir Robert Walpole: The Making of a Statesman* (London: The Cresset Press, 1956), p. 342.

8. TE 3, pt. 2, p. 96.

9. John G. Sperling, *The South Sea Company: An Historical Essay and Bibliographical Finding List*, The Kress Library Series of Publications, no. 17 (Cambridge: Harvard Univ. Press, 1962), p. 83.

10. [Sir John Blunt], *A True State of the South-Sea Scheme, as it was first form'd, etc. With an Enquiry into some of the Causes of the Losses which have ensued. As Also an Abstract of several Clauses of the Acts of Parliament, made against those Directors, and the Grounds of them: with some Remarks on the whole* (London, 1732), p. 106.

11. Erskine-Hill, *The Social Milieu*, p. 166.

12. Paul Langford, *The Excise Crisis: Society and Politics in the Age of Walpole* (Oxford: Clarendon Press, 1975), p. 45, reports that "it is also remarkable how late general interest was really fired by [the Excise Bill]. Even after *The Craftsman*'s articles in October and November there was little or no indication of the storm in the offing. In fact it broke quite suddenly at the end of the year." We must remember that while the *Epistle to Bathurst* was not published until 15 January, it had been at the press since at least 14 December. Pope's correspondence indicates that the poem may have been finished before the end of October; see Pope, *Correspondence* 3: 327, 335, 337. TE 3, pt. 2, pp. xxii–xxiii, summarizes evidence that Pope worked on some parts of the poem as early as 1730.

13. *The Journals of the House of Lords* 24 : 255. William Cobbett, ed., *Cobbett's*

Parliamentary History of England (London, 1806–20), 9:91, identifies Lord Bathurst as the speaker.

14. See Hervey, *Memoirs* 1:184–92, 197–200, for an account of the South Sea Company debate in the House of Lords. In Harold Williams, ed., *The Correspondence of Jonathan Swift*, 5 vols (Oxford: The Clarendon Press, 1965), 4:22 Gay tells Swift "I believe the Parliament next Year intend to examine the Southsea Scheme."

15. *Journals of the House of Lords* 24:295. Lord Hervey found "this protest . . . so very extraordinary" that he could not "help transcribing" the last two articles, one of which I quote (*Memoirs* 1:198).

16. In *The Social Milieu*, Erskine-Hill shows how accurate Pope's information is.

17. Ibid., p. 260. Mack, *The Garden and the City*, pp. 184–85, n.5, discusses the political implications of Quadrille.

18. In *The Craftsman*, no. 80 (13 January 1728), Walpole is the great magician "Signoir Roberto."

19. A manuscript of the poems indicates that the "watchful Ministers" were first ironically intended to be identified as the Earl of Sunderland and Walpole, the two ministers most often held culpable for the bubble. There is also evidence that allusions to the South Sea Bubble were originally even stronger in this passage than they are in the published version. See Wasserman, *Pope's Epistle to Bathurst*, p. 347.

20. Bateson is probably mistaken in identifying Turner as Richard Turner. Pope is more likely referring to Edward Turner, whose obituary in *The Gentleman's Magazine* (March 1737) reads: "Edw. Turner, Esq; a Bencher of *Grays-Inn*. He was one of the Proprietors of the *Charitable Corporation* and lost 70,000 £. notwithstanding which he died very rich." The sum of money lost and the association with the *Charitable Corporation* match details Pope noted in 1735.

Pope's use of the past tense to describe Turner in a note of 1735 does not necessarily indicate that Turner was dead when the note was written. In another footnote added in 1735, Pope describes Sir William Colepepper in the past tense (l. 53), even though Colepepper lived until 1740.

21. Cobbett, *Parliamentary History* 8:1049–51.

22. Mack, *The Garden and the City*, p. 88, identifies the allusion to Zeus's possession of Danae in Horace's sixteenth ode of the third book. See Marin Le Roy Gomberville, *Moral Virtue delineated, In One Hundred and Three short Lectures . . .* , trans. Thomas Mannington Gibbs (London, 1726), pp. 98–99, for a depiction of Horace's golden shower as an emblem of "Money corrupts all men." Walpole, as the minister "Dives," is associated with "Golden Showers" in *C{ourt} and Country. A Play of Seven Acts. In which will be review'd. the Entertaining Scene of the Blundering Brothers. To which is Added. The Comical Humours of Punch. The Whole concluding with the Grand Masque. call'd. The Downfall of Sejanus. Written by a Masquerader . . .* (London, 1735).

23. Paul J. Korshin, "The Development of Abstracted Typology," p. 151, notes the Balaam-Judas parallel.

CHAPTER 4: "The Snarling Muse"

1. Pope, *Correspondence* 3 : 345. Pope's description of himself as a "preacher" is important because the Balaam portrait may have been inspired by contemporary divines: see Howard H. Erskine-Hill, "The Lucky Hit in Commerce and Creation: Atterbury and Pope's Sir Balaam," *N&Q* 212 (1967): 407–8; Peter Dixon, *The World of Pope's Satires: An Introduction to the Epistles and Imitations of Horace* (London: Methuen, 1958), p. 147.

2. Lord Bathurst to Swift, *The Correspondence of Jonathan Swift* 4 : 132.

3. John Butt, TE 4 : xxxvi.

4. Joseph Spence, *Observations, Anecdotes, and Characters of Books and Men*, ed. James M. Osborn (Oxford: Clarendon Press, 1966), 1, no. 321a. Pope's account of how and when he began his political *Imitations of Horace* is corroborated by Bolingbroke: see Spence, no. 321. It should be noted, however, that, as John Butt points out, "Pope had been a translator and imitator all his life" (TE 4 : xxix).

5. The fullest discussions of the relation between Horace and Pope are Reuben A. Brower, *Alexander Pope: The Poetry of Allusion* (Oxford: Clarendon Press, 1959); and Mack, *The Garden and the City*. As Howard D. Weinbrot has recently shown us (see n. 11, below), the Horatian pose was not one Pope could long feel comfortable in. Perhaps Pope's recognition of Horace's less attractive side encouraged him to imitate Donne in his next poem.

6. Mack, *The Garden and the City*, p. 188.

7. Pope, *Correspondence* 3 : 11, 52n.

8. Mack, *The Garden and the City*, p. 121.

9. TE 4 : 3.

10. See the discussions of libel in C. R. Kropf, "Libel and Satire in the Eighteenth Century"; Robert Halsband, "Pope's 'Libel and Satire,'" *ECS* 8 (1974/75): 473–74; Richard Reynolds, "'Libels and Satires! Lawless Things Indeed!'" *ECS* 8 (1974/75): 475–77.

11. For important reconsiderations of how eighteenth-century writers viewed Caesar Augustus see Howard D. Weinbrot, "History, Horace, and Augustus Caesar: Some Implications for Eighteenth-Century Satire," *ECS* 7 (1973–74): 391–414; Malcom Kelsall, "Augustus and Pope," *HLQ* 39 (February 1976): 117–31; Weinbrot, *Augustus Caesar in "Augustan" England*.

12. See the account in Laurence Hanson, *Government and the Press 1695–1763* (London: Oxford Univ. Press, 1936), pp. 67–68.

13. ——— Gerard uses Pope's own imagery against him in *An Epistle to the Egregious Mr. Pope, In Which The Beauties of his Mind and Body Are Amply Displayed* (London, 1734):

The next Farce-Scene a Raree-Show affords,
It gives us *Pope* and Horace measuring Swords;
Our Poet now become an Errant-Knight,
May combat Windmills with a *Quixot's* Might   (P. 13)

14. Ronald Paulson, "Satire, Poetry, and Pope," in *English Satire: Papers Read at a Clark Library Seminar, January 15, 1972* (Los Angeles, 1972), p. 81.

15. See Cedric D. Reverand II, *"Ut pictura poesis."*

16. Mack, *The Garden and the City*, p. 182.

17. Ibid., p. 232.

18. See Perez Zagorin, *The Court and the Country: The Beginning of the English Revolution* (London: Routledge and Kegan Paul, 1969).

19. The discussions of the *Imitations of Horace* I have found most useful are Robert W. Rogers, *The Major Satires of Alexander Pope* (Urbana: Univ. of Illinois Press, 1955), pp. 66–93; Reuben A. Brower, *Alexander Pope: The Poetry of Allusion*, pp. 163–87, 282–318; Thomas E. Maresca, *Pope's Horatian Poems* (Columbus, Ohio: Ohio State Univ. Press, 1966); John Butt, TE 4:xiii–xliv; John M. Aden, *Something Like Horace: Studies in the Art and Allusion of Pope's Horatian Satires* (Knoxville: Vanderbilt Univ. Press, 1969); and Howard D. Weinbrot, *The Formal Strain: Studies in Augustan Imitation and Satire* (Chicago and London: Univ. of Chicago Press, 1969), pp. 129–64. The most recent treatment of Pope's imitations of Donne is Aubrey L. Williams, "What Pope Did to Donne," in Donald Kay, ed., *A Provision of Human Nature: Essays on Fielding and Others in Honor of Miriam Austin Locke* (University, Ala.: Univ. of Alabama Press, 1977), pp. 111–19.

20. W. Walker Wilkins, ed., *Political Ballads of the Seventeenth and Eighteenth Centuries* (London: Longman, 1860), p. 265. It is possible that Pope's "Captain" was intended to be a conflation of George II and Walpole, satirized as Captain Macheath in the *Beggar's Opera* and often accused of commanding "like Law."

21. Foord, *His Majesty's Opposition 1714–1830*, p. 127.

22. Samuel Johnson, *Lives of the English Poets*, 2 vols. (New York: Dutton, 1968), 2:42.

23. Peter J. Schakel, *The Poetry of Jonathan Swift: Allusion and the Development of a Poetic Style* (Madison: Univ. of Wisconsin Press, 1978), p. 4.

24. Gay to Swift, 16 May 1732, in C. F. Burgess, ed., *The Letters of John Gay* (Oxford: The Clarendon Press, 1966), p. 122.

25. All quotations from Gay's poetry are taken from *John Gay: Poetry and Prose*, ed. Charles E. Beckwith and Vinton A. Dearing, 2 vols. (Oxford: Clarendon Press, 1974).

26. P. 5. Except for the addition of a new twelve-line opening, *The Dutchess's Epistle* is the text of *Mr. Taste's Tour from the Island of Politeness, to that of Dulness and Scandal* (London, 1733).

27. As if to counter Opposition attacks on the "Great Man," this ministerial print shows a tiny Walpole assailed by giants. When, in 1741, Walpole's political demise seemed imminent, the Opposition reduced the "Great Man" to the size of a pygmy in *The Protest* (B.M. 2488).

28. The fullest treatments of the political background to *Epistle* 2:1 are Manuel Schonhorn, "The Audacious Contemporaneity of Pope's Epistle to Augustus," *SEL* 8 (1968): 431–43; "Pope's *Epistle to Augustus*: Notes Toward a Mythology," *Tennessee Studies in Literature* 16 (1971): 15–33.

29. John, Baron Hervey, *Memoirs* 2:261.

30. Ibid.

31. *The Yale Edition of the Works of Samuel Johnson* ed. Allen T. Hazen, John H.

Middendorf, et al. (New Haven: Yale Univ. Press, 1958—), 6:48, 49, 53, 56, 60.

32. This shift is discussed in Isaac Kramnick, "Augustan Politics and English Historiography: The Debate on the English Past, 1730–35," *History and Theory* 6 (1967): 33–56.

33. Samuel Johnson, *Works* 6:60; 10:25.

34. Hervey makes the accusation in *Observations on the Writings of the Craftsman* (London, 1730) and repeats it in *The Conduct of the Opposition, and the Tendency of Modern Patriotism . . .* (London, 1734).

35. The three prints are reproduced in Mack, *The Garden and the City*, pp. 130, 142, 133.

36. James M. Osborn, "Pope, the Byzantine Empress, and Walpole's Whore," *RES* 6 (1955): 372–82, reprinted in *Essential Articles for the Study of Alexander Pope*, ed. Maynard Mack, rev. ed. (Hamden, Conn.: Archon Books, 1968), p. 585.

37. Pope, *Correspondence* 3:423.

38. Brower, *The Poetry of Allusion*, p. 312.

39. Reproduced in Paulson, *Hogarth: His Life, Art, and Times*, p. 75. Picart's engraving was apparently the model for both the 1742 print *Magna Farta; or, The Raree Show at St. J{ames}'s* (B.M. 2575) and the 1743 print *Faction Display'd* (B.M. 2603).

40. In addition to the article by Osborn, see the unconvincing source offered by John M. Aden, "Another Analogue to Pope's Vice Triumphant," *MP* 66 (1968/69): 150–51.

41. Mack, *The Garden and the City*, pp. 141–50.

42. Bolingbroke, *Works* 1:409.

43. Purvis E. Boyette, "Pope's *Epilogue to the Satires, Dialogue II*, 171–82," *Explicator* 24 (1965), item 46.

CHAPTER 5: **The Politics of Education in *Dunciad* 4**

1. Leo Braudy, "Recent Studies in the Restoration and Eighteenth Century," *Studies in English Literature* 17 (Summer 1977): 538; Braudy here is reviewing Goldgar, *Walpole and the Wits*, the most thorough discussion of the Opposition's view of the relationship between political and cultural decay.

2. The term "anti-epic" is from John E. Sitter, *The Poetry of Pope's Dunciad* (Minneapolis: Univ. of Minnesota Press, 1971). See also Aubrey L. Williams, *Pope's Dunciad: A Study of its Meaning* (Baton Rouge and London: Louisiana Univ. Press, 1955); Brower, *Alexander Pope: The Poetry of Allusion*, pp. 317–61; William E. Rivers, "Backgrounds to Pope's Satire of Education," Ph.D. diss., Univ. of North Carolina, 1976; and C. R. Kropf, "Education and the Neoplatonic Idea of Wisdom in Pope's *Dunciad*," *Texas Studies in Language and Literature* 14 (1973): 593–604.

3. For a discussion of the ways in which Pope extended the political implications in the first three books for the 1743 edition, see Mack, *The Garden and the City*, pp. 150–62.

4. James Sutherland, ed., *The Dunciad*, the Twickenham Edition of the Poems of Alexander Pope 5:339.

5. This phrase is borrowed from Alan Dugald McKillop, "Ethics and Political History in Thomson's *Liberty*," in *Pope and His Contemporaries: Essays Presented to George Sherburn*, ed. James L. Clifford, and Louis A. Landa (Oxford: Clarendon Press, 1949), pp. 215–29. See also Alan D. McKillop, *The Background of Thomson's Liberty*, Rice Institute Pamphlet, 38, no. 2 (Houston: Rice Univ. Press, 1951). Thomson's poetry is quoted from J. Logie Robertson, *The Complete Poetical Works of James Thomson* (Oxford: Oxford Univ. Press, 1908).

6. Mack, *The Garden and the City*, p. 161.

7. Ian Jack, *Augustan Satire: Intention and Idiom in English Poetry 1660–1750* (Oxford: Clarendon press, 1952), p. 124.

8. TE 5:269.

9. Mack, *The Garden and the City*, pp. 152–53.

10. See William Kinsley, "Physico-Demonology in Pope's 'Dunciad' IV, 71–90," *Modern Language Review* 70 (1975): 20–31.

11. For additional associations of the rise of opera and the decline of political freedom see James Miller, *Harlequin-Horace; or, The Art of Modern Poetry* (London, 1731), ll. 330–59; and Samuel Johnson, *London*, ll. 124–31.

12. Dulness's proclamation is literally a speech given from the throne, but on a more explicitly political level, it is a Speech from the Throne, the speech with which the monarch annually opens the new session of Parliament. Addressed to both Houses of Parliament convened in the House of Lords, the British Speech from the Throne is analogous to the American State of the Union Address. As is customary in the Speech from the Throne, Dulness describes the past, present, and future states of her realm. Not infrequently, the Country Interest saw the monarch as the spokesman for the minister: "Speeches from the Throne are always considered as the Speeches of the Minister, and have been more peculiarly so of late Years, as containing an Enumeration of his past, and a short Sketch of his intended Measures." [Thomas Carte?], *The Case Fairly Stated: In a Letter from a Member of Parliament in the Country Interest to One of his Constituents* (London, 1745), p. 14.

George Sherburn, "The *Dunciad*, Book IV," *Texas Studies in Literature and Language* 24 (1944), reprinted in *Essential Articles*, pp. 730–46, points out that "Book IV presents a grand drawing-room, appropriate for a royal birthday, at which titles or orders of merit are bestowed by the Queen of Dulness. The scene is chiefly that of such a drawing-room, but it unfolds in a slightly confusing dreamlike fashion into an academic meeting for the conferring of degrees" (p. 734). The "confusing dreamlike fashion" is increased by what I think is an allusion to the medieval visual topos of the presentation scene, in which a translator or author offers his work to his patron—as "Montalto" does in *Dunciad* 4:101–18. For a brief, illustrated discussion of this topos see Elizabeth H. Hageman, "John Foxe's *Henry VIII* as *Justitia*," *The Sixteenth Century Journal* 10 (1979): 35–43, esp. p. 36.

For the sources in Bolingbroke and Filmer of Dulness's speech see Oswyn Murray, "Divine Right in 'The Dunciad' (IV, 175–88)," *Notes and Queries* 213

(1968): 208–11. I believe that Murray is mistaken (p. 210) in not thinking George II as well as Filmer is alluded to.

13. Translated in the Loeb edition of Claudian, *On Stilicho's Consulship* (Cambridge: Harvard Univ. Press; and London: William Heinemann, 1963), p. 51.

14. Kramnick, ed., *Bolingbroke: Historical Writings*, p. 275.

15. Pope's note to line 176 cites the seventeenth-century historian Arthur Wilson.

16. Hervey, *Ancient and Modern Liberty Stated and Compared* (London, 1734), p. 51.

17. Paul de Rapin Thoyras, *History of England . . . Abridged in 2 Vols.* (London, 1732–33), 2:235. Pope, Bolingbroke, and Thomson all agreed with Rapin's judgement that the reign of James I caused the rise of parties in England.

18. See, for example, Howard H. Erskine-Hill, "The 'New World' of Pope's *Dunciad*," *Renaissance and Modern Studies* 6 (1962), reprinted in *Essential Articles*, pp. 803–24.

19. Joseph Spence, *Observations* 1, no. 337.

20. Robert Molesworth, Viscount, "Preface" to *An Account of Denmark, As It Was in the Year 1692* (London, 1694), unpaginated.

21. Alexander Chalmers, ed., *The Works of the English Poets, from Chaucer to Cowper* (London, 1810), 10:531.

22. Ibid., 14:174. The encouragement actually comes from Virgil's "awful form."

23. However, *Dunciad* 4:405–19 and Pope's note to line 409 contain pointed references to Queen Caroline, who died in 1737 from an umbilical rupture suffered in the birth of her last child. Pope wrote a notorious couplet on her death: "Here lies wrapt up in forty thousand towels / The only proof that C—— had bowels" (TE 6:390). Given the cause of death and Pope's known animus toward the queen and king, *Dunciad* 4:415–16 ("And lo the wretch! whose vile, whose insect lust / Lay'd this gay daughter of the Spring in dust") may contain a particularly vicious hit at George II. The king had at least once before been blamed for his wife's death. Egmont records in his diary on Wednesday, 26 July 1738, that "A vile libel was some days past affixed to Kensington Gate by some Jacobite, not yet discovered, and therefore there is not much spoken of it:

> Here lives a man of fifty-four,
> Whose Royal Father's will he tore,
> Who thrust his children out of door,
> Then killed his wife and took a whore.

Diary of the First Earl of Egmont (Viscount Percival), vol. 2 (London: Historical Manuscripts Commission, 1923): 503.

24. Bolingbroke, *Works* 2:23.

25. Quoted in Basil Williams, *Carteret and Newcastle: A Contrast in Contemporaries* (Cambridge: Cambridge Univ. Press, 1943), p. 151.

26. TE 4:332.

27. Pope, *Correspondence* 4:169.

28. Ibid., p. 250.
29. Bolingbroke, *Works*, 2:373.
30. Pope, *Correspondence* 4:365.
31. Ibid., p. 5.
32. Pope's comprehensive indictment of contemporary education, as I have described it, anticipates Catherine Macaulay's very similar attack in the "Introduction" to her *History of England* (London, 1763). Macaulay, too, sees the educational system that embraces grammar school, the universities, and the grand tour as inculcating the principles of tyranny and absolutism.
33. S. K. Heninger, Jr., *Touches of Sweet Harmony: Pythagorean Cosmology and Renaissance Poetics* (San Marino: The Huntington Library, 1974), p. 269. Heninger reproduces on p. 270 an emblem of "Hercules at the crossroads of the letter Y."
34. For a learned discussion of ape imagery see H. W. Janson, *Apes and Ape Lore in the Middle Ages and the Renaissance* (London: Univ. of London, 1952), esp. pp. 199–237.
35. James A. Freeman, *Milton and the Martial Muse: Paradise Lost and European Traditions of War* (Princeton: Princeton Univ. Press, 1980), pp. 186–99, discusses both positive and negative traditions of bee imagery. S. K. Heninger, Jr., *The Cosmographical Glass: Renaissance Diagrams of the Universe* (San Marino: The Huntington Library, 1977), pp. 31–81, shows us the universe Dulness upsets.
36. For a reproduction of Verrio's painting on the drawing room ceiling at Hampton Court of Queen Anne as Justice, see Green, *Queen Anne*, p. 137. For the tradition of Jove or Justice enthroned, see Jane Aptekar, *Icons of Justice: Iconography and Thematic Imagery in Book V of the Faerie Queene* (New York: Columbia Univ. Press, 1969), pp. 13–38.
37. The verses also accompany George Bickham's 1731 print *The Syren of the Stage: A Satire on Madame Cuzzoni* (B.M. 1882).
38. Paulson, ed. *Hogarth's Graphic Works* 1:260.
39. See Samuel C. Chew, *The Pilgrimage of Life* (New Haven: Yale Univ. Press, 1962), esp. pp. 12–34, 226–52, and the accompanying illustrations for the Renaissance representations of Time, Truth, Justice, and Death that Pope draws upon in *Dunciad* 4.

CHAPTER 6: **After the Fall**

1. James Sutherland, ed., *The Dunciad*, pp. 344–45.
2. See Robert W. Williams, "Some Baroque Influences in Pope's *Dunciad*," *British Journal of Aesthetics* 9 (April 1969): 186–94; and Teona Tone Gneiting, "Pictorial Imagery and Satiric Inversion in Pope's *Dunciad*," *ECS* 8 (1974/75): 420–30.
3. *The Idea of a Patriot King* (1749; reprint, Indianapolis: Bobbs-Merrill, 1965), pp. 6–7. Although Bolingbroke's *Idea* was not published until 1749, it was written circa 1738 and the manuscript was placed in Pope's keeping. See Mabel Hessler Cable, "*The Idea of a Patriot King* in the Propaganda of the Opposition to Walpole, 1735–39," *PQ* 18 (1939): 119–30; Giles Barber, "Bolingbroke, Pope, and the *Patriot King*," *The Library*, 5th ser., 19 (1964): 67–89; and Frank T.

Smallwood, "Bolingbroke *vs.* Alexander Pope: The Publication of the *Patriot King*," *Papers of the Bibliographical Society of America* 65 (1971): 225–41.

4. *The Idea*, p. 14. Oswyn Murray, "Divine Right in 'The Dunciad' (IV, 175–88)," *N&Q* 213 (1968): 208–11 cites Bolingbroke as a source for Pope's passage.

5. Bolingbroke, *Historical Writings*, p. 149.

6. The most detailed history of political events between December 1741 and June 1747 is John B. Owen, *The Rise of the Pelhams* (1957; reprint, New York: Barnes and Noble; London: Methuen, 1971). A good general survey of the period 1714–60 is W. A. Speck, *Stability and Strife: England 1714–1760* (London: Edward Arnold, 1977).

7. Quoted in Owen, *The Rise of the Pelhams*, pp. 15–16.

8. For example, Pulteney is an exemplar of shameful perfidy in Tobias George Smollett, *A Complete History of England, from the Descent of Julius Caesar to the Treaty of Aix la Chapelle, 1748*, 11 vols. (1757–60), 11:110–11.

9. *Diary of the First Earl of Egmont* 1:251.

10. *The Works, of The Right Honourable Sir Charles Hanbury Williams* (London, 1822), 1:132. All quotations from Williams's poetry are taken from this three-volume edition annotated by Horace Walpole.

11. Walpole to Sir Horace Mann, 24 December 1744, *Horace Walpole's Correspondence*, ed. Wilmarth S. Lewis, et al. (New Haven and London: Yale Univ. Press, 1937–), 18:549.

12. Walpole to Sir Horace Mann, 26 June 1747, 12 January 1748, 21 March 1746, in ibid., 19:418, 455, 229.

13. Williams, *Works* 2:198.

14. Walpole to Sir Horace Mann, 27 October 1755, *Walpole's Correspondence* 20:506.

15. Quoted in Speck, *Stability and Strife*, p. 261.

16. Horace Walpole, *Memoirs of the Last Ten Years of the Reign of George the Second* (London, 1822), 1:201.

17. Both poems are found in *The Foundling Hospital for Wit. Number III. By Timothy Silence, Esq.* (London, 1746).

18. See John B. Owen, "George II Reconsidered," in Anne Whiteman, J. S. Bromley, and P. G. M. Dickson, eds., *Statesmen, Scholars and Merchants: Essays in Eighteenth-Century History Presented to Dame Lucy Sutherland* (Oxford: Clarendon Press, 1973), pp. 113–34. In addition, I am indebted to conversations with Stephen Baxter for information on George II's dominant role in foreign affairs.

19. Atherton, *Political Prints*, p. 205.

20. Ibid., p. 121.

21. *Walpole's Correspondence* 18:33.

22. Gray, *Correspondence*, ed. Paget Toynbee and Leonard Whibley, with Corrections and Additions by H. W. Starr, 3 vols. (Oxford: Clarendon Press, 1971), 1:207.

23. In Kris, ed., *Psychoanalytic Explorations in Art*, p. 190.

24. See Atherton, *Political Prints*, pp. 51–60, for a discussion of Townshend and his work.

25. Ibid., pp. 228–51, mentions a number of animal prints that appeared at mid-century.

26. Walpole to Sir Horace Mann, 20 April 1757, *Walpole's Correspondence* 21:77.

CHAPTER 7: **The Writing of History at Mid-Century**

1. Lord Bolingbroke, *Historical Writings*, introd. Isaac Kramnick, pp. 28–29. All future citations of Bolingbroke's *Letters* in the text refer to this edition.

2. The full title of Warburton's pamphlet is *The Nature of National Offences Truly Stated: And the Peculiar Case of the Jewish People Rightly Explained: Shewing that Great Britain, in its Present Circumstances, May Reasonably Aspire to the Distinguished Protection of Heaven: A Sermon Preached on the General Fast Day, Appointed to be Observed December 18, 1745.*

3. There are a number of mid-century political verses, including some by Sir Charles Hanbury Williams, which parody the style but do little with the content of the Bible. Sacred history is rarely, if ever, used as the basis for sustained political fiction in the 1740s and 1750s in the way it had been a century earlier.

4. See Weinbrot, *Augustus Caesar in "Augustan" England.*

5. For much of the information in this paragraph I am indebted to Addison Ward, "The Tory View of Roman History," *SEL* 4 (1964): 413–56.

6. Ibid., p. 425.

7. Baron De Montesquieu, *The Spirit of the Laws*, trans. Thomas Nugent, introd. Franz Neumann (New York: Hafner Press, 1949), p. 315.

8. In a footnote to Hume's essay "Of the Protestant Succession," in *Essays Moral, Political and Literary by David Hume* (Oxford: Oxford Univ. Press, 1963), p. 491. Future references to this edition of Hume's *Essays* will be cited by volume and page number within the text.

9. In the past decade there have been a number of challenges to the long-standing misconception of Hume as a Tory historian: Leo Braudy, *Narrative Form in History and Fiction* (Princeton: Princeton Univ. Press, 1970), pp. 31–90; Constant Noble Stockton, "Hume—Historian of the English Constitution," *ECS* 4 (1971): 277–93; Duncan Forbes, *Hume's Philosophical Politics* (Cambridge: Cambridge Univ. Press, 1975); John J. Burke, Jr., "Hume's *History of England*: Waking the English from a Dogmatic Slumber," in *Studies in Eighteenth-Century Culture*, vol. 7, ed. Roseann Runte (Madison: Univ. of Wisconsin Press, 1978), pp. 235–50; James Conniff, "Hume on Political Parties: The Case for Hume as a Whig," *ECS* 12 (1978/79): 150–73.

10. David Hume, *The Letters of David Hume*, ed. J. Y. T. Greig, 2d ed., 2 vols. (1932; reprint, Oxford: Clarendon Press, 1969), 1:258. Future references to this edition of Hume's *Letters* will be cited by volume and page numbers within the text.

11. David Hume, *The History of Great Britain: The Reigns of James I and Charles I*, ed. and with an introduction by Duncan Forbes (Harmondsworth: Penguin, 1970), p. 251. The reprint of the first edition, superbly introduced by Forbes, is hereafter cited within the text as 1 (1754). Quotations from the volume of Hume's *History* covering Charles II and James II are hereafter cited within the text as 2

(1759). Because the two first published volumes created the greatest reaction, I choose to quote from them as they first appeared—before they were revised to take their place as the last two volumes of the 1763 collected edition. All other quotations from Hume's *History* are taken from the 1763 collected edition of 8 vols., as reprinted in 1803.

12. "Post-script" to *Moral and Political Dialogues* (London, 1761 ed.), quoted in Ernest Campbell Mossner, *The Life of David Hume* (1954; reprint, Oxford: Clarendon Press, 1970), p. 302.

13. Edward Gibbon, *Gibbon's Journal to January 28th, 1763*, ed. and with an introduction by D. M. Law (New York: Norton, 1929), p. 103. Gibbon is contemplating writing the history of Sir Walter Raleigh. One problem, among others, would be how to compete in English history-writing with "the original philosophic genius of *Hume*."

14. Horace Walpole to Richard Bentley, 27 March 1755, in Horace Walpole, *Horace Walpole's Correspondence* 35:214. For Walpole's less favorable reactions to the succeeding volumes of the History, see Walpole to George Montague, 22 September 1765; Walpole to Henry Zouch, 15 March 1759, *Correspondence* 10:176; 16:28.

15. David Hume, *New Letters of David Hume*, ed. Raymond Klibansky and Ernest C. Mossner (1954; reprint, Oxford: Clarendon Press, 1969), p. 69.

16. *The Philosophical Works of David Hume*, ed. T. H. Green and T. H. Grose, 4 (London, 1874–75): 68.

17. Richard Hurd, *Moral and Political Dialogues; With Letters on Chivalry and Romance*, 3d ed. (1765; reprint, Westmead: Gregg International, 1972), 2:328.

18. Catherine Graham Macaulay, *The History of England from the Assession of James I to the Elevation of the House of Hanover* (London, 1763), 6:vii.

19. See Reed Browning, "Samuel Squire: Pamphleteering Churchman," *Eighteenth-Century Life* 5 (1978): 12–20.

20. See Marie Peters, "The *Monitor* on the Constitution, 1755–1765: New Light on the Ideological Origins of English Radicalism," *EHR* 86 (1971): 706–25.

21. Scholars have almost completely ignored Smollett's *History*. For two recent treatments see: Donald Greene, "Smollett the Historian: A Reappraisal," in *Tobias Smollett: Bicentennial Essays Presented to Lewis M. Knapp*, ed. G. S. Rousseau and P.- G. Boucé (New York: Oxford Univ. Press, 1971), pp. 25–56; Robin Fabel, "The Patriotic Briton: Tobias Smollett and English Politics, 1756–1771," *ECS* 8 (1974): 100–114.

22. Edmund Burke, *The Works of Edmund Burke*, ed. S. U. Pinney (Boston: Little, Brown & Co., 1871), 7:478–79.

23. J. G. A. Pocock, *The Ancient Constitution and the Feudal Law: A Study of English Historical Thought in the Seventeenth Century* (Cambridge: Cambridge Univ. Press, 1957), p. 19.

CHAPTER 8: **Charles Churchill and Political Satire of the Early 1760s**

1. Atherton, *Political Prints*, pp. 263–64. The increasing role issues, principles, and parties had in post-1760 political history has been the subject of several recent important studies. See, especially, Frank O'Gorman, *The Rise of Party in*

England, 1760–1782 (London: Allen and Unwin, 1975); and John Brewer, *Party Ideology and Popular Politics at the Accession of George III* (Cambridge: Cambridge Univ. Press, 1976). Most historians would agree that after 1760 a politics of exclusion succeeded the Pelhamite system of comprehension.

2. Henry Fox to Sir Charles Hanbury Williams, 19 November 1751, quoted in Earl of Ilchester, *Henry Fox, First Lord Holland: His Family and Relations* (London: John Murray, 1920), 1:179.

3. Walpole to Sir Horace Mann, 27 January 1761, *Correspondence* 21:472.

4. Walpole to Sir Horace Mann, 2 January 1761, *Correspondence* 21:465.

5. Walpole to Sir Horace Mann, 20 June 1762, *Correspondence* 22:42.

6. Walpole to Sir Horace Mann, 31 July 1762, *Correspondence* 22:53.

7. Henry Fielding, *The Jacobite's Journal and Related Writings*, ed. W. B. Coley (Oxford: Oxford Univ. Press, 1975), pp. 211–12. The increased expectation of personal satire is excellently represented by the 1763 republication of a 1731 anti-Walpole play, *The Fall of Mortimer: An Historical Play: Dedicated to the Right Honourable John Earl of Bute.* The new dedication, attributed to Wilkes, ironically emphasizes the supposed sexual relationship between Bute and the king's mother. For a discussion of the political meaning of the play when it first appeared, see John Loftis, *The Politics of Drama in Augustan England* (Oxford: Clarendon Press, 1963), pp. 105–6.

8. Edgar Wind, "The Revolution of History Painting," *Journal of the Warburg and Courtauld Institute* 2 (1938–39): 116.

9. All quotations of Churchill's poetry are taken from *The Poetical Works of Charles Churchill*, ed. Douglas Grant (Oxford: Clarendon Press, 1956). Churchill's cruel treatment of Hogarth was soon challenged by the anonymous author of *The Patriot Poet, a Satire: Inscribed to the Reverend Mr. Ch——ll. By a Country Curate* (1764):

Ch——, stand forth; I dare thee to be try'd
In that great court where virtue shall preside.
Thus thou call'dst H—G—TH, but with brutal rage
To blame the poor poor weaknesses of age.   (P. 26)

10. Charles Press, "Georgian Political Prints and Democratic Institutions," *Comparative Studies in Society and History* 19 (1977), 216–38. Press underestimates the lingering importance of the emblematic tradition.

11. Churchill often deserves the mockery of *The Patriot Poet*:

And then, sonorous Ch——, teach my line
To flow exuberantly wild like thine:
And string with idle particles my lays;
That, one poor sentiment exhausted, *when*
The weary reader hopes a respite, *then*
I may spring on with force redoubled, *till*
I break him panting breathless to my will;
And make him, tir'd in periods of a mile,
Gape in deep wonder at my rapid stile.   (Pp. 13–14)

Very recently, Churchill has received the attentions of far more symphathetic critics: Neil Schaeffer, "Charles Churchill's Political Journalism," *Eighteenth-Century Studies* 9 (1976); pp. 406–28; Raymond J. Smith, *Charles Churchill* (Boston: Twayne, 1977), the best full-length study of Churchill's poetry; and Thomas Lockwood, *Post-Augustan Satire*.

12. Horace Walpole, *Memoirs of the Reign of King George the Third* (1894; reprint, Freeport, N.Y.: Books for Libraries Press, 1970), 3:121–22.

13. All quotations from *The North Briton* are taken from *The North Briton, from No. I. to No. XLVI. Inclusive, With Several Useful and Explanatory Notes, Not Printed in any Former Edition, to Which is Added, a Copious Index to Every Name and Article. Corrected and Revised by a Friend to Civil and Religious Liberty* (London, 1769).

14. For two examples of such charges see *The Crisis* (London, 1764) and *A Letter to the Earl of B——* (London, 1765).

15. Walpole to Sir Horace Mann, 9 November 1762, *Correspondence* 22:97.

16. [Sir John Dalrymple], *The Appeal of Reason to the People of England, on the Present State of Parties in the Nation*, 2d ed. (Edinburgh, 1763), accuses Pitt of using Churchill, Wilkes, and the Mob in his attempt to set up another Cromwell-style dictatorship.

17. We saw a more traditional example of the *paragone* in chap. 1 when Pope compared his poetry to Verrio's painting. For a discussion of *paragone*, see Hagstrum, *The Sister Arts*, p. 66.

Epilogue

1. Paulson, *Popular and Polite Art*, p. 101. Mary Dorothy George, in her excellent modern survey of English political prints in the eighteenth century, *English Political Caricature to 1792: A Study of Opinion and Propaganda* (Oxford: Clarendon Press, 1959), observes, "Only in the last three decades of the century was the transformation from the emblematical print to the political caricature complete. . . . But important progress towards this development was made in the mid-century" (p. 111). An earlier survey, unscholarly but still useful, is Thomas Wright, *Caricature History of the Georges* (1868; reprint, New York: Benjamin Blom, 1968).

Index

Italicized page references are to the illustrations.